Rethinking Attention Deficit Disorders

Rethinking Attention Deficit Disorders

Miriam Cherkes-Julkowski

Susan Sharp

Jonathan Stolzenberg

Brookline Books

ISBN 1-57129-037-0

Library of Congress Cataloging-In-Publication Data
Cherkes-Julkowski, Miriam.
    Rethinking attention deficit disorders / Miriam Cherkes-Julkowski, Susan Sharp, Jonathan Stolzenberg.
        p.   cm.
    Includes bibliographical references and index.
    ISBN 1-57129-037-0 (pbk.)
    1. Attention-deficit-disordered children – Education.
2. Attention.   3. Attention-deficit hyperactivity disorder.
I. Sharp, Susan.   II. Stolzenberg, Jonathan.   III. Title.
LC4713.2.C54   1997
371.93–dc21   97-6106
                                                      CIP

Interior design and typography by Erica L. Schultz.

Printed in the United States by Hamilton Printing Company.

10   9   8   7   6   5   4   3   2   1

Published by
BROOKLINE BOOKS
P.O. Box 1047
Cambridge, Massachusetts 02238-1047
Order toll-free: 1-800-666-BOOK

Contents

1

Attention or Behavior?

- Rachel does not follow directions. She may begin, but soon finds herself doing something else. When she is reminded, she may begin again, but without continual urging, Rachel does not stay on course. She does not hand in her homework. Teachers and parents become agitated and express their wishes that she become more independent and that she take requests more seriously. Rachel responds with confusion and protest when she is told that she must either do what she has been directed to do or suffer the consequences. Rachel most often seems to make the choice to socialize, to talk to the children sitting next to her. She is able to sustain this activity but not those related to school assignments. If teachers insist that she do her work, there is apt to be an angry or frantic outburst.

- David acts without thinking. He gets in trouble all the time. He is active, talkative, and incorrigible. He says provocative things to both teachers and peers. They, of course, respond to him negatively, either by ignoring him or by escalating the confrontation. He exhibits similar behavior when asked to do his schoolwork. He will hand in work that he has rushed through. He makes what appear to be careless errors. He has been corrected countless times, but reprimands bring no change in his behavior. When confronted about his rude, thoughtless, or slapdash behavior, David is defiant. He insists that he is not careless, that others provoke him.

- Lisa talks out loud as she attempts to do a workbook assignment. Her peers find this distracting. Her teacher finds her chatter, apparently without concern for others, inconsiderate and disruptive. Lisa is restless and fidgety. Teachers are continually telling her to settle down so that she can pay attention to her school work.

Although these three children think and act differently, each has a form of attention deficit disorder (ADD). It may seem that they suffer from behavioral difficulties, that they will need carefully constructed behavior management programs to set them on the proper course of development. In actuality, the problem is more complex.

There is a wealth of literature addressing the behavioral aspects of ADDs. Suggestions are made for how to manage disruptive behaviors and how to increase time on task, productivity, or socially appropriate action. Deficits in attention, however, impact the individual in far more profound ways. We use the term Attention Deficit Disorder(s) (ADDs) rather than Attention Deficit/Hyperactivity Disorder (ADHD) to place the emphasis on attention rather than on behavior (hyperactivity).[1]

The attentional system consists of a complex network of neurological sites influencing a number of cognitive functions. Attentional processes are essential in nearly all aspects of human activity, including thought, feeling, and action. The system is vast, dynamic, and complex. In this book we examine the nature of attention and attention dysfunction, focusing on their relevance to learning and understanding. Attention dysfunction makes learning difficult, particularly the learning of symbolic or complex information requiring sustained attention or execution of multiple steps. What is novel about the approach of this book is its interest in the neuropsychological and cognitive dynamics of attention dysfunction and their specific implications for personal and social development, for thought, and for the learning of reading, math, and writing skills. Attention is presented as a complex, self-organizing system that is nonlinear and recursive in its functioning. We demonstrate how the effects of dysfunction reverberate throughout the system (the self) and how the system, in turn, attempts to cope.

It is our basic axiom that all behavior represents an individual's best effort at adaptation. Given the challenges presented to an individual with ADD in the school setting, there is a great need for coping. The person with ADD will be motivated to self-organize for optimal levels of functioning. However, the cost of coping is large, and the coping itself can take on the aura of dysfunction. Behavioral interventions that attempt to control coping activity could be counterproductive. Rather than behavioral or top-down cognitive-behavioral management intervention, we describe an

---

[1] Our use of the plural term "ADDs" reflects a recognition of several variants of the disorder (see the material in chapter 2 about classification according to DSM-IV). Throughout the text, we use the singular term "ADD" to refer to the manifestation of attention dysfunction in a particular individual.

approach that facilitates the system's own efforts at dynamic self-organization.

In brief, we have written this book to emphasize that ADDs are truly disorders of attention, cognitive disorders based in neurological function, affecting all forms of thought — not simply a matter of behavioral disturbance. ADDs will affect learning in specific ways requiring specific instructional modifications. Our goal is to encourage teachers, parents, and practitioners of various kinds to view the behavioral manifestations of ADDs from a systems perspective, as the child's constructive effort at self-organization and adaptation.

The Children

Rachel. On a behavioral level, Rachel may appear to be immature, to need strict consequences for not handing in her homework and for doing it carelessly. She appears to be unmotivated, more interested in having a good time with friends than in meeting her responsibilities in school. Her outbursts when confronted with reasonable demands border on defiance and would receive quick, intense feedback such as being sent to sit in the principal's office, other forms of time out, loss of recess, or loss of another preferred activity. A behavior management plan and check lists might be used to coordinate home and school to ensure that Rachel handed in her homework.

In our view, all of Rachel's difficulties can be seen as reflections of her ADD. She can neither sustain attention long enough to capture instruction or directions, nor hold them in mind firmly enough to grasp their meaning. Since she is not clear about what the assignment asks of her, she does not know how to get started. If she can complete her homework, she may not be able to maintain a conscious awareness of the need to put it in her backpack so it will get to school, or to put it in the homework bin when she arrives there. Rachel's preference for socializing might serve the purpose of providing a more pleasant and more gratifying experience for her. She may have come to expect negative feedback and agitation from her teachers. In order to preserve some sense of self, she avoids the humiliation of school failure in favor of the rewards of socialization. She may find a more favorable level of arousal in fast-moving, multifaceted social interactions than in the strictly and narrowly confined focus of attention required for schoolwork. When compliance is enforced, frustration mounts. Rachel's outbursts may serve to discharge the energy associated with the resultant increase in frustration and in failed efforts to regulate attention. Rachel is on her way to school failure, a poor sense of self, and poor resilience in the face of a challenge. Confrontation causes the problem to escalate.

David. David's behavior may be seen as unacceptable. He is disrespectful to adults, argumentative, and unable to remain seated. He does not do well with peers and, what is more, takes no responsibility for his problems; it is always someone else's fault. David's behavior problems are so disruptive that he may be placed in a special program for behaviorally disordered children. From a behavioral perspective, wherever he is placed, David will need a tightly controlled behavioral program.

Our view suggests that David's undesirable behaviors, however maladaptive they may seem, are all efforts to cope with his ADD. His activity level may in fact help him to increase an otherwise low level of arousal. His cognitive impulsivity (slapdash, error-prone work) and behavioral impulsivity are essential parts of his ADD and may reflect the failure to inhibit responses or the desire to act on a thought or feeling before it is lost to inattention. He seems to perceive others as attacking him and rises rapidly to his own defense. His perceptions may be "justified" by a history of rejection by both teachers and peers, as well as general difficulties in social relationships from birth onward.

Lisa. So it is with Lisa too. Behavior by behavior she is disrespectful, fails to finish independent work, and is disruptive to others. In the view of ADDs presented here, all these behaviors are of a piece. Lisa may be highly motivated to meet the demands of school. She may be trying to compete with distractions by talking aloud as she works, which has a positive effect on her ability to narrow and sustain focus. But if Lisa achieves success on her assignments using these tactics, that success comes at the expense of peer acceptance and teacher approval.

ADDs: A Systems Perspective

Whereas the traditional view of ADDs includes them under behavioral disorders, the view presented here sees them as *dynamic interactions of behavior, cognition, and affect,* out of which emerge distinct and idiosyncratic ways of coping. We find that much of what is commonly emphasized in attention deficit disorder is the array of symptoms that represent a person's attempts to cope with this essential dysregulation. It is important not to be misled into thinking that the symptoms *are* the problem. The essence of attention dysfunction transcends the issues of behavior (e.g., failure to interact with peers appropriately) and function (e.g., failure to follow directions). It is inappropriate to place the emphasis on how to bring isolated behaviors to functional levels — how to help a child attend longer, talk out less, control distractibility more.

Focus on the behavioral manifestations of attention disorders, to the exclusion of the cognitive and affective components, erroneously emphasizes symptoms over underlying causes. Furthermore, even if motor functioning and affective functioning are spared in some cases of attention dysregulation, it is most likely that cognitive aspects of attention will not be spared.

All behavioral symptoms are not of equal concern. Some are superficially problematic, and some are important coping strategies. While overactivity or hyperactivity may well have a neurological basis, they must be seen from a broader perspective. For example, overactivity might be a moderately undesirable aspect of the biology of ADDs. Or it might serve the regulatory function of discharging energy (Zeskind & Marshall, 1991) and thus improving homeostasis. Or, alternatively, it might be an effort to cope with waning arousal with the goal of maintaining attention (much like what a drowsy person might do while driving a car: wiggle in the seat, turn the radio up, move hands and feet ...). These may be the dynamics that promote "misbehavior" in the cases of David and Rachel. It is important for treaters to discern what is driving the behavioral symptoms since, in each case, the appropriate supporting intervention will depend on the essential source of the problem — the function served by the behavior. In our examples, none of the proposed sources of dysfunction would be amenable to extinction or other behavior-shaping paradigms. *The behavior supports regulation, and regulation will need to be valued,* even if it is necessary to work with the individual to find more acceptable forms of self-regulation.

There is ample evidence that ADD is fundamentally a problem with the regularity, control, and fluency of attention. People with ADDs are not always able to balance the demands of sustained focus against the force of more visceral attractions (i.e., distractions), such as novelty, intensity, or strong affect-driven preferences. The disorder results in coping strategies that may or may not be helpful toward the control of attention, and that may cause additional problems of their own. For example, like Lisa, schoolchildren with ADDs often try to compete with their distractions by talking aloud as they work. This appears to have a positive effect on sustaining focus but can disturb others, and may seem to teachers to be inconsiderate, immature, or simply deviant. The child may have traded acceptance by her peers and teachers for success on her worksheets.

Attention deficits and their consequences are not discrete problems, each individually in need of fixing. Rather, they are part of a much more complex system. Deficits exist at essential levels of processing, often in conjunction with marked strengths or talents. Since the deficits are essential parts of the self-organizing properties of an individual, they shape (and are shaped by) experiences from the first moments of life. Effects of the disorder, then, are longitudinal and thus self-confounding and self-reinforcing — often to the detriment of the self. In the language of chaos theory, growth trajectories are initialized by and highly sensitive to early conditions.

Each aspect of development along the way enters into the equation and influences all subsequent events.

ADDs affect all aspects of a person's functioning. All information (input and output), experience, communication, personality development, and social interactions are vulnerable to maladaptive attempts at coping that present themselves as "problems." In the course of development, effects become causes of still other effects. Effects feed back on initial causes, and influence all facets of the system. As time goes on, if the disorder is not treated effectively, symptoms (dysfunctional coping behaviors) can become worse and more abundant. They can become significant problems in their own right. The person who sometimes *can* is seen as *not* performing and therefore as *not wanting to.* Her inabilities to meet expectations are seen by others, and often by herself, as being willful acts of refusal, laziness, or a lack of motivation. With the shift to a frame that holds "willfulness" as a cause rather than an outcome, the misperception of the disorder, and thus the person, is compounded: what was erroneously seen first and foremost as a "disruptive behavior" problem is now perceived as a moral issue as well. The irony is that behavior interpreted as "thoughtless" probably is a result of too much awareness and the desire to cope. Interventions, then, are important in the developmental course of the individual. They must be early, effective, and humane.

Certainly attention dysfunction brings disorder to the self and to the other systems in which it is located. But the positive aspects of attention dysfunction deserve to be seen as well. The creative benefits of disinhibition (Baum, personal communication) are obvious. The intensity of experiencing novel events, the search for arousal, and sometimes for risk and adventure, contribute to the making of interesting personalities whose poor adaptation to restricted environments, such as school classrooms, might portend much greater accomplishments.

THE BROAD BASIS OF ATTENTION

To understand our view of ADDs, it is necessary to understand the magnitude of attention itself. The ability to attend is critical to learning and to a person's well-being. Freud (1965) described attention as vital to consciousness: "Becoming conscious is connected with the application of a particular psychical function, that of attention" (p. 632). He sees attention as necessary for the process of knowing what is and what isn't real. What one attends to is the reality of that individual.

While many look at attention as a way of integrating "things out there," we see it also as an aspect of "things in here" — a view that embeds attention firmly in the individual's cognitive and affective system. Attention takes place in the context of all other cognitive processes. An individual learns to modulate behavior in response to experience. The effects of that experience are stored as patterns of association, memories, which will influence future behavior in unknown ways. As the individual learns and remembers, attention makes it possible to shift and maintain focus on new events in the context of previous experience. In complex environments, whether internal or external, the individual shifts back and forth among myriad foci and must keep track of her place in this process. Every step in learning and memory depends on active, self-regulating attention.

Attention is the process that holds discrete states long enough for them to be noted, processed, integrated, related, and acted upon in thought, feeling, and movement. Attention is not a linear system in which information is received, comprehended, and then stored. Rather, the process of attention is recursive. The mind abandons, postpones, returns to, or acts upon the information that attention has captured.

The intricacies of attention are far-reaching. The system must maintain arousal, not too much and not too little. It must be able to ignore irrelevant distractions, keep some on-line power in readiness for new relevant information that may appear, maintain attention needed to retrieve appropriate information from the knowledge store, shift attention when necessary, and still address the purpose of making meaning from the internal and external interactions that are its fuel. To this end, part of the attentional mechanism is a working memory "holding tank" that can temporarily store anything the brain does not want to lose while it works on other jobs, and that will not degrade the information while it is held.

The brain's ability to function in a goal-directed way is dependent upon, among other things, its ability to come to, maintain, and shift attention to thoughts, feelings, actions, goals, external sensations, and expectations. In this way, attention is not just the mechanism by which we can become conscious; it is also the mechanism through which we can examine consciousness itself, be introspective, have intentions — be aware not just of ourselves, but also of our selves in relation to all else (Varela, Thompson, & Rosch, 1993).

Attention as Consciousness

The focus of attention is the direction in which consciousness is turned. Thus attention, in its limitations, reveals the limitations of consciousness (Edelman, 1992). These limitations are well established (Kahneman, 1973). Edelman offers a convincing theory of biological conditions that make this so. In Edelman's view, learning itself, building knowledge out of which consciousness can emerge, is based in a process of neuronal group selection. Repeated experience creates associations among simultaneously activated neurons and thus selects neuronal group mappings that form the basis for concepts and automatic responding. Each neuronal group mapping consists of neurons in close proximity, as well as some neurons more remote. These same neurons in different combinations can participate in other neuronal group mappings as well — e.g., one neuron might be associated with the sight but also the touch of a given object. Mappings, therefore, are complex. Each involves considerable brain tissue. It would be impossible to invoke more than one or two of these mappings simultaneously without their being in competition with each other. What attention can bring into consciousness is controlled by competitive dynamics at this most microscopic of levels.

Edelman draws a further distinction between primary and higher-order consciousness. Primary consciousness reflects the animal's attention to things in the environment, co-opted by their salience (i.e., their intensity, novelty, and relevance for survival). With the emergence of language and planning skills, consciousness can be directed toward material that reflects the values, desires, and intentions of the individual. It can be directed toward the self as well, so that the self can be conscious of consciousness itself (or so it seems). It should be noted, however, that these desires, values, and intentions themselves emerge out of dynamic interactions at fundamental levels (more about this in chapter 5).

Those associations that get formed — which then form the basis of knowing, the material for consciousness — are *selected* by experience. Those neuronal groupings activated in the process of experience survive and are strengthened. Those that are not activated grow weaker and ultimately fail to meet the requirements for selection. In this way, consciousness emerges out of dynamic activity at the most local of levels to produce order at the global level. Rules for processing information are not given *a priori*; patterns of association are emergent based on experience. And, in this way, "adaptation takes place by selection, not instruction" (Edelman, 1992, p. 74).

We take Edelman's statement literally and in its broadest implications. Instruction is based on the premise that awareness is a top-down mechanism, that a higher-order plan can be put in place (instructed) to effectively "crank out" future, adaptive behaviors and concepts. From a developmental standpoint, such a rule-governed, instructional process has been construed as the epigenesis, or unfolding, of internal rules for making sense of the world (Piaget & Inhelder, 1969). From an educational standpoint, instruction has taken the form of providing information about the procedures and rules for operating and knowing. In the education of children with disabilities, ADDs included, instruction has taken the form of strategy training and overlearning of procedural rules.

If adaptation occurs by selection, then rule-based, top-down instruction must stand aside to allow and support the system to form itself. Education of this kind would provide opportunities for direct experience that would lead most effectively, in the context of the individual, toward a desired outcome, such as learning how to read, how to solve a time-distance problem, or how to communicate effectively. Giving good examples is critical, as is providing opportunities for action and personal engagement. The implications for teaching are enormous and shall be discussed throughout this book.

Attention as Regulation

The dynamic and complex nature of the self-system necessitates regulation among its components. At its best, attention maintains the proper balance between highly focused awareness and more implicit reception of the stimulus field. It maintains a balance between activation and arousal, between a search for novelty and distractibility, between disinhibition and overfocus.

The regulation of and by attention emerges out of the self-organizing properties of the system, the self in its context. It emerges out of the self-organizing balance among neurotransmitters, among patterned neuronal activity, among cognitive and affective processes that are emergent entities themselves. As with all complex, nonstatic systems, energy is required to create and sustain well-regulated organization, to resist the natural progression toward entropy. Thus energy and effort are also vital to the regulation of attention.

Attention Dysfunction

Problems with the dysregulation of attention can ripple through the entire system and cause more widespread disruptions. They can disrupt learning, memory, affect, and movement. Attentional dysfunction, like most things, falls on a continuum. It is also susceptible to situational constraints. When the situation facilitates attention regulation, the individual will appear to be "in control" of her attention. Such a situation might be one that is optimally arousing (not too boring, not too stimulating). However, on her own, faced with an over- or under-arousing situation, the same individual may find herself dysregulated, unable to maintain the proper balance within the system. Environments that value rapid, hyper-responsivity to novel stimuli are ones to which people with attention deficit disorders might adapt well. Those that value sustained, focal attention to repetitive tasks would be the most difficult.

Attention dysfunction can affect one or more of the basic classes of human endeavors (movement, affect, and cognition), producing an array of problems. One's movements may lose their focus, possibly resulting in the *dysregulation of motor behavior* observed in hyperactivity, graphomotor dysfunction, clumsiness, hypoactivity, and/or impulsivity. *Affective dysregulation* may also occur: emotions may be labile, with more than the usual ups and downs. Temper may be short. The individual may exhibit risk-taking behavior based on impulsive thoughts, or obsessive behavior when unable to shift attention off a particular focus. As mentioned earlier, *cognitive dysregulation* makes learning difficult, particularly the learning of symbolic information or of complex tasks requiring sustained attention or execution of multiple steps. Nowhere are the demands for well-regulated attention and conscious awareness more predominant than in the school environment.

Academic achievement tasks are particularly challenging to the attention-disordered individual. She may have insufficient attention to collect all the relevant information for the task, or she may be distracted by irrelevant information, resulting in an incomplete or incorrect response. She may have difficulties with information management and become overloaded with information; this overload can produce inappropriate coping in the form of either passive behavior (withdrawal, avoidance, refusal) or active behavior designed to hold onto whatever she can (impulsivity, rushing). The result is an insufficient or inefficient ability to find a dynamic balance in response to attentional demands. To be successful, the balance must be accomplished with synchrony at the levels of input, integration, and organization for output that is smooth, productive, and efficient, and at a reasonable, nonexhaustive cost.

The cost of coping is important to consider. Individuals with attention disorders are often able to muster great effort and "put it all together." Unfortunately, it is often the product of this effort that is noted and not the process that has accomplished it. Achievements are often misinterpreted as evidence that "he/she can, when he/she wants to" and signal a breakdown in morality (i.e., the work ethic) when the individual is unable to maintain the needed level of attentional effort all the time. But the true cost of such effort can be enormous. The individual may expend such huge amounts of energy to accomplish the slightest attention-intensive task that the resulting exhaustion renders her incapable of performing the next task, even if it is one that she could, under other circumstances, have managed quite well. Exhaustion resulting from extra effort can contribute to irritability and negative outbursts. Effort may go into appearing attentive, while nothing is understood or learned. The behavioral accomplishment could undermine the overall cognitive process and/or exact an affective cost that produces frustration and sadness.

It is a basic axiom that all behavior is an individual's best effort at adaptation (Murphy, 1962). Those behaviors that persist are those that serve adaptive functions for that individual. Given the challenges presented to all individuals with ADDs, particularly in the school setting, there is likely to be a great need for developing adaptive coping. The person with ADD will be motivated to self-organize for optimal levels of functioning. This might mean blurting out information, perhaps without regard for rules of polite behavior, in order to say something before it is lost to attention. It might mean shutting down in order to down-regulate as irritation and arousal mount. In the latter case, the coping looks like task avoidance, laziness, or lack of motivation, but may serve a larger adaptive function of maintaining systemic regulation and integrity. There would be an inherent, if subconscious, wisdom in this approach, since it would increase the total time in attention and maintain precious composure. It might mean choosing *not to try* in order to preserve self-esteem or homeostasis, in the face of what is perceived as an insurmountable obstacle.

Attention Deficit Disorder

Surely attentional deficits have been around for ages. Why all the attention to attention now? There is more awareness and increased diagnosis, fueled by the long-over-due recognition that hyperactive behaviors and overt behavioral impulsivity are not pathognomonic, diagnostically necessary features. The knowledge that environmental pollutants, such as lead, and in some cases dietary and allergic phenomena can *cause* attention dysfunction may have increased our awareness of the disorder, as might the survival of extremely premature babies or the increase of children with fetal exposure to abused substances. These are areas demanding more study. However, we believe that the concern about disorders of attention has arisen out of our increasing appreciation for the significant problems they raise for the individual.

Attentional deficits impact those functions of the self that are most necessary in our modern world: high-order, sophisticated learning; complex social interaction and understanding of expectation; selectively appropriate behavior, motivation, and goal orientation; self-awareness; and insight in order to enhance rapid and efficient adaptation to a changing world, environment, family, and personal universe. The demands are large, and there is little tolerance for poor fit.

Werry, Minde, Guzman, Wiess, Dogan, and Hoy (1972), in their study of the neurological status of hyperactive children, conclude that the condition represents a variant of reproductive casualty (Sameroff & Chandler, 1975); i.e., it has a clear and definitive neurological basis but is aggravated by the interaction of the original vulnerability with environmental demands. Werry et al. described the condition of hyperactive children (the term used at the time) as being "... in the majority of cases, a biological variant made manifest by the affluent society's insistence on universal literacy and its acquisition in a sedentary position" (Werry et al., 1972, p. 449).

The challenges of development from birth through the life span are formidable in and of themselves. For the attentionally deficient, those challenges are magnified. Attention deficits are pervasive *in the context* of the modern classroom and the modern world. A person with attention deficit disorder stands out (that is, his behavior is different from his peers') and is poorly tolerated by a demanding society. Often the true, underlying handicap cannot be seen. In the context of an otherwise intact organism, failure to attend — to adapt to the complex, higher-order demands of school and life — is seen as a flaw of character, motivation, the work ethic. It is important, however, that the disorder and the resultant attempts at coping be seen for what they are. We are at a point in our technology where we can begin to measure attention dysfunction to some degree, appreciate it to some degree, and treat its manifestations to some degree, however imperfectly. Given our current technology — including functional magnetic resonant imaging (MRI), positron emission tomography (PET), and single-photon emission computed tomography (SPECT) — as well as our increasing awareness of the nature of the attention network, we are at a point where we can begin to appreciate the complexity of the disorder, a complexity that dictates a multimodal intervention. Our knowledge base has grown and no longer allows reductionist views of the disorder or approaches to its treatment. Interventions that acknowledge the dynamic interactions within the biological, cognitive, affective, and social realms are not merely justifiable; they are imperative.

SUMMARY AND FORWARD LOOK

Attention deficit disorders are traditionally considered to be behavioral in nature. We take the view that attention dysfunction is not as simple as that. We will explain how complex and how deeply rooted in cognition the attention system is. In chapter 2, we describe the history of classification of ADDs, from the perspective of ADDs as *cognitive disorders.*

Problems with attention affect nearly all aspects of learning and thought. For this reason, when there is a disorder anywhere within the attention system, nearly all aspects of function are jeopardized. Once a problem exists, the person with ADD will try to adapt. She will invent ways of coping with the disorder that are motivated to maintain the best balance within the system at large. Sometimes the coping method itself will be mistaken for the problem. To help a person with ADD, it is important to understand the nature of the attention system. Chapter 3 describes the extent and complexity of the attention system. Because of extreme limitations in attentional capacity, a child with ADD requires special instructional supports.

Like all complex systems, attention must find a balanced coordination among all its components. This regulation arises out of the biochemistry and cognitive components of attention. Interventions, whether instructional or pharmacological, must complement the individual's own efforts at self-regulation (chapters 4 and 6).

Motivation is very much a part of the attention system (chapter 5). It emerges, with attention, out of fundamental cognitive, emotional, and physiological processes. We contend that motivation is not under simple, conscious control and cannot be manipulated through behavioral interventions.

The remaining chapters provide practical suggestions for supporting the ADD child in school. Of course, these suggestions rest on our model of the attention system as explained in the preceding sections. The attentional demands of classroom functioning, social adjustment, reading, math, and writing are described. We illustrate how breakdowns in attention interfere with functioning in each of these areas and offer practical suggestions for interventions.

In the last chapter, we remind the reader that the focus on *behavior* is insufficient and misplaced. Attention dysfunction takes place within the cognitive system and affects all aspects of self-regulation.

2

Attention Deficit: The Disorder

The history of Attention Deficit/Hyperactivity Disorder (ADHD) is mysterious and circuitous. It is at once a phenomenon in search of an accurate and proper name, and a named diagnosis in search of a phenomenology. Although the syndrome of ADHD has been identified since early in the twentieth century, it has been given numerous labels, and the constellation of symptoms needed for diagnosis has varied. This chapter reviews the history of the disorder over the past century, with particular emphasis on the evolving role of cognitive, attentional, and personal dysfunction in its formulation.

The Pre-DSM Era

The 19th-century German physician Heinrich Hoffman wrote a clinical description of ADD/hyperactive behavior and family dynamics in his collection of moral tales for children. The verse below tells of fidgety Phil, the obnoxious dinner-table nightmare who so infuriates:

> "Phil, stop acting like a worm,
> the table is no place to squirm."
> Thus speaks the father to his son,
> severely says it not in fun.
> Mother frowns and looks around,
> although she doesn't make a sound.

But Philip will not take advice,
he'll have his way at any price.
He turns,
and churns,
he wiggles
and jiggles
Here and there on the chair;
"Phil, these twists I cannot bear."

(Garfinkel & Wender, 1989)

Phil's problem is a behavioral one presented as having a moral etiology. Notice the emphasis on *will*. He could do better, but he "won't." He's a bad boy: he "will not take advice," "he'll have his way." Notice also the impact on the family and parenting dynamic. Father is stern, Mother is depressed and avoidant, there is inconsistency and no follow-through, and Phil learns nothing of how to improve his behavior.

At the time of this moral tale, there would have been little question about the best treatment for Phil's problem: severe discipline. Today, it would be recognized that his behavior needs to be managed and modified through reinforcement, limit-setting, counseling, cognitive training, and parent and family therapy. Pharmacological intervention aimed at normalizing neurotransmitter function would be added as a treatment option. If his behavior can be controlled, we are told, he will learn (Silver, 1990). This is the modern, "enlightened" approach. But there is something missing.

The "enlightened" treatment has primarily focused on modifying the external manifestations of Phil's attention disorder and hyperactivity: issues of behavior. Phil himself — how he thinks, how he learns, how he feels, his ability to learn — has been ignored. The modern approach emphasizes the observable dysregulation and dyscontrol. It may, perhaps inadvertently, help Phil's poor regulation and control of emotion and help heal his weakened sense of self-worth. But it does not directly address, and potentially neglects, the impact of an attentional deficit on his poor regulation and control of cognition itself. It also fails to address the impact of this poor regulation and control on every aspect of his personal system. To treat the behavior alone would be to ignore the full complexity of the problem.

The correlation between learning and attentional problems has been recognized since very early in this century. The first description of the "attention deficit disorder" syndrome is credited to Still (1902), who described a group of 20 children in his clinical practice who were aggressive, defiant, resistant to discipline, and often overactive; they had impaired attention and showed little will to inhibit, relative to their same-aged peers. Still described the syndrome as a "defect in moral control" (p. 1009) and believed it to be a chronic condition. He suggested that deficiencies in moral control, sustained attention, and inhibitory volition were related to one another, and to some underlying neurological deficiency. Although he had no empirical evidence (this would come later from other researchers), he theorized about a lower threshold for reaction to stimuli, or a cortical disconnection between "thought" and "will." Although Still's terminology, with its connotations of morality, is somewhat distressing, he did not intend to suggest that this syndrome was a flaw in a person's character, controllable with improved motivation. Rather, he provided the theoretical foundations for ADHD as a neurobiological disorder accompanied by behavioral symptoms.

Support for the brain connection was provided by a number of researchers in the early decades of the twentieth century. Von Econonmo's encephalitis, which emerged as a part of the influenza pandemic that followed World War I, left a number of child survivors with behavioral and cognitive symptoms that included impaired attention, impulse control, and memory, as well as difficulties with activity level, self-regulation, and social skills (Hohman, 1922). The syndrome was referred to as "postencephalitic behavior disorder" and was attributed to damage to the central nervous system. The infection had produced a decrease of dopamine in the basal ganglia.

Other causes of brain injury were also studied, such as childhood central nervous system infections (Bender, 1942; Meyer & Byers, 1952), birth trauma (Shirley, 1939), lead toxicity (Byers & Lord, 1943), epilepsy (Levin, 1938), and traumatic brain injury (Goldstein, 1936; Meyer, 1904). Children suffering from these evident injuries to the brain often displayed the attentional, behavioral, and cognitive impairments associated with ADHD. Furthermore, research on primates (e.g., Levin, 1938) noted similarities between the behaviors of severely hyperactive children and those of primates who had frontal lobe lesions.

As a result of this correlational evidence, it became common practice to attribute ADHD symptoms in all children to brain injury, regardless of whether brain injuries could be validated through clinical histories. The behavioral symptoms, in and of themselves, were considered to be evidence of underlying central nervous system damage, or of Minimal Brain Damage [MBD] Syndrome, a term coined by Strauss and Lehtinen (1947). Strauss also believed that in some individuals these behaviors might emanate from biological, inherited factors, rather than from pre- or postnatal brain injury.

Diagnostic and Statistical Manual (DSM)-II Era

Strauss's work was extremely influential and contributed significantly to the idea that specific behavioral problems imply brain damage. The further suggestion was that these behaviors could exist as distinct neurological problems, separate and independent from cognitive and emotional functioning. Strauss also developed guidelines for classroom and environmental modifications.

In the 1950s and 1960s, investigators who became uncomfortable using the term "brain damage" to describe individuals who showed little or no evidence of actual damage modified the term to "Minimal Brain Dysfunction." The concept of "soft" versus "hard" neurological signs was developed, with the latter signifying actual brain involvement. "Soft" signs were presumed to indicate less tangible neurological involvement. A U.S. government-sponsored task force defined the application of the term "MBD" as follows:

> children of near average, average, or above average general intelligence with certain learning or behavioral disabilities ranging from mild to severe, which are associated with deviations of function of the central nervous system. These deviations may manifest themselves by various combinations of impairment in perception, conceptualization, language, memory, and control of attention, impulse, or motor function. (Clements, 1966, p. 9)

In order of frequency (Silver, 1990), the ten characteristics of MBD were:

- hyperactivity,
- perceptual-motor impairments,
- general coordination defects,
- disorders of attention (e.g., short attention span, distractibility, perseveration),
- impulsivity,
- disorders of memory and thinking,
- specific learning disabilities (e.g., reading, writing, arithmetic, and spelling),
- disorders of speech and hearing,
- equivocal neurological signs, and
- electroencephalographic (EEG) irregularities.

Thus, currently acknowledged symptoms of learning disabilities and attention deficit disorders were seen as running together in varied combinations, mainly being evidenced by "soft" neurological signs.

Near the end of the 1950s, the MBD terminology was replaced by terms that were considered to reflect more specific and observable cognitive and behavioral traits. By

1960, terms such as *dyslexia, dysgraphia, dyscalculia, language disorders,* and *learning disabilities* were used to describe the learning and cognitive deficits previously included under MBD, while the syndrome of attention deficit disorder was reduced to a single, cardinal feature: that of hyperactivity. Chess (1960) and others (Laufer & Denhoff, 1957; Werry & Sprague, 1970) focused on excessive activity level — a feature that was observable and could be objectively measured — as the defining characteristic. In a 1967 psychiatric textbook, Laufer stated that learning disabilities and hyperkinetic impulse disorder may occur together or separately. He proposed a brain-based dysfunction (diencephalic) that

> ... could make the individual unusually sensitive to stimuli flooding in both from peripheral receptors and viscera .... Others have proposed that the rostral portions of the reticular activating system are concerned with the ability to respond differentially to stimuli, to inhibit, to establish, and to alter set — all of which seem important in the production of this syndrome. (Laufer, 1967, p. 1445)

There was also a new optimism about long-term prognosis, as experts noted that the symptoms involving activity level alone were often resolved by puberty. The Diagnostic and Statistical Manual of Mental Disorders (DSM-II; American Psychiatric Association, 1968) created the diagnostic label "Hyperkinetic Reaction of Childhood" to describe the syndrome, and focused primarily on excessive activity level rather than on attention or other associated symptoms. Since the DSM has, across all of its editions, been the primary handbook used by medical and psychological professionals to diagnose disorders, the emphasis taken by the DSM at any given time has profound effects on how a disorder is conceptualized and treated, and on who gets identified.

The DSM-III Era

It wasn't long before investigators realized that the ADHD syndrome encompassed much more than just a high activity level. "Attention Deficit Disorder" emerged as a better descriptor as researchers recognized that attention, rather than activity level, was the core symptom of the disorder (Cantwell, 1988; Douglas, 1972; Douglas & Peters, 1979; Dykman, Ackerman, Clements, & Peters, 1971; Whalen & Henker, 1976). The defining characteristics of the hyperkinetic syndrome were broadened to include inattention and impulsivity, along with hyperactivity. Specific criteria were developed from the consensus of experienced investigators (not yet empirically determined), and "symptom" lists for inattention, impulsivity, and hyperactivity were created.

The criteria for diagnosis of ADD in the DSM-III manual (American Psychiatric Association, 1980) included specific cutoff scores for symptoms in each area (at least 3 in the Inattention category, at least 3 in the Impulsivity category, and at least 2 in the Hyperactivity category), as well as guidelines for age of onset, duration of symptoms, and exclusion of other psychiatric disorders as causes. Furthermore, DSM-III recognized that some individuals may have attention deficit disorder without hyperactivity. They described subtypes: ADDH for those who had symptoms in all three categories, ADDnoH for those who had inattention and impulsivity without hyperactivity, and ADD–Residual Type (ADD-RT), for those whose inattention and impulsivity persisted although hyperactivity subsided. The ADD-RT designation was an important one because it legitimized the concept that individuals who would once have met the criteria for ADDH could suffer continued social and occupational impairment in the absence of overt hyperactivity. The persistence of the disorder into adulthood and its successful treatment with drugs were described in the 1970s (Huessey, 1974; Wood, Reimherr, Wender, & Johnson, 1976). What DSM-III did not acknowledge was that when those children with ADD without hyperactivity grow up, *they too* can experience the painful personal consequences of persistent inattention, impulsivity, and cognitive and biological dysregularity and dyscontrol.

ADD was completely separated from learning disabilities in DSM-III. ADD was classified as a mental disorder, while LD was classified as a developmental disorder under Axis II. ADD was listed under its own category of "Disorders Usually First Evident in Infancy, Childhood, or Adolescence" (Axis I). Conduct Disorders were also listed under their own category, and Oppositional Defiant Disorder was not listed at all until a subsequent revision (DSM-III-R). Contrary to what some researchers have stated (Epstein, Shaywitz, Shaywitz, & Woolston, 1991), DSM-III did *not* list attention deficit disorders and conduct disorders together under the heading of "Disruptive Behavior Disorders." This invention did not appear until DSM-III-R and was short-lived. However, both ADD and conduct disorder were meant to be seen in DSM-III as having overt "behavior" as their "predominant area of disturbance" (Spitzer & Williams, 1980). DSM-IV continues this perception by combining ADD, conduct disorder, and oppositional defiant disorder under an all-encompassing classification of "Attention Deficit and Disruptive Behavior Disorders."

With the publication of DSM-III came a rash of validation and other studies exploring every aspect of these disorders and their comorbidities (i.e., other disorders that frequently appear in conjunction with them). Key issues included whether or not ADD without hyperactivity existed and, if it did exist, whether or not it and ADD with hyperactivity were subtypes of the same disorder.

DSM-III-R

The revised edition of DSM-III (DSM-III-R), published in 1987, came too soon to reflect the building evidence from the research efforts in the field. To the consternation of many clinicians, researchers, parents, teachers, and patients, DSM-III-R changed the name of the disorder and the diagnostic criteria once again.

The new nomenclature, "Attention Deficit Hyperactivity Disorder," was chosen because at the time there was little empirical evidence to substantiate separate subtypes for ADDH and ADDnoH. (The subtype of "Undifferentiated Attention Deficit Disorder" was included in DSM-III-R, with a recommendation for further research.) Although DSM-III-R included the word *hyperactivity* in the new label, it continued to emphasize that attentional deficits, more than motoric activity, defined the disorder. The three categories of symptoms in DSM-III were combined into a single list, and the diagnostic criteria changed so that the presence of any 8 of the 14 symptoms in the areas of impulsivity, inattention, and/or hyperactivity would indicate a positive diagnosis. An index of severity was also added: more symptoms indicated a more severe case of ADHD; fewer symptoms, a milder case. The list of symptoms, now based on a body of empirical evidence, spurred the publication of a number of behavior rating scales tailor-made to the diagnostic criteria.

A review of the behaviors described, however, indicates a significant problem: they are characteristic, primarily, of elementary school-aged children. What of preschoolers, preteens and teens, or younger and older adults? The clinician must extrapolate, and the researcher must be very creative. This problem was well addressed in a paper describing the tasks of the DSM-IV work group (Shaffer et al., 1989):

> When applied to much younger or much older age groups, the criteria (for ADHD in DSM-III-R) take on a humorous quality. How many 3-year-olds can wait their turn in line or do not speak out of turn? ... we estimate that fewer than half of the ADHD symptoms are applicable for adolescents or the young adult. (p. 833)

The behaviors are listed in descending order of discriminating power, based on field trials. At least one highly respected researcher and clinician in the field described these trials as being poorly organized, with small numbers of patients and "capricious" selection of cases that did not cover the whole taxonomic domain (Werry, 1988). In the same piece, Werry notes that DSM-III-R invalidated much of the research on ADD based on DSM-III criteria.

Cantwell and Baker (1988) state a similar opinion of the reformulation of ADD to ADHD and its field trials. They further note that recent evidence runs counter to

DSM-III-R's position that the diagnosis of ADDnoH is rarely made — and that ADD with and without hyperactivity are unlikely to be separate subtypes of a single disorder; the literature in only a few years since DSM-III's publication "... has provided a surprising number of cases" that illustrate the association of the two forms. DSM-III-R did not provide a way to differentiate those with hyperactive symptomatology, many of whom meet the "8 out of 14" criteria, from those who are not behaviorally impulsive. This makes subtyping research, which is pervasive in the literature, extremely difficult to interpret. It is important to reemphasize, however, that as odd as it may seem, one may be easily diagnosed as having Attention Deficit Hyperactivity Disorder without being hyperactive! And, in cases for which that doesn't work, but in which attentional dysfunction is a significant impairment to behavioral and social functioning, the Undifferentiated ADD category is available. In fact, Lahey and his colleagues (Lahey, Pelham, et al., 1988; Lahey, Piacentini, et al., 1988) found that 13 of the 15 children in their study who met the criteria for ADDnoH under DSM-II also met the criteria for ADHD under DSM-III-R.

Despite the criticisms reported here, many experts believed that DSM-III-R was an improvement over earlier versions. In a report of the 1985 field trials of the DSM-III-R diagnostic criteria, reported three years after its publication, Spitzer, Davies, and Barkley (1990) state:

> Using as a standard the diagnosis of these disorders made by expert clinicians with experience with these disorders, the diagnostic criteria that were finally included in the DSM-III-R demonstrated high sensitivity, specificity, and internal consistency. (p. 690)

Two other important changes also occurred between the DSM-III and the DSM-III-R versions. First, under DSM-III-R, affective disorders could coexist with ADHD. Second, ADHD was moved out of mental disorders and included as a developmental disorder, under the category of disruptive behavior disorders (along with Oppositional Defiant Disorder and Conduct Disorder). Clearly, ADHD continued to be considered as a behavioral disorder, rather than a cognitive disorder. In fact, the association with Oppositional Defiant Disorder and Conduct Disorder suggests that ADHD is on a continuum with antisocial behavior.

The manual relegates Undifferentiated ADD to a sort of orphan category called "Other Disorders of Infancy, Childhood, and Adolescence." Its listing is separated from that of ADHD by 45 pages. Undifferentiated ADD is defined as follows:

> This is a residual category for disturbances in which the predominant feature is the persistence of developmentally inappropriate and marked inattention that is not a

symptom of another disorder such as Mental Retardation or Attention Deficit Hyperactivity Disorder, or of a disorganized or chaotic environment. Some of the disturbances that in DSM-III would have been categorized as Attention Deficit Disorder without Hyperactivity would be included in this category. Research is necessary to determine if this is a valid diagnostic category and, if so, how it should be defined.

(American Psychiatric Association, 1987, p. 95)

This seems to imply that in Undifferentiated ADD, one does not find significant symptoms of impulsivity or hyperactivity (Cantwell & Baker, 1988). Thus Undifferentiated ADD *could* capture those individuals who are ADD and not hyperactive, as well as those disenfranchised adults and adolescents who were once hyperactive but no longer have those symptoms. The one positive feature of UADD is that it, unlike ADD-Residual Type, does not require any past signs of hyperactivity.

Cantwell and Baker (1988) point out that ADHD is somewhat similar in form to Wender's (1971) concept of "minimal brain dysfunction." For this category, no specific single symptom or set of symptoms would be necessary criteria for the diagnosis (Cantwell & Baker, 1988).

DSM-IV

The most recent revision of the Diagnostic and Statistical Manual of Mental Disorders includes ADHD under a superordinate category of Attention-Deficit and Disruptive Behavior Disorders. Field trials for ADD/ADHD were conducted on a national sample of 440 children, ages 4-17, who were referred to child-study clinics as psychiatric inpatients or delinquents. Follow-up assessments were held every 12 months for four years. Based on this information, three subtypes of attention deficit disorders are described: one with predominant characteristics of inattention, one with predominant characteristics of hyperactivity/impulsivity (which were loaded together on factor analysis studies), and one that is a combined type. When hyperactivity and impulsivity are the major characteristics, the attention deficit disorder is primarily one of disinhibition: the individual has difficulty controlling his/her impulses and applying his/her skills. Inattention exists as difficulty with persistence and effort. When inattention is the major characteristic, the attention deficit disorder primarily involves selective and focused attention. The individual has difficulty knowing what to pay attention to, or sustaining that attention without losing focus.

THE DOUBTERS

There is not universal acceptance of ADHD as a legitimate disorder. In the mid-1970s, some suggested that hyperactivity was a myth created by intolerant teachers and parents and an inadequate educational system (Conrad, 1975; Schrag & Divoky, 1975). In the late 1980s (1987-1988), the Church of Scientology and its Citizens Commission on Human Rights waged a massive public campaign against ADHD's status as a disorder and its treatment with Ritalin (see Barkley, 1990a, for a review).

ADHD as a Motivation Deficit Disorder

Since the 1980s, a camp of investigators has pursued yet another line of analysis to explain the behaviors that characterize attention deficit disorder. Noting that problems with sustained attention were not always observed in different conditions, Barkley (1984) hypothesized that motivation deficits may be at the core of the attention deficit disorder syndrome. Neurologically based deficits in rule-governed behavior, and/or impaired responsivity to behavioral consequences, were reported to account for the impulsive, inattentive, and hyperactive behaviors associated with ADHD (Barkley, 1984, 1990a; Sergeant, 1988). Some support for this theory is found in neuroanatomical studies. Lou and associates (Lou, Henriksen, & Bruhn, 1984; Lou, Henriksen, Bruhn, Borner, & Nielson, 1989) found decreased activation of brain reward centers and their cortico-limbic regulating circuits. Beninger (1989) found that dopamine pathways were involved in regulating locomotor behavior and incentive learning.

Barkley (1984) summarized the support for his concept of Motivation Deficit Disorder as follows:

(1) its greater explanatory value in accounting for the more recent research findings on situational variability in attention in ADHD;
(2) its consistency with neuroanatomical studies suggesting decreased activation of brain reward centers and their cortical-limbic regulating circuits;
(3) its consistency with functions of dopamine pathways in regulating locomotor behavior and incentive or operant learning; and
(4) its greater prescriptive power in suggesting potential treatments for ADHD symptoms. (p. 26)

Yet the motivation deficit theory did not receive wide acceptance, and Barkley himself seems to have abandoned it in favor of labeling disinhibition and impaired executive functions as more central defining features. In fact, cognitive, neuropsychological, and neurobiological concepts of the attentional system and its function and dysfunction account very well for issues of dysregularity, dyscontrol, and variability across time, contexts, and different task demands. In a paper published in 1990, Barkley states that "the more complicated the task and hence the greater demand for planning, organizing, and executive regulation of behavior, the greater likelihood ADHD children will perform more poorly on the task than normal children" (Barkley, 1990a, p. 348).

Attention, as we discuss throughout this book, is a limited capacity system. The phenomenon of decreasing performance as information load increases in complex situations is readily explained by the model of a constantly and strictly limited attentional capacity. Decreased motivation might best be seen as a reflection of the dynamics of an attention system trying to cope with more than it can handle (Tucker & Williamson, 1984).

It is well documented that motivation and effort are embedded in the attentional system of the human brain (Kahnemann, 1973; McGuiness & Pribram, 1980; Mesulam, 1990; Tucker & Williamson, 1984, etc.). While motivation and other forms of attention influence each other in critical ways, this does not justify isolating motivation from its neurobiological and cognitive place in the attentional network (Mesulam, 1990). To isolate any contributing factor would be to ignore the centrality of the larger self-organizing system — in this case, the attentional system.

ADHD as a Cognitive Disorder

Throughout their storied history, attention deficit disorders have been called by diverse clinicians, researchers, and other interested parties by a variety of names — *minimal brain damage, minimal cerebral dysfunction, minimal brain dysfunction, hyperkinetic reaction, hyperkinetic impulse syndrome, hyperkinesis,* etc. — that were applicable to a broad population of children with diverse problems and multiple presentations. A sort of Tower of Babel has resulted. Cantwell (1977) states, "Since these terms have been used in widely divergent ways by different investigators, the same children have been described by different terms and different children by the same terms" (p. 524). In spite of the more scientific approaches used recently, there has not been much improvement in clarifying the situation Cantwell describes. Besides the problem of changing names, diagnostic criteria and validation studies describe a wide variety of individuals whose characteristics vary by the setting in which they were identified (e.g., those referred to mental health clinics vs. those referred to pediatricians, psychologists, neurologists, or schools; Epstein et al., 1991).

Further muddying the waters is the schism between the medical community and the educational community that developed in response to the minimal brain dysfunction era. According to Shaywitz and Shaywitz (1988),

> there developed a schism in the way the medical and the educational communities viewed the disorder. The medical literature accepted the term minimal brain dysfunction and incorporated the entity into a medical model. In contrast, the educational literature focused more on the findings of a learning difficulty and preferred to describe affected children as having a specific learning disability. (p. 374)

Initially, this divide served a functional purpose: educators did not practice medicine and physicians did not try to teach. Ideally, approaching the same problem from different perspectives might have led to sharing information and further understanding. In reality, a great separation developed, with each camp proceeding with research and interventions and dismissing the contributions of the other. There exists a perception that learning disabilities and attention deficit disorders represent distinct disturbances, although they exist in sometimes overlapping populations.

The range of symptoms covered by the inclusive term of minimal brain dysfunction was overwhelming. For that reason, it was divided up, and the idea that deficits in attention and disabilities in learning were intimately related was lost. In the ensuing efforts to divide and subdivide into more manageable groupings, and to avoid the association with the old terminology, relationships between attention deficit disorders and learning disabilities have been overlooked. For example, most everybody describes learning disabilities and attention deficit disorders as being neurologically based. Yet there seems to be an aversion to referencing minimal brain dysfunction and the possibility that learning and attentional disabilities are different parts of a unified phenomenon.

The definition of learning disabilities provided by U.S. law (IDEA, Part B) states:

> ... specific learning disabilities means a disorder in one or more of the basic psychological processes involved in understanding or in using language, spoken or written, which may manifest itself in an imperfect ability to listen, think, speak, read, write, spell, or to do mathematical calculations. The term includes such conditions as perceptual handicaps, brain injury, minimal brain dysfunction, dyslexia, and developmental aphasia. The category does not include children who have learning problems which are primarily the result of visual, hearing, or motor handicaps, or mental retardation, or emotional disturbance, or of environmental, cultural, or economic disadvantage. (Individuals with Disabilities Education Act, 1990)

Thus, according to the U.S. definition, a disorder characterized by a significant deficit in attentional function is a learning disability, on the basis of several inclusion criteria. Given that attention is "an underlying psychological process," and that it is "involved in understanding language, spoken or written," and that a disorder in it "may manifest itself in an imperfect ability" to perform the tasks and skills listed, then surely an attention deficit disorder qualifies as a learning disability (Cherkes-Julkowski & Stolzenberg, 1991). Some have disagreed, on the grounds that ADD/ADHD represents an emotional disturbance and thus is excluded from the above definition. This is an untenable position. Emotional disturbance may certainly be co-incidental, or comorbid, to ADD, and it may clearly be a secondary phenomenon, a response of the person to his difficulties in managing his behavior. But it is not at the center of the disorder. Emotional disturbance can coexist with learning disability as well.

A review of the handling of ADD/ADHD in the Diagnostic and Statistical Manuals reveals an ironic disregard for the cognitive component of attention. Initially, the syndrome named "hyperkinetic syndrome of childhood" was defined by the core symptoms of inattention and distractibility. Then the name shifted to "attention deficit disorder," to reflect the central deficit in attention — but the syndrome continues to be described and diagnosed on the basis of hyperactive behaviors. Nowhere, in any of the lists of symptoms, is its full impact on cognition acknowledged.

For all the above reasons, we prefer to take the broad path, lumping all "subtypes" of attention deficit disorders into one large, diverse group for the purpose of studying their fundamental common characteristic: neurologically-based cognitive dysfunction (Baumgaertel, Wolraich, & Dietrich, 1995). To maintain the emphasis on the cognitive aspects of the disorder, we shall use the term *attention deficit disorder* (ADD) or *disorders* (ADDs).[1]

The following is our definition:

Attention deficit disorders are neurobiologically based disabilities that have pervasive, variable, and potentially lifelong effects. Implicated areas of human functioning include self-regulation, organization, neuromotor integration, coordination, judgment, rule-governed and reward-response behavior, self-worth, school, work, and interpersonal performance.

The effects of this disorder are situation-dependent and reflect difficulty with the maintenance of consistency over time. Not all individuals have the same problems or to the same degrees. Attention deficit disorders are, first and foremost, characterized

---

[1] When we incorporate the term "ADHD," it is in recognition of the fact that a particular individual under discussion was diagnosed using that term, or in reference to other studies that use the term.

by attentional processes that are inadequate for coping with the demands of development, and for successful age-, context-, and abilities-appropriate functioning. The abilities to come to, stay at, and shift attention to internal and external stimuli are all affected to different degrees in different individuals, in different contexts, at different times.

As we noted in chapter 1, we believe attention is critical to all that is involved with learning. The DSM criteria have failed to acknowledge the impact of attention deficit disorders on thinking and learning. It is time to refine our conception of attention deficits to include problems in the regulation, control, and fluency of attention that affect individuals with this disorder, impeding higher-order and complex cognitive and social behaviors.

Summary of Nosology and Definitions

The nosology of attention deficit disorder has progressed through several stages, from moral disorder to brain damage to disruptive behavior disorder, with continued discussion of the role of activity level. The difficulty of systematic classification is enough to lead one to wish this disorder would just go away. It hasn't, and it won't, because it is real, and no serious investigator or clinician doubts its validity as a syndrome — cognitively, behaviorally, and biologically.

The varying definitions, depending on the criteria, have identified separate populations. The important point, and our point of departure, is that this is a disorder that has as its primary problem *an attentional deficit* with major impacts on cognitive functioning and therefore, on one's personality.

Etiology

Substantial research over the past quarter century has explored numerous possible etiologies for ADDs. Some of these have been disproved quite thoroughly, while others appear more promising. Barkley (1990) notes that much of the research completed to date is plagued by methodological problems and provides inconsistent and conflicting results. However, it is highly probable that a disorder as complex as attention dysfunction will have multiple etiologies. Nonetheless, many continue to hope that evidence from multiple lines of research, using different methods of measurement, will ultimately reveal the common neurological pathway(s) involved in this disorder.

Environmental Substances Factors. In the 1970s and 1980s, much attention was directed to the role of environmental toxins in producing hyperactivity and attention deficits. Feingold (1975) claimed that the majority of hyperactivity was due to food additives such as dyes, preservatives, and salicylates. Later, the focus shifted to refined sugar as the villain (Smith, 1975). Despite continued acceptance by the public, including many public school teachers, these theories have never been substantiated with scientific research. A recent, exquisitely well-controlled study by Wolraich and his colleagues (Wolraich et al., 1994) failed to find any correlation between refined sugar, artificial sweeteners, or placebos, and hyperactive or inattentive behavior.

Cool-white fluorescent lighting was also suggested to cause hyperactive behavior (Mayron, Ott, Nations, & Mayron, 1974). However, the study was refuted by the findings of a methodologically superior one (O'Leary, Rosenbaum, & Hughes, 1978), and this theory also appears to be at a dead end.

There is correlational evidence that connects cigarette smoking during pregnancy (by both mothers and fathers) with ADHD children (Nichols & Chen, 1981). It is possible that exposure *in utero* to cigarette smoke may contribute to some anoxic injury to the developing brain. Similarly, alcohol use by mothers during pregnancy is also associated with hyperactivity in the child (Shaywitz, Cohen, & Shaywitz, 1980). It is notable, though, that ADHD individuals are more likely to smoke and drink than non-ADHD individuals as adolescents and young adults. Given the genetic link in ADHD, it is also possible that the correlation between drinking and smoking is due to a genetically linked ADHD in both parent and child. Finally, there is some correlational evidence that body lead levels are associated with hyperactivity and attention problems (Thomson et al., 1989), although to a very limited degree.

Family Functioning and Conflict Factors. Several studies have shown a correlation between poor parental management and childrearing practices and ADHD behavior in the parents' children. While there was a tendency in the 1970s to blame the child's behavior on that of the parents, more rigorous study of the interactions between parents and child confirmed that there is, in fact, a certain synergy at work here. The ADHD children tended to be more difficult, disruptive, and noncompliant, while the mothers were more commanding and negative. The mothers' tendencies toward highly directive and critical behavior were reduced when their ADHD children were on stimulant medication, and increased when their children were on placebos.

Genetic Factors. A number of studies have examined the heritability of attention deficit disorders, with the most promising studies using monozygotic and dizygotic twin pairs (e.g., Goodman & Stevenson, 1989; O'Connor, Foch, Sherry, & Plomin,

1980; Willerman, 1973). These studies show a very high concordance (from 51% to 100% for monozygotic pairs, and from 17% to 33% for dizygotic pairs) for hyperactivity and inattention. Goodman and Stevenson (1989) suggest that heritability for ADHD may be as high as 30% to 50%.

Biological Bases for Attention Deficit Disorders

The role of brain damage or dysfunction has been a suspected cause of attention disorders since the very beginning of its conceptualization. New technologies that allow brief and indirect peeks into the functioning of the central nervous system — such as Positron Emission Tomography (PET scans), X-Ray Computed Tomography (CT scans), Magnetic Resonance Imaging (MRI), and Electroencephalography (EEG) — let researchers explore the neurological underpinnings of attention deficit disorders.

We must remember, though, that attention is embedded, in a complex way, into a larger cognitive system (Benson, 1991; Mesulam, 1990; Voeller, 1991). Colby (1991) states:

> While specific brain systems seem to be responsible for arousal of the organism, attention cannot be pinned down to a simple set of structures. Indeed, there is hardly any region of cerebral cortex beyond the primary and motor regions that cannot be shown to participate in some kind of attentional process. (p. S 90)

The attention network is complex and involves a number of brain areas, including the premotor cortex (Zametkin et al., 1990), the right parietal area (Mesulam, 1981), the reticular activating system (McGuiness & Pribram, 1980; Mesulam, 1990), and others. Attention influences varied cognitive functions, too, including activation and arousal (McGuiness & Pribram, 1980; Tucker & Williamson, 1984), vigilance, focused and sustained attention (Mirsky, Anthony, Duncan, Ahearn, & Kellam, 1991), inhibition, distractibility (Mirsky et al., 1991), and executive functions (Benson, 1991; Mirsky et al., 1991; Reader, Harris, Schuerholz, & Denckla, 1994; Schachar & Tannock, 1995).

The frontal areas are believed to be a major neuroanatomical site for executive function (Benson, 1991; Damasio, 1994; Stuss & Benson, 1986). However, frontal areas have multiple, reciprocal connections — both direct and indirect — with many other cortical and subcortical systems (Fuster, 1989). Therefore, any dysfunction that affects frontal areas is likely to have a negative influence on a wide range of functions based in other areas of the brain.

Communication within the brain depends on neurotransmitters, biochemicals that enable impulses to jump the synaptic gap between neurons. Pathways in frontal areas are rich in two neurotransmitters, dopamine and norepinephrine. Biochemical disturbances in these neurotransmitters have been implicated as a source of attention deficit disorders (Rogeness, Javors, & Pliszka, 1992; Shaywitz & Shaywitz, 1988; Tucker & Williamson, 1984).

Further evidence for the brain-biological basis for attention deficit disorders is provided through neuropharmacology. The central nervous system is responsive to both internal and external mechanisms for regulation of neurotransmitters at synaptic sites, and there are pharmacological agents that alter the function of neurotransmitters at various stages of activity (Rogeness et al., 1992). Pharmacologic interventions for attention deficit disorders, particularly as they affect a child's functioning in school, are discussed more fully in chapter 6.

3

The Nature of Attention

The concept of attention is a very large and complex one that encompasses nearly all aspects of human functioning. But while it is an essential component of human activity, attention is a limited-capacity system. This condition, *infinite demand* on a system with *finite resources,* creates a vulnerability to dysfunction and reveals the need for dynamic management or regulation of attention. We have emphasized the very broad nature of attention and its intricate embeddedness in the larger system of cognition. We will attempt to demonstrate what is central to the concept, particularly as it affects school learning and adaptation in general, without isolating attention from its essential cognitive context. In doing so, we are rooting our thoughts in systems theory (von Bertalanffy, 1968), self-organizing systems theory (Barton, 1994; Nicolis & Prigogine, 1989), and theories of neural networking (Courchesne, Chisum, & Townsend, 1994; Mesulam, 1990; Thatcher, 1989).

As part of the complex process of cognition, attention serves to maintain arousal and to fine-tune or highlight some aspect of thought or experience. Directing attention to an object is nothing less than becoming conscious of it. Objects of attention can be events or experiences in the external world — what we have come to call "things out there," as well as events, thoughts, or sensations internal to the self — "things in here" (Stolzenberg & Cherkes-Julkowski, 1991a). There has been some suggestion in the literature that attention is a shallow process, a fleeting experience that precedes cognition. Considering attention as it relates to sentience and consciousness lends it a far more profound status, if also a vulnerable one. In writing of waking from sleep, Freud (1965) said:

Becoming conscious is connected with the application of a particular physical function, that of attention — a function which as it seems, is only available in a specific
quantity, and thus may have been diverted from the train of thought in question
onto some other purpose. (p. 632)

THE WORLD OF ATTENTION IS ROUND

In the study of attention dysfunction, attention has been treated as if it were a
subcognitive process (Silver, 1990) that hands its contents over to deeper-level cognition (Craik & Lockhart, 1972), at which point thinking or learning can take place.
Earlier information-processing models of attention (Schneider & Shiffrin, 1977) depicted attention as the first step in the process of thinking. According to these models, attentional mechanisms bring in impressions; other, higher-level forms of thinking then act upon these impressions and give them meaning. This proposed system is
neat. Things happen one at a time. Everything is in its place, and there is a place for
everything. Upon closer inspection, however, it is clear that the model cannot explain
how attention and thinking actually work.

To begin with, there are an infinite number of things to attend to in the world —
even if we disregard the aspects of a person's internal world that demand attention.
Limitations in attention require repeated samplings of information to create some
representation of an entire context. The more complex the notion, the more information it contains and the more intricately that information is intertwined. Thinking,
then, involves a well-regulated rhythm, perhaps a juggle, of attending–interpreting–
attending–embellishing–attending–reinterpreting, and so on, ad infinitum. Attention
is a *recursive* process creating a continuous loop that can and must encompass increasing amounts of information.

Since there are an infinite number of things to which one could attend, limitations in attentional capacity create the need for controlled and modulated attention.
Sequencing is one device for segmenting experience into manageable units. As James
(1902) points out, sequencing is not a cognitive process in its own right (as is often
assumed in educational interventions for people with learning disabilities), but a
manifestation of attentional limitations. That is, since we lack the attention to sweep
an entire stimulus field at once, we are forced to deal in segments, sequenced over
time. In our view, these segments are not points along a linear trajectory, but a single
pass in the recursive process, a single lap through the cycle.

Despite the dominance of linear models in traditional approaches to artificial
intelligence (AI), current AI models (Hofstadter, 1995) argue that *no* aspect of cognition is linear. Many processes are active simultaneously. Attention would thus be one

aspect of a dynamic, parallel processing system. The system uses internal and external resources to continually evolve in nonpurposive, only vaguely predictable ways (Thelen & Smith, 1994).

In cognition, nothing comes "first." The process of attention is a dynamic one in which all subsystems relay messages back and forth in order to generate a complete thought or to orchestrate a complete response (Hofstadter, 1985). A cognitive event is influenced by both past and future events. The idea of hierarchy is one with which educators and developmentalists are all too familiar. They understand, for example, that a child needs to have trunk strength and control before she can walk, and needs to master object permanence before she can be aware of symbolic representation (Piaget & Inhelder, 1969). Addition precedes multiplication. But the reverse in each case is also true. The act of walking will help build trunk strength and control. And awareness of advanced algebra changes one's view of basic whole-number operations — much as the view from the top of a mountain is quite different from the one on the climb to the top (Bruner, 1985).

Thoughts, including their attentional demands, are assembled in real time, organized in cooperation with their situation (Thelen & Smith, 1994). Unlike what early behaviorists and information processing theory suggested, cognition is not based on gathering temporally discrete bits of data which are subsequently associated (Alkon, 1989). Rather, information is initially perceived (Gibson, 1979) and stored as integrated patterns. In fact, pattern storage has been identified both at the neuronal level of the brain and in computer simulations of human intelligence. Temporally related events that form a pattern are associated with changes in the flow of potassium ions from the cell cytoplasm to the cell membrane. The change is permanent when the information has been stored. The system is then ready to respond when confronted with aspects or analogues of the original pattern; in some sense the system is kindled (Leventhal, 1990). What has actually been stored — or, more accurately, potentiated — is a metaphoric "template" against which further experiences can be mapped. The system has gained the potential to reassemble a *pattern* rather than temporally or sequentially discrete events:

> Pattern storage — which is to say memory formation — is governed by a rather simple rule: pieces of a pattern will become linked together in a memory if the pieces are perceived more or less simultaneously. A pattern is formed and stored when a group of pieces or elements is associated in time. (Alkon, 1989, p. 42)

In summary, the cognitive system is a nonlinear, self-organizing system that requires attention to regulate itself adaptively. By perceiving, storing, and knowing in a more integrated way — i.e., at the level of the pattern — a cognitive system can consolidate information, and thus spare attentional resources. Without such consolidation, these resources might have been deployed across all the separate aspects of the information field.

Limited Capacity of the Attentional System

In a complex cognitive system that operates in a dynamic and multidirectional way, limitations upon attentional resources create a need for selection, focus, shift, deployment, and regulation. Difficulty in managing one's attentional resources leads to distractibility, a short attention span, and an inability to maintain sustained attention, vigilance, or controlled, effortful attention. In an infinite-capacity system, distractions would not matter. There would still be adequate attention to select and focus on a central theme, to coordinate all relevant cognitive processes, and to attend to more subtle nuances. But of course, this is not the case. In essence, all problems of attention are problems of regulating limited resources in response to infinite demands (Hallowell & Ratey, 1994).

Selective Attention

Understanding the limited capacity of the processing system is central to understanding attention (Kahneman, 1973; Navon & Gopher, 1979). It is this capacity limitation that necessitates efficient and effective deployment of attention. There is greater stimulus complexity in the world than we can know (Meldman, 1970; Posner, 1978), and our attentional and processing resources are limited.

One challenge is to select out those aspects of the environment (internal and external to the individual) that are relevant to the topic at hand. Choices must be made, and each choice comes at a cost, in terms of what is *not* attended to and in terms of the attention allocated to making and monitoring the choice itself. Choices are made in concert with what has been learned in the past, how it is structured, and therefore what a person is likely to recognize as salient, or — by virtue of developmental status and experience — to recognize at all (Chi, 1985; Piaget & Inhelder, 1969). In addition, choices are further determined by anticipated reward in interaction with the effects of novelty and habit (Levine, 1989). Choices do not happen at a discrete point in time; the act of selection requires a continual scanning or reading not only of internal frames of reference but also of the external stimulus world. All of these data need to be compiled and recompiled to determine what is the relevant dimension for selection (Zeaman & House, 1979) in an ever-changing stimulus field (internal and external).

Choices about the selected focus of attention rarely occur at a conscious level. Rather, competition arises among neural subsystems of cells, which code different properties of external stimuli. The excitatory and inhibitory competition among these subsystems determine which aspects of the stimulus world will be represented in working memory, where they are held on-line for further processing (Levine, 1989). Subsystems establish their interconnections as a result of repetitive experience. Neural networks that are strongly, possibly automatically, associated will be activated simultaneously and will dominate in the competition of what gets selected and submitted to working memory. Patterned excitation comes at the cost of inhibiting other, related networks of association and losing their input to working memory (Alkon, 1989). Also, any recently excited subsystem, however dominant, is less receptive to subsequent excitation. Thus novelty is a powerful determinant of what is selected for attention. And thus, the excitation-inhibition mechanism is one of the many examples of a self-organizing dynamic system in search of dynamic stability.

Levine (1989) argues that competitive events of this kind, at the neuronal level, explain, in part, why reinforcement schedules do not always have the power to control behavior. The forces that control behavior are far more fundamental — i.e., at the neuronal level — and come far earlier in the chain of events. These dynamics, which take place below the level of consciousness, indicate that *"no one is in charge here."* This is an essential principle of self-organizing systems and is explored throughout this book as a way of understanding attention and its role in cognition.

THE ATTENTION/WORKING MEMORY SYSTEM

The challenge for the attentional system is in highlighting various aspects of the internal or external world so that sense can be made of them within the larger context of cognition. To do so, attention must work in harmony with working memory and with previous experience.

Working memory, attention, and knowledge store (what one already knows) have been somewhat arbitrarily marked off and identified as separate systems (Wagner, 1996). Each feeds back and feeds forward to the others and to different aspects of the larger system. Each overlaps with other, related systems. For the purposes of this discussion, however, we will treat each as a separate element so that the dynamic relationships among them can be discussed.

Working Memory

Working memory has been defined in a number of ways. Some have claimed that it collects internal thoughts (memories, previously learned knowledge) and holds them on-line so that they can be seen in relationship to each other and manipulated in novel ways (Goldman-Rakic, 1992; Hofstadter, 1995). Others (Swanson, 1994; Tannock, Ickowicz, & Schachar, 1995) have emphasized that working memory comes into play whenever active processing is necessary to maintain information on-line. In this sense, working memory is distinguished from a hypothetical short-term memory store, which would allow for passive storage. Working memory can be thought of as a temporary holding area for partial solutions as complex information gets compiled gradually (Carpenter, Just, & Shell, 1990). In its role of information management, working memory overlaps with executive functions, which collaborate with many other functions to coordinate higher-level cognitive processes and strategic thinking. These processes keep information alive or "on-line" in working memory while releasing it to deeper-level analysis and to the permanent, integrated knowledge store.

The process of coordinating attention in the cognitive system is not a simple, unidirectional procedure. Knowledge structure helps determine what is relevant or novel and to what, therefore, an individual should or could attend. For this reason, there needs to be continual communication between current awareness and thought (mediated attentionally) and the deepest layer of potentiated memories and conceptualizations. In complex stimulus situations, executive functions serve to set and maintain goals, to plan and organize, to inhibit competitive or noncontributory processes, and to monitor all of these functions. All communications must pass through working memory. Whether information comes in from the outside world, or up from one's internal world, it must be held and managed temporarily in working memory.

Clearly, the boundaries among the components of the cognitive system are indistinct. The distinctions among attention, working memory, and executive function are particularly problematic. As stated by Mirsky et al. (1991), "the boundaries between 'attention' and 'executive function' are rather indistinct" (p. 130). Limitations originating in one system would automatically impose limitations on the others.

The limitations of working memory are extreme and well documented (Goldman-Rakic, 1992; Miller, 1956; Spitz, 1966). Studies done on very young children (Chi & Koeske, 1978) and on adults with mental retardation (Belmont & Butterfield, 1971) have established that basic capacity is no more than three bits of information at a time. It is true that functional capacity can be increased in adults with no identified cognitive disorder by chunking or clustering small bits into a larger, more cohesive unit (Miller, 1956; Hofstadter, 1995). Nevertheless, there are limits to how much capacity can be optimized for anyone, at any age. When some proportion of resources is devoted to optimizing or managing information, less is available for processing the information itself. There is a constant juggle to get information in, managed, analyzed, and out in order to make room for the next set of information. If the attentional-cognitive system is out of sync, it will overload or underestimate capacity, resulting in some degree of cognitive-attentional disorganization.

It is within the context of working memory limitations that attention is called upon to do its work. In its *highlighting* function, attention allocates working memory resources to some subset of information. The attention/working memory system is intimately interconnected and subject to the constraints of finite capacity. Because of resource limitations, attention and working memory create a metaphoric bottleneck (Kahneman, 1973), which becomes a source of vulnerability whenever cognition is at issue (Cherkes-Julkowski & Stolzenberg, 1992). Ideally, working memory and attention work in harmony, with attention transmitting just the right amount of information to working memory. Too much would mean overload, confusion, and frustration; too little would underestimate the optimal representation of complexity, bog down fluid processing, and add extra demands in terms of piecing things back together again.

Whenever there is a weakness anywhere in the system, it is likely to show up as a dysfunction in working memory and attention. Much like a runner's knee, it is the site that receives the most stress and is most vulnerable to excess demands or to any dysfunction anywhere within the system. You can't run without bending your knee. Cognition cannot take place without the regulatory contribution of attention/working memory. Capacity is most limited in a function that is vital and always in play (Cherkes-Julkowski & Stolzenberg, 1992).

Working memory requires active and controlled processing in order to maintain information on-line until meaning can be found. Requisite to specific activation strategies (such as rehearsal or other mnemonic devices) is generalized vigilance. We discuss this futher in chapter 4 as the regulation of activation and arousal.

INFLUENCES ON ATTENTION

Experience, Knowledge Structure, and Attention

Knowledge structure strongly influences attention. In Chi's (1985) view, it determines what is salient and creates an integrated frame for managing information. The more you know about something, the more likely that knowledge is to be intricately interconnected, and thus the faster access you have to relevant frames. As with a road system, the more access routes there are, the easier and quicker it is to travel back and forth between points of origin and destination (Cherkes-Julkowski & Gertner, 1989). Speed frees up limited resources, as does the integration and organization of information, which allows more information to be considered. Experienced chess players, regardless of their age, remember more about the board and remember more intricate configurations than novices who are older (Chi & Koeske, 1978). Deeper and better-integrated knowledge stores allow for informed and flexible decisions about relevance, which create the context for selective attention.

A lack of relevant frames for interpreting new information and experiences creates a drain on attention. This happens because the attentional system is uninformed about the optimal "cut" or subdivisions that should be made in the data. Without appropriate frames, the attender is likely to overfocus on what may be less relevant features, or to rely on literal acquisition of detail, probably resulting in overload and inefficiency. Alternatively, the attender might cope with the lack of a relevant frame by *under*focusing, trying to relieve the effort system by achieving a more holistic impression. This strategy is likely to end in vagueness, an overly broad interpretation, and nonretention. In a problem situation for which there are few previously learned reference points, adaptive functioning appears to consist of a well-regulated (attentional) oscillation between these two poles: taking a broad sweep and collecting more focal information (Hofstadter, 1995).

Experience, Cell Assemblies, and the Coordination of Attention

Support for the critical role of experience in selective attention comes from studies of neural networking. Levine (1989) takes issue with the position that reinforcement drives learning or behavior. He argues that attention selection is driven as much by existent patterns of neural activation as by the control induced through reinforcement schedules. Any stimulus situation activates multiple cell populations that are responsible for coding different kinds of stimulus properties — color, form, etc. Networks of cell assemblies develop as a result of repeated experience, repeated interconnection (Hebb, 1949).

While these cell assemblies enhance their own networked excitation, they inhibit other cell assemblies (Alkon, 1989). Since attention and working memory have limited capacity, there is continual competition for space in conscious awareness. The version of the event that enters working memory represents the dominant or selected part of the input, at least for that moment in time. What is attended to, then, depends upon previously stored knowledge structure in the form of cell assemblies, as well as upon immediate competition for excitation. The cycle self-organizes into transient patterns of activation and inhibition. When one set of synapses is activated, there is an increased production of neurotransmitters in that area. That set dominates. Eventually, however, transmitter release ends in depletion and the opponent channels become dominant. Thus novel stimuli demand attention, habituation takes place, and a new set of stimulus characteristics becomes novel.

The coordination of the effects of novelty and habit (reinforced behavior) on selective attention is thought to take place in the frontal cortex. In cases of animal or computer-simulated frontal damage, reinforcement effects can be weakened, perseveration may occur in unrewarded trials, or novelty may dominate reinforcement (distractibility) as a determinant of attention selection (Levine, 1989).

The implication is that some coordination, if not a control center, is necessary to manage the overwhelming and often conflicting demands on attention. According to this conceptualization, the attentional system, left to its own devices, would be at the mercy of novelty; its form would be determined by networks of cell assemblies which are associated over time and which interact capriciously with the effects of novelty. In fact, attention *is* capricious in the unschooled preschool-age child — and, of course, in the population of people with attention deficits.

Experience, in the forms of recent activation/novelty effects, associated cell populations, and reinforcement-based expectations, always affects attention. Again, a breakdown in any of the contributing processes will manifest itself as an alteration both in patterns of selective attention and in the resultant message sent to working memory. This is the beginning of the problem. Since the information or misinformation that enters working memory provides the content for further information processing, all of cognition is affected.

Novelty and Habituation

Novelty is a primary, involuntary, and powerful determinant of attention. An unexpected sight or sound will command immediate attention. At the earliest stages of development in infancy, novel stimuli appear to have nearly total command over attention (Fagan, 1982). Novelty orientation is a trait so reliable among infants that it is used repeatedly to study how infants process information and what aspects of a situation afford them generalization. Habituation is the flip side of novelty orientation. Once an individual has habituated (learned about) the stimulus, it ceases to be novel, and attention is freed up for the next, more novel experience.

Novelty is a primary source of arousal and orientation at all ages (McGuiness & Pribram, 1980; Tucker & Williamson, 1984). Orienting toward novel stimuli serves the adaptive function of alerting the individual to any change that might signal danger or a need to alter one's response mode. Rapid habituation facilitates novelty orientation by allowing the organism to recover quickly from a novel occurrence in order to be ready for the next. In this way the novelty–habituation cycle naturally drives a self-organizing scan of the stimulus field. Left to its own devices, this search for continual novelty would prohibit more narrow, sustained, and focal attention. In school environments, teaching styles provide decreasing novelty with increasing grade level. A particular student's need for more novelty is labelled as 'distractibility.' The search for continual novelty can manifest further as arousal-seeking and risk-taking — key symptoms of deficits in the attention system.

As an individual matures, a dynamic self-organizing regulation evolves to meet demands for more focal and sustained attention. Activation of a more focal kind serves as a check on the draw of novelty. This dynamic self-regulation has clear roots in the neurochemical system. The dynamic interaction between novelty and habituation is discussed extensively in chapter 4 and receives some attention as the basis for motivation in chapter 5.

Automaticity and Capacity Utilization

Well-integrated, highly associated knowledge networks are one mechanism for enhancing limited capacity; *automaticity* is another. Automaticity, or non-effortful attentional processing, stands in contrast to controlled, effortful attention. Control processes themselves consume some part of limited capacity (Kahneman, 1973) and can thus contribute to a breakdown in the attention-working memory system.

For schoolchildren, the effects of a lack of automaticity are seen most vividly when complex processing is required. A child must decode efficiently in order to spend all her available capacity on interpreting complex, embedded language as a part of reading comprehension (Cherkes-Julkowski & Stolzenberg, 1991b; Perfetti & Lesgold, 1977). This efficiency is necessary for reading lengthy passages while retaining the cognitive capacity necessary for building mental models (Carlisle, 1989; Johnson-Laird, 1983). Likewise, automatic access to number facts in arithmetic frees a child to process complex problem information, track his work during multistep procedures, or attend to the logic and linear progression of algebraic permutations.

Problems with automaticity and with attention are mutually reinforcing. As previously mentioned, a lack of automaticity decreases the availability of attention/working memory capacity. At the same time, children with impaired attention systems have a difficult time learning skills and arbitrary associations at an automatic level. Building automaticity requires sustained and vigilant attention in order to maintain and control arousal for the purpose of repeated associations (e.g., "2 plus 3 is five, 2 plus 3 is five ..." or "*a* is /a/"). Thus, it draws upon two of the central deficiencies of a child with an attentional disorder: (1) controlled, vigilant attention and (2) redundant, repetitive processing (Tucker & Williamson, 1984).

The fewer relevant automatic components available for a job, and the less automatic (more effortful) each is, the greater the drain on total capacity (Shiffrin & Dumais, 1984). Resources are likely to be consumed by lower-level processes — such as retrieving number facts or letter sounds — that would normally be handled by automatic responding. There is little left over for higher-level processing or thinking. The result appears to be a problem in tracking, abstraction, integrating information, or, most broadly, thinking. But is it? Treatment of executive functions such as self-monitoring or cognitive control strategies is not likely to work if the problem lies at the level of allocation of attentional resources to underdeveloped lower-level processes.

Allocation of Resources

The challenge for the limited capacity attentional/working memory system is to regulate the allocation of resources. It is only in the context of "attention-demanding tasks" (Porges, 1983) that the regulatory system is challenged at all. In a relatively unaroused state of simple wakefulness, there is little challenge to the limited capacity of attentional processes. All aspects of selective attention, however, require mental effort. Even when attention is captured involuntarily by novel stimuli, mental effort may be implicated in the act of focusing (Kahneman, 1973; Shiffrin & Dumais, 1984). The issue of voluntary vs. involuntary attention refers only to how the subject matter of attention is determined, not to the effort inevitably involved in focus (James, 1902).

When the stimulus world is too complex for a limited-capacity system to receive, the challenge for that system is to deploy resources efficiently and with the greatest return (Navon & Gopher, 1979). Ideally, attentional resources should be invested in the most cost-effective way, achieving optimal return (awareness, success in school, learning, communicating ...) while maintaining a well-regulated homeostasis.

Describing the challenges of the attentional system, Navon and Gopher (1979) use the metaphor of a manufacturing plant. Decisions about optimal output/functioning must be made with regard to the limitations of material and personal resources and the degree of stress on the entire operation. The challenge is to reach maximal performance without placing undue stress on machinery or personnel, so that the entire operation doesn't "burn out." For this reason, factories do not generally work at full capacity. So it is with the attentional system. Kahneman (1973) uses a different metaphor to describe the possibility of "burnout":

> Consider again the electrical analogy. In that analogy, the concept of a limited capac-
> ity has a precise meaning. The generator can only supply a certain amount of power.
> When the demands exceed that amount, the addition of one more toaster or air
> conditioner to the circuit no longer results in a corresponding increase of electrical
> output. In some systems, overload actually causes the total power supplied by the
> source to decrease. (p. 15)

In human beings, the result may be shutdown, oppositional behavior, or decrease in
motivation.

Attention Deployment

The issues of allocation of resources, selective attention, and attention deployment
are intricately interconnected. Selection and deployment become issues because of
resource and capacity limitations. In order to continually monitor whether or not
attention is placed correctly, it is necessary to reserve some attentional resources to
continually scan a situation, look for alterations, and judge whether attention is
being used most effectively.

Problems of attention selection and deployment are exacerbated whenever the
stimulus world is changing at a rapid pace. The need to make rapid attentional shifts
is most dramatic when stimuli enter through the aural channel. Spoken words or
sounds disappear, evaporate. Visual stimuli can remain available to be taken in at a
self-determined pace or to be reexamined if attention flags. The difference between
performance based on visual input and that based on auditory input has been a
major theme in the understanding and treatment of learning disabilities. Typically,
the difference has been attributed to differences between auditory and visual perceptual processing. We believe, however, that the difference is due in large part to the
different demands made on working memory and attention deployment.

The demand for well-deployed attention increases with the complexity of the situation. Simply put, the richer the information field, the more one must attend to. Of
course, these demands refer to external as well as internal stimuli. From this perspective, efficient attention regulation is most critical at higher levels of cognitive function. At the base of fluid and creative problem solving, there seems to be an attention
system that facilitates a dynamic swing between a broad sweep of the stimulus field
and a more focal sampling of more refined, specific attributes (Hofstadter, 1995).

It is the dynamic swing between these two extremes that is likely to protect the system from overload. Getting stuck at the point of collecting details that do not cohere is overwhelming from the perspective of information management. Getting stuck at the point of looking for the broad view or underlying principle could also be overwhelming, particularly when the relevant concepts are elusive.

Efficient attention deployment is particularly crucial whenever there is a need for rapid, responsive attentional shifts. Nowhere is this need greater than in the context of interpersonal relationships and communication. Social dynamics are complex and unpredictable. They emerge out of the idiosyncratic dynamics of the moment and thus demand spontaneous, immediate, and creative responses. For example, a conversational topic can change instantly, creating a need for attentional shift. Gestural and verbal allusions require an individual to make further rapid associations. It is important to attend to where the eyes are focused when a communication partner says, "Watch out for *him*." And one must attend to tone, prosody, intonation, syntax, word choice, etc., to fully appreciate communicative intent.

Attention dysfunction, then, is likely to manifest as an "auditory processing" problem or as difficulty with communication and social interaction (Cantwell & Baker, 1991; Goldstein & Goldstein, 1990). These are important areas to monitor whenever attentional difficulties are suspected. Conversely, when social, communicative, or "auditory" processing problems are noticed, it is important to consider the potential role of attention in their breakdown.

The Role of Executive Function

As we have discussed, the challenge for the attention/working memory system is to coordinate complex thinking and functioning despite capacity limitations. The notion of executive function (similar to metacognition) has been invoked as a site and an agency for central, internal coordination of the many aspects of cognition (Fuster, 1989). The executive agency regulates and orchestrates the smooth management and association of information, ultimately aiming to optimize capacity. Other executive functions include forming, maintaining, and shifting set; enhancing mental effort; setting and adhering to a goal; invoking foresight; planning; monitoring or tracking; and inhibiting prepotent responses. The regulatory aspects of executive function are discussed further in chapter 4. In this section, we focus on goal-related functions and on inhibition.

Instruction sets goals and provides supports so that the learner can maintain the goal and progress toward it. The purpose of goal-setting is to narrow the relevant information field and thus constrain the degrees of freedom in both behavior and attention. A learner who is able to internalize the goal and the concomitant constraints is said to have learned (Cherkes-Julkowski & Mitlina, submitted for publication; Shaw, Kadar, Sim, & Repperger, 1992). In children with ADDs, breakdowns in executive functions threaten this process at each point along the way.

The executive function of *inhibition* plays a major role in the regulation of attention. Inhibition of prepotent responses allows for maintenance of goal-directed thought and activity and helps maintain information on-line, active in the mind, when there are response delays. Without adequate inhibition, each feeling and thought that had immediate potency would compete for attention and limited working memory resources, disrupting focus and goal-directed behavior. This state of distractibility is often at the heart of attention disorders.

Structural vs. Functional Limitations

As we have mentioned before, the attention/working memory component depends upon previous experience and previously associated networks of information. Early in the study of short-term memory (STM; Spitz, 1966), the prevalent theory held that there were initial structural limitations to capacity and that structural changes accompanied development (Piaget & Inhelder, 1969). Higher-level structures and greater capacity were thought to unfold through neuromaturation triggered by experience. Later thinking suggested that span limitations were less structurally determined and were due instead to deficiencies in the production of strategic thinking generated by the mythical "executive homunculus" (Edelman, 1992; Flavell, 1985). Again, it was believed that young children and populations with disorders in learning were most seriously limited. More recently, attention/working memory has been conceptualized as a function of domain-specific knowledge, depending on the amount of information stored and the degree to which it is interconnected (Chi, 1985). Current theories of schema (script, frame, or other relational terminology) and span limitations also address the role of patterned environmental events in providing pre-organized, consolidated information and thus reducing the information load in working memory (Caron & Caron, 1981; Rogoff, 1990). Well-regulated processing (executive function) has also assumed an important role in coordinating challenging amounts of information (Breslin & Weinberger, 1991; Carpenter, Just, & Shell, 1990).

Attentional Limitations and Language Functions

As illustrated above, *span* or attentional capacity is in part reliant on a well-integrated knowledge store. Children who lack experience will have more limited functional capacity. A further limitation on attentional functioning can be caused by a disorder in language processing. Language is a mechanism for sustaining activation of information. It facilitates controlled working memory strategies, directing mental effort in the form of rehearsal or other controlled verbal mediation strategies. Children who are deficient in rapid automatic naming (RAN) — or, stated otherwise, who lack efficient (phonologically driven) access to their lexical and semantic networks — are likely to manifest attentional limitations that are atypical for their developmental status. In our work we have found an interaction between attention disorders and language disorders, which renders children's efforts to cope with capacity limitations nearly nonfunctional and causes them to experience extreme difficulty adapting to typical instructional supports. In fact, Wood (1991) has found that together ADD and deficiencies in RAN are the greatest predictors of negative academic outcomes, including unresolved dyslexia and fewer years of education.

Multidirectional Influences among Component Processes

We do not mean to imply anything about the direction of causality, i.e., whether attention problems cause deficient knowledge or deficiencies in the knowledge store cause attention problems. Limitations in attention/working memory/executive function contribute to difficulties with incidental learning and knowledge acquisition in general. Impoverished knowledge stores fail to create the efficient retrieval and convenient frames for chunking, compressing, organizing, associating and elaborating upon information; all of these processes would have helped maximize span and decrease capacity allocations to control, strategy selection, and usage processes. In the end, the problems are *integrated* attentional/working memory/executive function problems. Our question concerns how the problems should be treated.

Certainly some part of intervention will have to address the complex of many attentional and other cognitive correlates that surround "the problem" and that *become* the problem regardless of its source, if indeed a single source can be conceptualized (Cherkes-Julkowski & Stolzenberg, 1992). Even when they are probably not the source of the problem, attentional manifestations should be treated, perhaps even pharmacologically (Davy & Rogers, 1989). Because everything is connected, there is no wrong place to start. Relief for the system can be given at any point along the way with the hope of freeing up more resources to yield improved functioning. However, because everything is connected, multimodal interventions are most efficacious.

Manifestations in School

Attention dysfunction is bound to have widespread effects in school and elsewhere. The most obvious and frequently cited concerns associated with ADD, distractibility and inattention, are often described in schools as off-task behavior, failure to complete assignments in a timely manner, difficulty working independently, failure to do homework, failure to participate in group discussions, and/or lack of motivation.

Table 3.1a–c compiles a series of behavioral ratings, grades, and teacher comments that appear in the elementary school report cards of a child identified later as having Attention Deficit Disorder. The reports come from a year in kindergarten (3.1a), a transitional first-grade year (3.1b), and then a year in a regular first grade (3.1c). Nearly all this student's work habits are of concern at one point or another. Social development is also an area of serious and consistent concern. The teachers make further comments about his problems with obeying rules and his need for structure and reinforcement. And of course, there is the inevitable lament, "If he would only pay attention." Note, too, the wide discrepancy among grades for academic progress. This child has a full-scale IQ of 124 and would ordinarily not be expected to have difficulty achieving in the early elementary grades.

Distractibility/Disinhibition

Distractibility is an essential part of attention breakdown. It seems based in an inability to resist novelty, an active seeking-out of arousal in the form of novelty, and, simply, a lack of focal attention. Since all schooling (at least traditional schooling) requires sustained and focused attention, distractibility has extreme effects on school adjustment as well as on others' perceptions of the person in question. Distractible students will often not hear portions of lectures or discussions. Distraction is also a problem while performing repetitive, low-arousal tasks, such as computation practice drills or assignments that call for finely tuned analyses involving repeated readings or careful, systematic presentation of an idea. Once a child or adult with attention deficits has an intuition and a vague feeling of knowing, the task ceases to offer the kind of arousal necessary for sustained focus. The person with attention deficits is off (and very possibly running) in search of something else. It should come as no surprise that people with ADDs often complain of boredom. Many children and young adults have developed the fine art of actually doing the work while never attending to it at all, much like driving a familiar route and having no conscious awareness of where you have been.

Distractibility can disturb internal thought processes as well. One eighth-grade

Table 3.1a

KINDERGARTEN

CODE: MATH — LANGUAGE ARTS

NO MARK INDICATES THAT INSTRUCTION HAS NOT BEGUN.
/- INDICATES THAT THE STUDENT IS RECEIVING INSTRUCTION BUT ASSESSMENT HAS NOT OCCURRED.
A- INDICATES THAT AN INDIVIDUAL ASSESSMENT HAS OCCURRED BUT THE STUDENT HAS NOT PERFORMED THE SKILL CONSISTENTLY.
X- INDICATES THAT AN INDIVIDUAL ASSESSMENT HAS OCCURRED AND THE STUDENT CONSISTENTLY PERFORMS THE SKILL.

CODE: SCIENCE, SOCIAL STUDIES, ATTITUDES, WORK HABITS, MOTOR DEVELOPMENT AND FINE ARTS

S- SATISFACTORY
I- IMPROVING
N- NEEDS MORE TIME AND HELP

MATH

	TERM 1	2	3
NUMBER			
IDENTIFIES NUMBERS 0-10	X	X	X
SEQUENCES NUMBERS 0-10	X	X	X
MATCHES WITH ONE-TO-ONE CORRESPONDENCE			
MATCHES SETS AND NUMBERS	X	X	X
IDENTIFIES ORDINAL POSITION			
ACTS OUT ADDITION AND SUBTRACTION STORIES	X	X	X
COUNTS BY 1's TO 130	20	30	134
COUNTS BY 10's to 100		60	100
GEOMETRY			
IDENTIFIES AND NAMES SHAPES	X	X	X
COMPARES OBJECTS BY LENGTH			
MEASURES THE LENGTH OF OBJECTS			
COPIES GEOBOARD DESIGNS			
COVERS TANGRAM DESIGNS			
OTHER SKILLS			
SORTS OBJECTS AND IDENTIFIES A SORTING RULE			X
COPIES AND EXTENDS PATTERNS			X
CREATES A REAL GRAPH			
NAMES THE DAYS OF THE WEEK			
IDENTIFIES COINS			

COMMENTS

J behavior has progressed nicely. If he paid attention more his academics would improve highly. I would like to Make an appointment to improve. I discuss J progress.

LANGUAGE ARTS

	TERM 1	2	3
DEMONSTRATES ENJOYMENT FOR LISTENING TO STORIES AND POEMS			
TALKS ABOUT BOOKS/STORIES			X
MAKES PREDICTIONS OF STORY EVENTS			
RECALLS MAIN TOPIC, CHARACTER, AND IMPORTANT DETAILS FROM A STORY			
SEQUENCES STORY EVENTS		X	X
DRAWS A PICTURE TO TELL A STORY ABOUT A PERSONAL EXPERIENCE			X
WRITES A STORY USING INVENTED SPELLING			X
NAMES LOWER CASE LETTERS OUT OF SEQUENCE			
NAMES UPPER CASE LETTERS OUT OF SEQUENCE			X
RECOGNIZES AND SUPPLIES RHYMING WORDS			
RECOGNIZES THE INITIAL CONSONANT LETTER OF A SPOKEN WORD			X
PRINTS FIRST NAME			X

SCIENCE

	TERM 1	2	3
DEMONSTRATES INTEREST	S	S	S

SOCIAL STUDIES — Computer

	TERM 1	2	3
DEMONSTRATES INTEREST	S	S	S

COMMENTS

J is doing better. He still needs to work at paying attention. I still believe his academics would improve if he paid more attention.

ATTITUDES AND WORK HABITS

	TERM 1	2	3
WORKS AND PLAYS WELL WITH OTHERS			
ACCEPTS CONSTRUCTIVE CRITICISM AND DISAPPOINTMENT	X		
DEMONSTRATES SELF-CONFIDENCE			
MANAGES CLOTHING	X		
TAKES CARE OF PERSONAL NEEDS	X		
KEEPS HANDS AND MATERIAL OUT OF MOUTH	X		
FOLLOWS DIRECTIONS			
PAYS ATTENTION	X		
LISTENS WITHOUT INTERRUPTING	X		
SHOWS EFFORT IN HIS/HER WORK			
WORKS INDEPENDENTLY	X		
CONTRIBUTES TO CLASS DISCUSSION	X		

MOTOR DEVELOPMENT

	TERM 1	2	3
DEVELOPING FINE MUSCULAR CONTROL (CUTTING, COLORING, PRINTING, ETC.)	S	S	S
DEVELOPING LARGE MUSCULAR CONTROL (HOPPING, SKIPPING, RHYTHMIC STEPS, ETC.)	S	S	S

FINE ARTS

	TERM 1	2	3
SHOWS INTEREST IN MUSICAL ACTIVITY	S+	S+	S
USES VARIOUS ART MATERIALS APPROPRIATELY	S	S	S
KNOWS COLORS			

COMMENTS

J has come a long way since the beginning of the year! I am so very proud of him! Keep it up. I know you can!

QC 0111

Table 3.1b

CLASS: TRANSITIONAL

NOTICE TO PARENTS

THIS REPORT OFFERS AN OPPORTUNITY FOR BETTER UNDERSTANDING OF YOUR CHILD'S CURRENT ACHIEVEMENT. ITEMS NOT NOTED WERE NOT EVALUATED AT THIS TIME. FEEL FREE TO COMMENT ON BACK OF REPORT.

EVALUATION KEY

I—Improving
S—Satisfactory
N—Needs Improvement

COMMENTS SHOULD BE READ CAREFULLY TO FULLY UNDERSTAND YOUR CHILD'S ACADEMIC PROGRESS.

LANGUAGE ARTS

	Period 1	Period 2	Period 3
RECOGNIZES NAME IN PRINT			
IDENTIFIES LOWER CASE LETTERS			
IDENTIFIES UPPER CASE LETTERS			
RECOGNIZES COLORS			
RECOGNIZES RHYMING SOUNDS			
UNDERSTANDS LEFT TO RIGHT PROGRESSION			
RECOGNIZES SOUNDS OF LETTERS			
BLENDS SOUNDS INTO WORDS			
RECALLS SEQUENTIAL ORDER			
REMEMBERS MAIN IDEAS			
RECOGNIZES LIKENESSES AND DIFFERENCES			
ABLE TO EXPRESS IDEAS IN A COMPLETE SENTENCE			
REPEATS RHYMES FROM MEMORY			
KNOWS NAME, ADDRESS AND PHONE NUMBER			
SPEAKS CORRECTLY			
PARTICIPATES IN DISCUSSIONS AND ACTIVITIES			
FORMS LETTERS CORRECTLY			
FORMS NUMBERS CORRECTLY			
PRINTS FIRST AND LAST NAME			
WRITES NEATLY AND LEGIBLY			
Listens to a story			

SOCIAL STUDIES/SCIENCE

	Period 1	Period 2	Period 3
UNDERSTANDS PRESENTED CONCEPTS			
PARTICIPATES IN DISCUSSIONS			
Science			
Computer			

MOTOR DEVELOPMENT

	Period 1	Period 2	Period 3
LARGE MUSCLE CONTROL (HOPPING, SKIPPING, JUMPING)			
SMALL MUSCLE CONTROL (CUTTING, DRAWING, PRINTING)			
ART			
MUSIC			
Gym			
Journal Writing			
Sight Vocabulary			
Homework			
DAYS ABSENT			

SOCIAL and EMOTIONAL DEVELOPMENT

	Period 1	Period 2	Period 3
COOPERATES WITH OTHERS			
DEMONSTRATES SELF CONTROL			
DISPLAYS RESPONSIBILITY			
LISTENS WITHOUT INTERRUPTING			
DISPLAYS SELF CONFIDENCE			
CLAIMS ONLY HIS/HER SHARE OF TEACHER ATTENTION			
ACCEPTS SHARING AND TAKING TURNS			
ACCEPTS & RESPECTS AUTHORITY			
RESPECTS RIGHTS AND PROPERTY OF OTHERS			
RESPONDS FAVORABLY TO CORRECTION			

WORK HABITS

	Period 1	Period 2	Period 3
DISPLAYS PRIDE IN WORK			
COMPLETES TASK TO BEST OF ABILITY			
WORKS ACCURATELY AND INDEPENDENTLY			
FOLLOWS VERBAL DIRECTIONS			
PARTICIPATES IN VARIETY OF ACTIVITIES			
HAS AN ADEQUATE ATTENTION SPAN			
WORKS WELL IN A GROUP			
USES TIME WISELY			

PROMOTED TO: Grade 1.   ROOM 6.

FIRST PERIOD COMMENTS

Although J_____ has shown progress in most academic areas, he still has difficulty in conforming to school and room rules. When J_____ settles down, he does better work. However, his work habits are disruptive and often distract the other children. I'd be happy to meet with you about J_____ progress at anytime.

PARENT SIGNATURE _____

SECOND PERIOD COMMENTS

J_____ continues to show progress in most academic areas. Small muscle control has shown a great deal of improvement but can be inconsistent. Social skills and work habits have come a long way this period. J_____ has been trying very hard to do his best and he really seems excited about his progress.

THIRD PERIOD COMMENTS

J_____ is a sweet little boy. He has really come a long way this year, ☺ (especially this past month). It has been a pleasure working with J_____, it was exciting to watch his growth and progress. Have a wonderful!

Table 3.1c

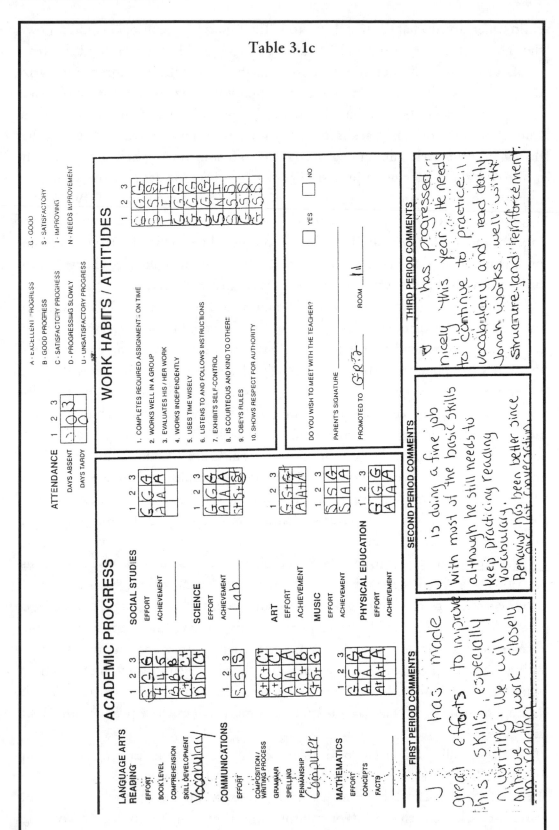

child, when asked what her first day taking Ritalin was like, replied, "I could follow a thought all the way to the end." Evidence of the jumble of ideas resulting from unplanned, triggered associations can be seen in the way these children summarize their thoughts, whether in speech or in writing. Ideas come out as bursts of information. Sentences can be rambling or run-on. Peripherally related thoughts often intrude. Often the original track is lost altogether, as one association leads to another that is even less relevant, and so on. Letters and sometimes whole words may be omitted in the transcription process. Figure 3.1 (p. 51) provides a writing sample in response to the picture stimulus on the Test Of Written Language-2 (TOWL-2) of a second-grade child who has an attention deficit disorder. In addition to the bursts of thought and the poorly controlled phonetic spellings, there are significant graphomotor problems and apparent attentional neglect of the left visual field. (See chapter 10 for further discussion of the writing problems associated with ADD.)

In our teaching experience, we have found that distractions can be reduced and sustained focus enhanced by using a number of techniques to increase arousal. A traditional recommendation is to switch tasks frequently. Providing environments that block out potential distractors is *not* helpful, since those environments also tend to reduce arousal/vigilance. Of course, the tasks that hold the most meaning for the learner will be more arousing (interesting) and therefore less vulnerable to distraction. Unfortunately, this dynamic often works against the child, since teachers can interpret distraction as a lack of motivation. The child *can* do a task when he is interested; failure to complete a task, therefore, is assumed to happen because the child didn't care or didn't want to. We have urged teachers to substitute the word "aroused" for *interested* or *motivated* so that the emphasis is placed, appropriately, on biology and not on character.

Perhaps the best way to maintain arousal, and thus the best defense against distraction, is to keep the child physically active. Any kind of hands-on activity or activity requiring gross motor movement would fall into this category. To teach letter names to a young child, hide the letters and ask the child to find them. Even writing, using letter tiles, or cutting out letters to practice letter names and sounds is incorporating some kind of action. More generally, allowing a child some motor activity while she is working is likely to enhance her sustained and focused attention. The old saying "sit still so you can pay attention" is simply *wrong* where people with ADDs are concerned.

Pedagogically, action has held an important position in learning. Piaget and Inhelder (1969), and later the followers of Gibson (Adolph, Eppler, & Gibson, 1993; Thelen & Smith, 1994), have made a strong case for the fact that our actions and perceptions affect each other. (For example, an organism that locomotes on two legs

Figure 3.1

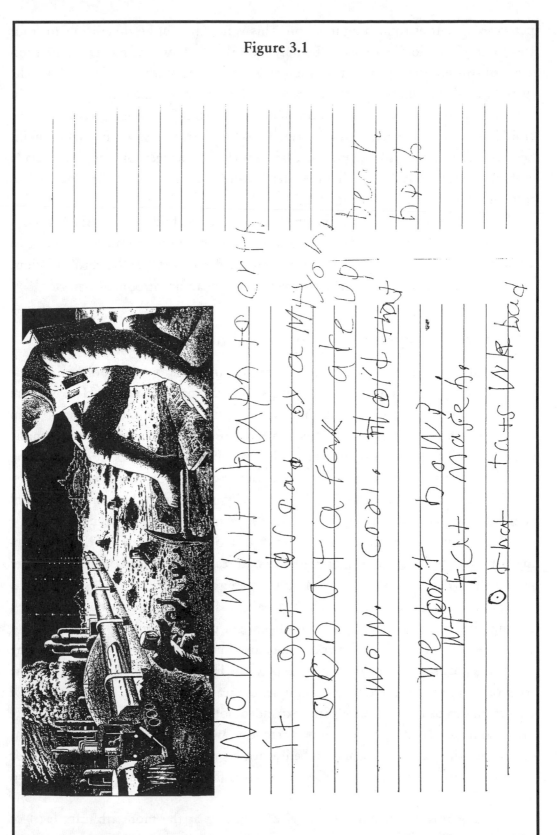

perceives a chair as something to sit on. This is not true for an organism with four legs.) But action does not have to be only motoric. Any form of mental prehension also constitutes activation and thus enhances focus and wards off distraction. The instructional challenge is to create this activation. Much like the way a parent might teach a child how to swim — by holding the goal close but far enough away so that the child has to swim one more stroke to reach it — the instructional environment might be designed to constantly require that last stretch. The danger, of course, especially with children with ADDs, is that the stretch will be too much and the rapid rise to frustration will interfere with learning.

Distraction is no less of a problem socially. Because children with ADDs do not always follow what their classmates are saying, they are prone to misinterpret or to ask annoyingly for repetitions. As speakers, furthermore, they can be hard to follow, since one uncompleted thought gets crowded out by an unintroduced new one.

Working Memory and Conscious Awareness

Perhaps the most undermining aspect of attention dysfunction in schools is the negative impact it has on controlled and active working memory processes. Here is where controlled focus is most essential, since strategies must be invoked in order to keep information actively on-line until deeper meaning (or less conscious, more automatic responding) is achieved. Any time a child has to make arbitrary associations, working memory is a critical factor. This is true in all out-of-context learning — which conceivably includes all in-school learning. It is especially needed when memorizing symbol systems, routines, or formal procedures that have not been rooted in meaning.

One might, then, expect children with ADDs to have histories of difficulty learning letter names, letter sounds, or math facts. In reading they might not notice letter patterns (-ough, -cient, ph-, and so on) or associate them with the sounds they make. Later, in math, algorithms for which the meaning is not immediately obvious — such as long division or division by a fraction — might prove difficult.

To reduce the burden on working memory, instruction must provide meaning when it is possible. Algorithms can be explained. They do not need to remain in the zone of arbitrary associations. For example, the reason underlying the long division algorithm can be demonstrated using expanded notation. A picture can demonstrate the meaning of dividing a fraction by a fraction. Awareness of orthographic patterns can reduce the number of words to be learned by sight and reveal something about more patterned systematic principles of decoding (as with *sight, might, right, fight,* and *flight*).

It is not possible to find this level of meaning at the more arbitrary level of symbol systems. In the case of symbol learning, the approach would have to ensure vigilance and active attention while practicing skills (i.e., memorizing that *3* stands for the amount • • •, or that *B* makes the sound of /b/). Tactics that might improve a child's vigilance include rehearsing with an adult, saying the associations aloud, saying and writing them simultaneously, or playing computer games which maintain well-modulated arousal. It might also help for teachers to vary the form of practice drills, and to provide spaced rather than massed practice.

Teachers and children alike often express their primary complaint as one of forgetting. The children may forget classroom routines (putting homework into the homework bin), or they may feel as if they know something immediately after a lesson, then later — perhaps on a test — find that they cannot recall the information. It is likely that the problem lies within the attention system rather than in memory *per se*.

In the case of "forgetting" to hand homework in, to bring proper materials to class, or to perform any other routine responsibility, the problem seems to be one of conscious awareness. More arousing distractions co-opt attentional space. Contingency systems that reinforce appropriate behavior *consistently fail to improve the situation*. Nevertheless, they continually appear in educational plans as nearly the sole approach to solution.

Given the nature of the problem, an effective intervention would need to bring the issue to the child's conscious level of attention. The teacher might leave a note or picture representation on a child's desk asking him to list his morning responsibilities or to list what he must bring to class. If he has routine responsibilities, he can be asked to tell what three things he is supposed to do each morning as he enters school — or, for that matter, each morning before he leaves for school, or each afternoon when he returns home. The emphasis here is not simply on giving the child a checklist. This strategy uses the teach-the-child-to-swim metaphor, as the child must actively bring his responsibilities to conscious awareness and rehearse them with full attention. Only then might he have a real memory of what they are.

Similarly, in preparing for a test, a student might read or review her notes and be able to understand them as she goes. This does not mean, however, that she has done the active coding that would make her understanding explicit and thus more likely to be freely retrieved at test. Consciously and explicitly processed information is easier to retell on a test, since linguistic form has already been given to it. Students with ADDs are often surprised when the information seems to have disappeared in the testing situation. Ironically, they can often tell much more if prompted with nonsubstantive clues such as "Tell me more" or "Anything else?" Prompts such as these, therefore, are an important test-taking accommodation.

Coping with Being Overwhelmed

Dysregulation in the attention system can contribute to the feeling of being over-whelmed. Since children with ADDs express their frustration filtered through fewer controls, they are more outspoken about their frustration and thus more annoying to others. Being overwhelmed, then, can be especially debilitating for them. Teachers can help their students avoid being overwhelmed by providing supports at the level of attention regulation. They can orchestrate that swing between gist and detail which the children cannot manage on their own. The teacher might ask the child just to describe what she can notice about a situation. When the string of information bits is getting too large, the teacher might provide the impetus for a switch to a broader sweep. This might be done through a series of questions that invoke analogues to be used as organizing, condensing frameworks. For example, the teacher might ask, "What does this remind you of?" Alternatively, the teacher can model the process, saying, "This reminds me of a _____" or "This reminds me of the time we _____." Any prompt that switches processing to a more fluid form could be effective. With infor-mation consolidated in this way, the child could be led back to a more focal examina-tion, and so on.

Knowledge Comes From Knowledge

A well-integrated knowledge store reduces attention demands to the extent that mean-ing comes more efficiently and the information field is functionally condensed. Thus, less of a demand is made on effortful, controlled attention and working memory processes. Less of a demand is made on limited capacity. The more a child with attention deficits can be taught, the less likely it is that his attentional difficulties will interfere with processing, at least in that subject area. In this sense, *teaching* is a key support for optimizing attention.

Coping: "The Problem" Is Not the Problem

In our view, the biggest threat to effective school supports for attention deficits is failure to remember the *systemic aspects of attention* and their implications for how a child copes with the problem. Since attention is a large network affecting many as-pects of function, ranging from arousal to focal attention, the disorder will manifest in many ways in many different contexts. It will be important for teachers, parents, and interventionists of any sort to view the child in her entirety, as a system, rather than to fall into the seductive behavioral trap of treating each issue in isolation.

When function has been disrupted by attention disorder, children will try to cope. At times, the coping can present a problem more critical than the actual, underlying condition. Children with ADDs are likely to want to be more "social" and less inclined to focus on academics. Some of this tendency is part of the essential search for arousal, but some might also be due to the immediate gratification brought by social interactions; social activity might thus become a way of coping with a more negative self-assessment where schooling is concerned. Refusal to work or oppositionality might also be seen as a way of coping with the difficulty of complying with attentional demands — just saying "No" in self-defense. Viewing a child's resistance in this way does much to avoid hopeless confrontation and to help teachers maintain a more positive attitude toward the child. It puts the child and her teacher on the same side of the issue. More importantly, however, it allows for the possibility of a meaningful intervention that supports the breakdown in the attention system rather than intervenes at the level of the coping mechanism.

SUMMARY

Attention is needed in nearly all forms of learning and thinking. The many aspects of attention must work together and in harmony with the rest of cognition. Limitations are imposed on attention from a number of sources: its own limits on sustained attention and attention span, working memory capacity, previously stored knowledge, and degree of automaticity. Since attention is constantly required for thought, and since there are serious limitations to attentional capacity, the attention system is a highly vulnerable one.

Schools value controlled and focused attention. Children with ADDs, then, are bound to require support in order to meet school expectations. Instructional interventions will need to consider the nature of the attention problem (i.e., distractibility, poorly controlled working memory) and will need to provide appropriate supports. Interventions need to identify the essential attentional problem and support the child at that level. Behavior management techniques insist on behavior change but fail to support the attentional deficits; thus, they are not likely to succeed.

4

Attention as
Self-Regulation

The attention system is dynamic, multifaceted, and multiphasic. The key to its functioning is modulation or regulation. Our view of regulation, however, clearly does not include governance from the top down. Ours is very much a self-organizing, nonlinear, nonhierarchic view of systems regulation.

It is the notion of balance, of regulation, that characterizes the neurochemical basis of attention. Just as attention is not a discrete, unified whole, neither is each subcomponent of the attention network a simple entity. Each has its own components and its membership in other networks (Mesulam, 1990). Each subsystem undergoes its own regulatory processes. For example, the dynamic aspects of stimulus/noise ratio involve the dual function of norepinephrine in inhibiting neural response to background noise while increasing excitation to foreground (Robbins, 1984). Heilman, Voeller, and Nadeau (1991) emphasize the competition and regulation within right and left frontal and striatal areas. Others have stressed the dynamics of emotion regulation as they affect the direction and level of vigilance (Derryberry & Reed, 1996). Functioning is a result of the balance among many such processes. What gets measured as attention is the behavioral manifestation of these dynamic transactions, which has very little relation to any localized or stable aspect of brain function (Tucker & Williamson, 1984). The reality is that the complexity and variability of attentional functioning are simply too great to unravel in any linear, algorithmic form. In our ensuing discussion, we would like to bow to the enormous complexity of the biological aspects of attention regulation while doing our best to describe what comprises the system and its regulation, with particular emphasis on arousal and activation.

Because the attention system is so complex, a basic guide to neurotransmitters, cognitive functions, and medications is provided in Appendix A. The appendix is meant to simplify the information. However, the reader is cautioned that any simplification of this material is necessarily an oversimplification.

BIOLOGICAL ASPECTS OF ATTENTION REGULATION

Arousal and Orientation

Arousal serves the general, global function of increasing alertness and orienting the individual toward the environment. It is now well established that even very young infants are aroused by and will orient attention to novel stimuli (Fagan, 1982). Arousal of this kind enables one to receive a good deal of information about the world. The arousal mechanism is designed to maintain a nearly continuous scan of the external stimulus context, a readiness for input. The scan is driven by the rhythm of orient–habituate–reorient, etc.

Without protection, the arousal system might promote a frenetic orientation to the next new, novel stimulus and then back to the old, which becomes relatively novel again. However, once the brain has built a neuronal model of repetitive input, it is protected from reorienting to that which matches the model and is free to orient to only those stimuli that differ. As we have discussed already, such a "template" for recognition also serves as a basis for generalization and analogical mental extensions.

Continuous scanning is further facilitated by the arousal system's bias toward rapid habituation. Rapid habituation is possible because stimuli are not analyzed in all of their detail and various nuances. Such analysis would demand and attract more active, controlled attention. By receiving, instead, the whole, integrated, Gestalt-like entity, it is possible to achieve rapid habituation and move on to the next novel experience. The necessity of such a novelty-driven arousal mechanism to the survival of the species seems obvious.

Reception or holistic processing of the kind just described is associated with the right hemisphere of the neocortex, where integrated and unanalyzed awareness becomes possible. Attentional pathways activated by norepinephrine have been found to be extensive in right hemisphere centers associated with orientation, global awareness, perception, and certain aspects of affect (McGuiness & Pribram, 1980; Mesulam, 1990). Forms of thinking that have been associated with arousal, novelty, and holistic processing include implicit awareness (Damasio & Damasio, 1992), simultaneous processing (Kaufman & Kaufman, 1985), parallel processing, imagery, and concept formation (Semrud-Clikeman & Hynd, 1990) and metaphoric, analogical thinking

(Edelman, 1992).

The orientation subsystem of the attentional network has been documented by Mesulam (1981) and others (McGuiness & Pribram, 1980; Voeller, 1990). In Mesulam's model, initial attentional functions result in an internal representation of external events. Based on this internal representation, attention is oriented toward those aspects of the stimulus situation that are within "grasp." Monkeys whose arms are restrained will not orient toward objects beyond their grasp. They will attend to what is relevant, and to what is within reach.

The animal's attention is directed toward what is motivating, a classification based in turn on the relevance, prehensibility, or comprehensibility of an object or situation. Action, positive affect, orientation, or approach are directed by the animal's assessment of graspability. The model invites the interpretation that a similar mechanism participates in the motivation of human attention (more about this in chapter 5). What is personally or cognitively relevant, what is comprehensible, and what is within cognitive grasp will motivate action, carve out the attentional field, and promote positive affect. That which is outside one's sensory or cognitive grasp ceases to exist as meaningful, and therefore simply ceases to exist. Mesulam (1981, 1990) sees inattention of this kind as a form of neglect.

The right parietal area, which contributes to the orienting function, is situated in close proximity to and connection with subcortical limbic structures and areas affecting mood and affect expression. Thus, orienting is literally rooted in emotional charge (Damasio, 1994; Mesulam, 1990). Furthermore, because of the dynamic multidirectional influences within the attention network, other attention functions are imbued with emotional charge as well. When the animal perceives an object as irrelevant, its dispassionate attitude is obvious. In schools this appears as lack of task commitment and poor persistence in pursuit of a goal. In extreme cases, there can be total, unconscious neglect of a stimulus field (Mesulam, 1981).

Dynamic Regulation of Effort, Arousal, and Attention

It has become customary to describe arousal as a unitary phenomenon that exists in an inverted U-shaped relationship with performance (Eysenck, 1982; Yerkes & Dodson, 1908). According to this view, performance improves with increasing arousal, to a point. After this point, any further increase in arousal would decrease performance level. The expenditure of effort, both cognitively and by the sympathetic nervous or endocrine systems (Hockey, 1984), creates a state of arousal, which in turn increases attentional capacity (Kahneman, 1973; Pliszka, McCracken, & Maas, 1996). When the surge of effort becomes too great, however, the result is a condition of burnout, which Kahneman (1973) compares to overloading electrical circuits (see chapter 3, p. 42).

Effort is the force that mobilizes the system to regulate its arousal/attentional resources. More is not necessarily better. The "best" response is an adaptive one which allows the animal/person to find stable points as the system self-organizes and reorganizes toward greater complexity. One has to assume that what goes for arousal goes for activation as well: each is multidimensional, and each reflects the regulation of subprocesses. The complexity of each subsystem adds exponentially to the total complexity of achieving and maintaining regulation.

In a multidimensional model of arousal, the question becomes how effort affects the distribution or relative activation of the various components of attention/arousal: alertness, selectivity, speed, accuracy, and working memory capacity (Hockey, 1984). It is not, then, only or mainly the *level* of arousal that is relevant to performance, but its "qualitative patterning" (Hockey, 1984, p. 467) across bodily and cognitive states. The challenge for the attender is to find the best fit between the distribution of attentional resources and the demands of a specific event.

The greater the challenge presented by a task, the greater the need to mobilize all attentional resources, each in synchrony with all others and all with the ability to sustain their own regulation, as well as their role in the regulation of the larger system. This is, of course, where the system becomes highly vulnerable. One form of coping might be to try harder, to exert more energy. But this is the beginning of the dip in the U-shaped curve, when too much effort results in diminished performance. In the terms of Kahneman's metaphor, this exertion behaves like a surge of energy in a poorly wired system that cannot distribute its energy in a well-regulated way to all terminals: the system may crash. Another form of coping, of course, is to retreat. This form of behavior has been called *learned helplessness* and, not surprisingly, is associated with norepinephrine depletion and the resultant dysregulation of the noradrenergic system's attempts to coordinate "response to stress over a range of different behavioral and physiological functions" (Robbins, 1984, p. 16).

In the end, exerting too much effort disrupts the delicate balance of the regulatory system. Teachers might keep this in mind when inspired to exhort their students to "try harder." Although retreat impedes successive reorganizations toward greater complexity — at least in the short term — it helps preserve homeostasis. In our opinion, retreat is likely to be less damaging than effort overload to the stability and regulation of the system at large. Remember the monkeys: what was out of their grasp ceased to exist as meaningful.

Activation and Controlled Focus

In complement to the more global, receptive attentional functions observed when right-hemispheric norepinephrine pathways are noticeably activated, attentional functions based in left anterior activation contribute to controlled, effortful focus and detailed analysis (Pliszka et al., 1996). Working memory and executive functions are thus supported by dopamine enhancement in left frontal regions. We stress one more time that neither neurotransmitter pathways nor any other aspect of function can be considered localized or independent. What is relevant is how the regulatory system manifests itself, or which pathways appear energized in relationship to which others (Rogeness, Javors, & Pliszka, 1992).

Dopamine is known to increase activation (Robbins, 1984; Tucker & Williamson, 1984) and to drive repetitive motor patterns. In contrast to norepinephrine-driven arousal, habituation bias, and redundancy reduction, dopamine-affected left frontal areas are associated with redundancy and repetition (Tucker & Williamson, 1984) and eventually with automaticity (Courchesne, 1989). Because of their potential for activation and for repetition, dopamine-driven centers of the brain provide the complement to the lack of redundancy of right-brain arousal mechanisms. In fact, it is possible that the elaborative function of detailed analysis associated with left-lateralized dopamine activation serves to prolong novelty by noticing different aspects of a stimulus situation, thus maintaining the arousal associated with right-hemispheric functioning.

In a well-regulated system, when too much information is accepted and working memory resources are spread too thin, the system can switch to "intuition." In a not-so-well-regulated system, excessive, repetitive, active focusing on discrete components of the stimulus context has a pathological appearance: perseveration, overfocusing, fragmentation, and obsession (Kinsbourne, 1990). In this case, dopamine-enhanced left-hemisphere function would be in complete opposition to the more integrated quality of norepinephrine-based right-hemisphere function. In order to repair the fragmentation of the highly focused, redundant left-hemisphere bias, language processes are required to embed the repetitive activation in meaning, in conscious awareness (Tucker & Williamson, 1984). Language labels and reconnects those components of experience made discrete through the focusing process. In fact, executive functions frequently depend on verbal mediation for explicit, controlled processing (Denckla, 1996a; Luria, 1966).

Language is needed to maintain activation of information in working memory (Shankweiler & Crain, 1986). Because of severe limitations in working memory capacity and the limited duration of trace in working memory, language-based processing — using verbal rehearsal (verbal repetitive action) or another form of verbal mediation — is necessary to capture information that has no immediate meaning. In contrast, when information is condensed in its holistic form, the language function is less needed for the purpose of cohesion. If the language-analysis-fragmentation-redundancy connection is called into play, but is not well modulated, it may lead to the fragmentation associated with schizophrenia, a fragmentation that has been attributed to dopaminergic imbalance (Breslin & Weinberger, 1991).

A Cognitive Parallel to Arousal/Activation: Implicit/Explicit Awareness

In cognition, and especially in school learning, the challenge is always to find the proper balance between a general, implicit sense of things — the level of insight/intuition — and a more explicit, analyzed, controlled and sequential awareness. Cognition at its best is a delicate balance, a dance between the two. Often, the first level of awareness is a vague, fuzzy set (Cherkes-Julkowski & Gertner, 1989; Rosch, 1977). Continued experience in combination with an established frame of reference, however vague, brings in additional detail, exceptions, and contradictions, thus creating the need for more active, conscious analysis to debug the concept and its relationship to other concepts. The next, perhaps higher level of awareness is developed only to set the original dance in motion again.

It is important for the learner to maintain some of the fuzziness that characterized her initial concept or awareness. It is this unanalyzed form, associated with habituation bias and orientation toward novelty, that allows for the flexibility and creativity associated with competent problem solving (Cherkes-Julkowski & Gertner, 1989; Hofstadter, 1995). Ironically, many interventions designed to help children or adults become better problem solvers are based in routinized verbal scripts, steps that are offered as universally reliable solutions (Meichenbaum & Goodman, 1971). Interventions such as these appeal to left-hemispheric analytic functions and, quite possibly, not at all to the source of flexibility in thinking. Certainly such an approach makes no allowance for the dynamic effects of right and left hemisphere interactions.

Effective attentional and cognitive states reflect a dynamic equilibrium of antithetical processes. No process can be viewed or treated in isolation. The activation/arousal feedback loop has always to be thought of in its entirety. The literature on attention and its regulation tends to emphasize the arousal system and has thus ignored some of the more intricate processes of analytical, language-based cognition as integral components of active, controlled attention (Denckla, 1996a; Stolzenberg & Cherkes-Julkowski, 1991). In contrast, intervention approaches tend to emphasize activation processes (Abikoff, 1991), this time ignoring the contributions of arousal and self-regulation.

Models of Attention Dysfunction Based in Self-Regulation

Rogeness et al. (1992) emphasize the mechanisms for self-regulation within and among neurotransmitters. The effectiveness of each neurotransmitter is dynamically influenced by precursors — phenylalanine and tyrosine in the cases of dopamine (DA) and norepinephrine (NE); by synthesizing enzymes; catabolic enzymes; storage issues of release and reuptake; and by dynamics at the pre- and post-synaptic sites. The balance among neurotransmitters can affect behavioral manifestation. Since the neurons affected by various neurotransmitters connect with each other, the activity of any neuron is influenced by other neurotransmitter systems.

In a model that parallels the activation/arousal dynamic, Rogeness et al. (1992) describe the self-regulatory aspects of a behavioral facilatory system (BFS) and a behavioral inhibitory system (BIS; Gray, 1987). The BFS is described as being dopamine-driven and related to behavioral activation such as reward approach, aversion avoidance, aggression, or extraversion. The BIS would provide the counterbalance mediated by norepinephrine and serotonergic (5HT) systems. The relative strength of each component would contribute to a person's greater or lesser ability to inhibit impulse. The model becomes more complex as one considers relative strength and balance among the three neurotransmitters with which the authors are concerned.

This model has implications for understanding and treating the subtypes of ADD. Low norepinephrine and low serotonin levels interact with high dopamine levels to influence aggressive conduct disorder (CD) and ADD with hyperactivity. Low dopamine levels in this context would not necessarily produce disruptions in attention — the child's functioning would be generally normal — but might appear as low motivation or schizoid manifestations. The combination of high norepinephrine, low serotonin, and high dopamine would produce aggressive conduct disorder with mild hyperactivity and adequate attention. Low norepinephrine, high serotonin, and high dopamine might result in nonaggressive conduct disorder, mild ADD and mild hyperactivity. With low norepinephrine, high serotonin, and low dopamine, there might be inhibition and ADD without hyperactivity. There are additional permutations, but none with immediate relevance to attention dysfunction. Depending upon the relative strengths and weaknesses within and among these systems, an attention deficit disorder would manifest itself differentially as learning difficulties, overactivity, impulsivity, aggression, various aspects of social maladaptation, or under- or overarousal.

Patterns of Attending

A child develops patterns of attention regulation that become a part of her temperament (Schwartz, Snidman, & Kagan, 1996). Regulatory patterns emerge out of initial biological conditions in interaction with experience (Derryberry & Reed, 1996). A highly aroused, anxious child may avoid novel, strange situations and thus narrow her knowledge base and fail to prepare herself for subsequent stressors. Of course, the essential arousal/anxiety could either be part of the child's original biology or have been induced through stressful or traumatic events. In these children, attention may be diverted to internal states, increasing self-awareness but further contributing to a narrowed information field. Attention to external events can be biased in the direction of threatening or negative information. In contrast, children with strong approach tendencies may be motivated by external factors such as rewards, social approval, and positive cues. Extreme manifestations would include impulsivity, hyperactivity, or conduct disorder. A well-regulated child can find a balance within this dynamic (Derryberry & Reed, 1996).

For children whose biology and/or early experience bias their regulatory systems toward one of these poles, how they cope becomes an issue. Avoidance — in the form of shifting attention to a less negative, more relieving stimulus — can effectively reduce anxiety in the short term, but again, it also narrows the information field. Schools often view avoidant coping as noncompliance or lack of motivation. Insistence that the child attend to the assigned topic would intensify the problem. Furthermore, anxiety can divert attention to worry, thereby interfering with the content to be learned (Derryberry & Reed, 1996). In any case, cognitive flexibility is likely to be sacrificed. Children with stronger approach tendencies may cope by diverting their attention away from school work to more immediately reinforcing social situations. For example, "socializing" is often seen as a cause of attentional problems, but it can certainly also be an effect.

When child study teams confront these profiles, they are often confused about whether learning problems are due to cognitive or emotional factors. In the self-regulatory view, cognitive and emotional symptoms are simply different reflections of the same dynamic. Attentional patterns get established at a neurological level through neural sculpting modulated by the neurochemistry of the attention system. Cooperative, mutually enhancing assemblies of cortical cells are formed that stabilize behavior and form the foundation for temperamental dispositions (Derryberry & Reed, 1996). Early experience is vital in setting the course of development.

STATE REGULATION IN INFANCY

The problem of optimal levels of arousal and stimulation has been studied in the infancy period. Very young children are susceptible to overstimulation (Sroufe, 1990; Thoman, 1987). Their efforts to maintain optimal levels of arousal, or to maintain an alert state, are at the mercy of an immature central nervous system which is itself struggling to maintain and regulate homeostasis at an autonomic level. The vulnerability of the system is that much more extreme in infants at risk for developmental delays: those born into environments that are potentially disorganizing, born prematurely, and/or born with other kinds of biological risk.

The infancy period, then, is an important one from the perspective of understanding the challenges of a well-regulated attention/arousal system. Primary to the organization of an attentive response is the ability to regulate state. The infant must be able to maintain and regulate arousal. If stimulation becomes too excitatory, an at-risk infant will avert her gaze or otherwise shut down, recoup her resources, and then return for further involvement (Karmel, Gardner, & Magnano, 1991; Sroufe, 1990). Infants, as well as vulnerable older children, are dependent on their caregivers to facilitate their own efforts at self-regulation. Caregivers who are sensitive to the rhythms and self-regulatory efforts of children, and who adjust their own behaviors to suit the child's state, facilitate self-regulation (Thoman, 1987). Those who cannot interpret the child's state, or who fail to adjust to it for any other reason, tend to disorganize the child and to debilitate his efforts at self-regulation (Foley & Hobin, 1981).

The more vulnerable the child, the more dependent he is on the caregiver's ability to help in the regulation and modulation of state or arousal. Thoman (1987) has demonstrated this nicely in her Blue Bear study of self-regulatory efforts in prematurely born infants, a study that capitalizes on the mobility available to the fetus. A soft, blue teddy bear is placed in the preterm infant's isolette. The bear has a mechanical heart that is set according to the pattern of the child's own heart and respiratory rhythm. As such, the bear can serve to entrain or set the infant's rhythmicity based on her own best-regulated periodicity. The bear is placed in such a way that the infant can choose to approach it or not, depending on her need or desire for assistance with self-regulation. Thoman has established that when vulnerable infants can receive responsive feedback, based in self-initiation and attuned to their own rhythms and needs, they achieve better and more periodic state regulation; as a result, their attentional resources are more available to attend to, interact with, enjoy, and learn from their interpersonal and object worlds.

It would be a mistake to conclude that the crucial aspects of self-regulation are all internal or all dependent on maturation of the central nervous system. Thoman's

Blue Bear makes the point that environmentally supported regulation can help to entrain CNS regulation. Similarly, Thelen's work involving walking behavior in infants (Thelen & Smith, 1994) points out that the system regulates itself based on multiple influences including central nervous system maturation, biomechanics, and specific environmental affordances. Behaviors assemble themselves in the context of the dynamic organization of all these components.

The implication for children in schools seems clear. When a child is dysregulated in school, she will not be able to regulate her own state for optimal levels of arousal/activation. An effective intervention might be modeled after the Blue Bear:

- Respect the child's effort at self-regulation.
- Work within the child's ability to regulate and achieve activated attention.
- Do not further disorganize the child with overstimulation.
- Utilize environmental resources to bring about dynamic processes that can result in optimally alert states.

Such intervention would not insist that the child "try harder" to stay in active attention. It might allow her, instead, to take periodic breaks in order to down-regulate. It would respect down-time as an important part of the regulatory process and use optimal moments of attention for instruction.

Studies of preterm infants have established the effects of poor state regulation (Thoman, 1987). The prematurely born infant is not able to maintain a quiet arousal state for any extended period. Nor can she maintain quiet arousal in the face of nonoptimal conditions such as noise, environmental disorganization, or any other potentially overstimulating event (Sroufe, 1990). It is difficult for such a child to self-soothe and shift state into quiet sleep, which is then hard to maintain. Preterms have been described as the prototype of children at risk for central nervous system dysfunction (Parmalee, 1989). Longitudinal study of preterms at mild risk (mean weight at birth 4.14 pounds, standard deviation 1.87) confirms the high incidence of learning and adjustment problems at school age. Of these preterms, 17.8% were identified as having ADD, 17.8% as having LD, 3.5% as language impaired, and 7.1% as otherwise neurologically impaired. An additional 28.5% had been referred due to concerns but had not been formally diagnosed at the time of follow-up (Cherkes-Julkowski, in press). It should be noted that neither birth weight nor degree of prematurity was a determining factor for classifying children as having a developmental disorder.

Because of the central nervous system vulnerability of preterm infants, they utilize many of their resources for autonomic regulation. Little remains for quiet, alert interaction with the environment. When the infant fails to regulate state, the problem is not just that "things" are not learned and experienced. The very foundations for self-regulation — which are essential to functional attention, mastery motivation, and personal and interpersonal growth — are not laid down.

External Regulation, Attachment, and Mastery Motivation

The more poorly regulated or poorly organized the child, the more dependent she is on "external" sources of regulation. When it is most effective, regulation in the context of a dyad is apparently not perceived by the child as external at all. The essence of the attachment relationship is that the dyad forms a unit that creates an intersubjectivity out of its two individuals. In that kind of relationship, the child is able to appropriate the actions of another as if they were her own (Foley, Passalacqua, & Ratner, 1993). In this way, adult efforts at organizing a child are literally internalized. Creation of an intersubjective system, however, is critical to the transmission. Foley et al. (1993) establish that the adult need not be a mother or even a long-term teacher. They found evidence of appropriation even within the short-term examiner–child relationship.

The growth process for all children during the birth-to-three period involves a move from initial *symbiosis* and other-regulation to a state of *self* and self-regulation. For children with early indications of central nervous system dysfunctions such as ADDs, this process is that much more challenging, and the demand on others for external regulation is that much greater. The process of evolving out of intersubjectivity to achieve self-regulation (Kaye, 1982; Rogoff, 1990) is a delicate one and is never complete. For many individuals with ADDs, the process extends well beyond the infancy period and remains a biological challenge throughout the life span. As we have mentioned before, each child develops his own rhythms and periodicity. Those adults who can capitalize responsively on the child's efforts at self-regulation, rather than impose some arbitrary rhythm, have been found to be most facilitative in helping children achieve regulation of their own states (Thoman, 1987).

The advantages of *responsive,* rather than *directive* or *intrusive,* parenting styles have been established for preterms as well as for normally developing children (Hess & Shipman, 1965). It seems that responsive interactions foster the child's own efforts to regulate arousal, homeostasis, and rhythmicity (Sroufe, 1990). According to this model, the child sets her own goals: to eat now, to attend to that toy, to make eye contact, to avert her gaze, and so on. The parent or caregiver responds by sharing the child's focus, adapting to her rhythm and helping her regulate within that rhythm. In this way the dyad entrains itself. The mother becomes the pacesetter and provides a control parameter that influences points of stable functioning.

The caregiver's role as regulatory agent does not stop with biological functions or directly after the most basic symbiotic stage (Mahler, 1979). The caregiver continues to influence regulatory and attentional processes directly, through continued (if more distant) regulation of everyday activities. Through the initial attachment relationship, the mother or primary caregiver indirectly influences the child's ability to regulate, to persist, to tolerate frustration, and to maintain motivation in the face of a challenge. Out of this primary relationship grows the child's sense of self and resiliency (Arend, Gove, & Sroufe, 1979).

The caregiver–child relationship is not independent of biological influences. Well-organized infants who clearly signal their state and their needs can be treated responsively far more easily than those who cannot do so. When the child's current state is not clearly discernible, as with many preterm infants, it is difficult for the caregiver to modulate stimulation. In the end, biological and psychosocial systems (neither of which is fully independent of the other) contrive to promote or interfere with the mother's ability to be responsive.

Thus, motivation toward mastery, a critical ingredient of school success, has its roots in the attachment relationship — which in turn is influenced by, and is an influence on, the biological integrity of the child. To say that a child has a problem with motivation is to describe a complex biopsychosocial disorder. There are lessons here for teachers. We shall return to them later in this chapter.

COGNITIVE SELF-REGULATION

The Need for Cognitive Regulation

Since the attentional system is so complex and so multifaceted, it is highly vulnerable, susceptible to perturbation (Nicolis & Prigogine, 1989). Because of the differentiated centers and functions that need to remain in well-regulated connection, the possibilities for breakdown are vast, and a controlling or regulatory function becomes essential to homeostatic functioning.

Principles of self-regulation allow homeostasis to emerge out of local dynamics. Traditionally, however, the idea of a control center has been invoked to account for the coordination among processes. Nowhere has this been more true than in the area of cognition. The mental faculty that has been posited as the center for the regulation of cognitive processes is the *executive function.*

Neuropsychological studies have placed the site of executive function bilaterally in the frontal area (Benson, 1991; Denckla, 1996b; Fuster, 1989). Recent neuropsychological findings have established further that attentional pathways directly involve frontal regions (Mesulam, 1981; Reader, Harris, Schuerholz, & Denckla, 1994; Trexler & Zappala, 1988; Zametkin et al., 1990), as well as other areas.

Executive function has been found to be reliant on verbal mediation (Denckla, 1996a) and activation centers in the left temporal lobe. Activation maintains information on-line so that the trace is not lost and thus more complex awareness, novel perceptions, or deeper meaning can be appreciated (Carpenter & Just, 1989; Hofstadter, 1995; McGuiness & Pribram, 1980; Tucker & Williamson, 1984). Verbal mediation, or internal use of language, also facilitates activation and serves the further functions of strategic management, compression, and elaboration of what is to be processed (Luria, 1966). Without inner language of this kind, it would be difficult to achieve the explicit, conscious awareness requisite to the intentional production of a plan for information management and to its systematic, monitored execution.

The suggested executive function system consists, then, of many subsystems. Primary among them is a feedback loop between frontal areas and left-temporally-based language processes of all kinds. Left temporal involvement is supported indirectly in the literature concerning the training of executive control strategies. Many executive function (or *metacognitive*) intervention strategies involve training verbal mediation, self-talk, self-instruction, and self-monitoring techniques (Kendall & Braswell, 1982; Meichenbaum & Goodman, 1971).

The lack of direct documentation of language-based temporal processes as part of the executive function seems to be a result of the inability of current research to address the issue. Studies with monkeys, which are a source of a good deal of our knowledge about neural networks, certainly cannot uncover language–attention–executive function connections. Studies with humans (Zametkin et al., 1990) tend to use nonlinguistic stimuli. This is likely an attempt to avoid confusion between language functions and attention functions. Nevertheless, such an approach makes it impossible to uncover a possibly essential or facilitative linkage.

Regulatory Role of Executive Function

Fuster (1989) points out that the frontal lobes are connected reciprocally to almost all areas of the brain. A connection that seems particularly relevant to the dysfunction of attention in people with ADDs is the frontal-striatal one which, when well regulated, makes possible the gating of behavior. Motor arousal and restlessness may originate in striatal regions and need to be controlled, or *gated*, in the frontal areas (Heilman, Voeller, & Nadeau, 1991). What is identified as impulsivity and hyperactivity might be a reflection of a "pathologically low threshold for gating behavior defined largely by external stimuli" (Heilman et al., 1991, p. S80) and characterized by premature or precocious shifts in attention mediated by the right hemisphere. Methylphenidate (commercially known as Ritalin; see chapter 6) appears to give priority to the internal controls, mediated by the left hemisphere, that make task-relevant, sustained focus possible. Heilman et al. (1991) further assert, "Methylphenidate improves behavior by ameliorating the hemispheric asymmetry in frontal-striatal function" (p. S80) — that is, by resetting the balance.

The role of frontal areas in inhibition has also been established. Dopamine-enhanced frontal pathways have been posited as major components of the behavioral inhibitory system (Breslin & Weinberger, 1991; Denckla, 1996a). We have already discussed the dynamic aspects of the inhibitory function in ADDs.

In its dynamic relationship with the rest of the intellective functions, executive functions must be viewed as the culmination of a series of mental, neuropsychological, and behavioral events that self-organize and stabilize at attractor points.

Self-Control vs. Self-Regulation

Executive function is implicated whenever an individual is involved in any purposive or self-directed activity. Such activities include the orchestration of thinking, self-control, self-direction, and self-regulation of affect and attention (Lezak, 1983). Motivation, goal-directed behavior, and reinforcement learning also come under the direction of attention and executive areas (Barkley, 1990; Mesulam, 1990). The original view of executive function envisioned a homunculus in the brain that handed down commands to all subsystems. The application of this view has taken the form of cognitive-behavioral therapies such as those suggested by Meichenbaum and Goodman (1971) or Kendall and Braswell (1982). The purpose of such interventions has been to train an internal executive agent that can instruct the rest of cognition in planning what to do and when to do it, in deciding what and how much to attend to, in keeping track of the initial goal and all the subroutines in service of that goal, and in maintaining a continual error search. This seems to be an overwhelming charge even for the omniscient homunculus.

In fact, the charge is self-defeating. There have been many exhaustive reviews of metacognitive or executive control training (Abikoff, 1991; Brown, Bransford, Ferrara, & Campione, 1983; Cherkes-Julkowski & Gertner, 1989). All have reached a similar conclusion. As long as the experimental intervention is in place, children can be helped to plan, monitor, and check their work, to invoke strategic processing, and to be more aware of what they are doing. However, regardless of how much or how thorough the training, as soon as experimental prompts are removed, training effects dissipate as well. Executive training that follows the little-man-handing-down-orders control model *simply doesn't work*. Most probably it doesn't work because it fails to consider the dynamic, multidirectional and self-regulatory qualities of cognitive processing (Cherkes-Julkowski & Gertner, 1989; Thelen & Smith, 1994).

Mental Governance: Democracy or Autocracy?

With two very apt metaphors, Hofstadter (1979; 1985) creates a different view of executive function. He first (Hofstadter, 1979) points out that the homunculus idea simply can't work. In his allegory, the Tortoise and Achilles become trapped in an Escher drawing. They can't, of course, tell which way is up or down, what is out or in. They find a lantern, rub it, meet a genie, and ask for directions out of their problem. The genie informs them that she is in charge of only one small section of the drawing; for a more complete orchestration of their way out, they will need the *meta*genie. Dutifully the characters call upon the metagenie, who in turn informs them that she can only manage her small quadrant of the drawing and that appeal must be now made to the *meta*metagenie — and so on in an infinite regress. The point is made vividly that *no one is in charge here*. No single agent can solve the problem, allocate resources, or do anything else without communicating with the entire complex of higher-level and lower-level subsystems.

Later, in an article entitled "Who Shoves Whom Around Inside the Careenium?" (1985), Hofstadter creates the image of a reverberating or oscillating system. Such a system is governed by a compilation of events. Like a series of balls careening around in a pinball game, or like neural firings, some of the connections made are based initially in sheer probabilities. Each connection, however, changes the probability for subsequent ones. In this way interconnections or subsystems emerge. There is no omnipotent governance here, only the selection of patterns of behavior (Edelman, 1992) which emerge out of the dynamics of lower-level activity. In Hofstadter's words:

> Those lower-level items feel to the top level as if they bubble up from nowhere. But in reality they are somehow formed from the churning, seething masses of interacting neural sparks — just as patterns of [ideas, bits of information] motions emerge out of the chaotic Brownian motion of the many tiny [ideas, bits of information].
>
> (Hofstadter, 1985, p. 619)

Decisions get made according to the same dynamic. Conflicts are not necessarily resolved through systematic equations applied from the top down. Again, in Hofstadter's words,

... conflicts of ideas are like wars, in which every reason has its army. When reasons collide, the real battleground is not at the verbal level (although some people would love to believe so); it's really a battle between opposing armies of neural firings, bringing in their heavy artillery of connotations, imagery, analogies, memories, residual atavistic fears, and ancient biological realities .... Would you now be inclined to say, Achilles, that your molecules push *you* around, or that *you* push *them* around?

(Hofstadter, 1985, p. 621)

We restate our point: Nothing happens first and no one is in charge here. In a dynamic system governed as much by the laws of probability, pattern creation, and detection as by anything else, the idea of a static attentional system that relays information to a center where it can be controlled is not workable. As a part of its role in executive function, attention/working memory takes part in the effort to orchestrate thought, but not to control it completely.

School Interventions: Problems with Cognitive-Behavioral Modification

Because of concern about the effects of difficulties with self-regulation and self-control on learning, cognitive-behavioral modification (CBM) therapies have seemed an appealing treatment for children with ADDs. What characterizes CBM interventions is the goal of modifying problem-solving ability, academic or social, through the combined influence of behavioral and cognitive change. The theory contends that a motivating contingency system can shape behavior, and that behavior can in turn shape cognition.

The goal of CBM interventions is to increase an individual's meta-awareness of and metacontrol over his or her own thought processes. The child is taught strategies that help him manage his thinking and procedures. He is encouraged to make a problem-solving plan, to enumerate each step in the process, and to talk himself through each of these steps systematically. Often the plan or plan-making process is modeled for him. In the end, the child is expected to internalize the procedure and to extend it, or generalize it, to novel domains. The belief is that once a child is trained to be aware of the metaoperations that control thought, she can take charge of her thinking to make herself more directed, controlled, and productive.

Yet CBM seems to be a particularly inappropriate model for the instruction of children with ADDs. In the first place, it presumes that cognitive controls can be learned through modeling and contingency systems, ignoring the biological, self-regulatory processes which facilitate or impede control of this kind. Given the biological basis for poor regulation (what CBM proponents might prefer to call *lack of control*) in children with ADD, learned control through CBM is an unlikely outcome. Second, CBM assumes that there is an identifiable control function. We have presented evidence to suggest that control itself emerges out of dynamics at far lower levels. Third, CBM offers a purely linear algorithm for thought. Since thought does not proceed in this way in its most productive form (Hofstadter, 1995) or possibly at all (Thelen & Smith, 1994), this is an ill-supported proposition. There is a fourth assumption that talking through a thought process is facilitative. Given capacity limitations, it is possible that *prescribed* self-talk becomes another drain on finite resources. Further, the prescription itself fails to encourage the active, self-generated process of labelling experience in the context of one's own frames of reference — i.e., the process of making meaning.

It is not our intent here to review in careful detail the CBM literature as it relates to ADD. Such reviews have been done quite well already (Abikoff, 1991; Douglas, 1980). We would like to consider its theoretical basis and effectiveness in the light of a dynamic attention network. CBM interventions are grounded in the belief that there is a metacontrol aspect of cognition and that this metacenter can manage thinking. We have questioned the feasibility of purely top-down mechanisms. A top-down theory fails to account for systemic effects. Evidence and reason argue strongly for a view of the mind as a system of top-down, bottom-up, and side-to-side influences, one in which order emerges out of interactions at the local level (Hofstadter, 1979, 1985; Thelen & Smith, 1994).

The Question of Metacontrol and the Efficacy of CBM

It has been found that deficiencies in strategic behavior in younger children or persons with mental retardation could be eliminated simply by training the group with those deficiencies to use specific strategies (Belmont & Butterfield, 1971; Brown, Campione, & Murphy, 1977). Unfortunately, however, subjects could only maintain strategic approaches in the presence of examiner prompts. Although training effectively increased strategy use and cognitive performance on the trained task, it was impossible to effect a permanent change in strategic performance.

These findings encouraged the interpretation that, in well-functioning individuals, there is some central control mechanism that invokes effective strategies. Cognitive impairment would be characterized by a "production deficiency" — a metaprocedural failure to call up the strategies needed. We remind you of our previous comments about metaoperations of any kind. It is logically inconceivable that there should be any all-knowing, autonomous, omnipotent control agency whose role is to hand down orders. Little wonder that there is a long history of disappointment with meta-cognitive interventions. Whenever the approach is attempted with populations char-acterized by cognitive impairments (mental retardation/MR, learning disability/LD, or ADDs), it fails. Failure in this case refers to the potential of cognitive-behavioral therapies to produce long-term and cross-situationally generalized results.

As the aforementioned literature concerning mental retardation demonstrated, interventions that train self-instruction or strategy usage for a particular task result in improved performance *on that task*. It has even been possible to maintain the training effect for a period of weeks. This was true for populations with retardation (Brown, Campione, & Murphy, 1977), with learning disability (Deshler, Alley, Warner, & Schumaker, 1981; Harris, 1986); and with ADDs (Hinshaw, Henker, & Whalen, 1984; Kendall & Braswell, 1982; Meichenbaum & Goodman, 1971). Beyond this, however, the only population that appears to sustain training effects is one comprised of chil-dren who manifest no cognitive dysfunction in the first place — "purely" behaviorally disordered children (Swanson, 1985). It is important to realize that even in this re-gard, ADDs are more like cognitive than like behavioral disorders.

Although the CBM school of thought holds that the key to improved generaliza-tion lies in improved reinforcement schedules and more systematic transition to novel stimuli, long-lasting effects of CBM training have yet to be substantiated. Even with an added emphasis on self-instruction, self-monitoring, and self-reinforcement, there has been little "generalization" to academic gains (Abikoff et al., 1988). The pure concentration on a single aspect of process — in this case metaoperations — fails to acknowledge the dynamic systemic aspects of mental process, and the dynamic aspects of knowledge itself. Strategies, processes, and self-awareness grow out of do-main-specific knowledge structures as much as they grow *down* from any omnipotent control center (Chi, 1985; Thelen & Smith, 1994). To the extent that content and process influence and define each other, the concept of generalization based in top-down process applications is simply wrong.

Nonlinear, Dynamic Organization of Thought

CBM would give the child a step-wise plan by which to conduct her thinking. She would be taught a series of steps which could then be applied as an algorithm for mental computations. The assumptions underlying CBM appear to be in conflict with what we are coming to understand about the dynamic nature of thought. It is evident that novel solutions would not be possible within this computational frame-work. The child would only be able to run the program as given. It should come as no surprise that trained top-down strategies do not generalize.

The dynamic view works from the pole opposite that of CBM. Top-down computational procedures are not acknowledged *a priori*. All thought emerges out of dynamics at a microscopic, local level. As elements in the world are experienced through perception and direct action, dynamic interactions occur in parallel at a neuronal level. Events that occur together (e.g., cats and whiskers, birds and feathers) activate a spatial contiguity of neuronal associations. Groups of neurons get selected and form patterns, which are the bases for concepts and categories. In this sense, *knowing* self-organizes out of reciprocal interactions among groups of neurons and reciprocal interactions of self and context. A thought or concept is formed out of the competitive dynamics of neuronal group selection (Edelman, 1992).

It is this on-line, dynamic, ever-active self-organizing process that makes change and growth, as well as variability, inevitable. It provides the flexibility necessary for generalization. An approach such as CBM would have the effect of discouraging the bottom-up dynamics out of which generalization might emerge. Little wonder that concept instruction has been found to be superior to CBM process-based instruction at follow-up (Kendall & Wilcox, 1980).

Fail-Safe Approaches to Learning

CBM would have the child do it the teacher's way. The message seems to be, "Watch me, do it my way, and you will be successful." We take serious issue with the assumption implied here, that the best strategy for learning is the one that reaches a correct solution most directly by avoiding error (Cherkes-Julkowski & Gertner, 1989). Error is part of the self-organizing process out of which knowing emerges. The CBM approach of modeling and affixing a script to the child's thinking has the potential to dysregulate the more essential process of building associations at a personally relevant, local level — those associations emerging out of the individual's own trajectory of past and present experiences (Thelen & Smith, 1994).

In the emergence of one's own thinking, there must be some degree of self-generated experimentation (Adolph et al., 1993; Bruner, 1985; Thelen & Smith, 1994; Vygotsky, 1962), which means there will be errors along the way. These errors are valuable, not only in refining the growth of a workable concept, but also because they feed back to an infinite number of frames called up along the way and thus affect many aspects of knowledge and knowing. In fact, there is some evidence that, in a population with developmental disabilities, the number of errors made during training correlates positively with strategy generalization to a slightly modified task (Cherkes-Julkowski et al., 1986).

Problems with Self-Talk: Capacity and Language Competence

CBM attempts to make a child explicitly aware of effective cognitive processes through self-talk, self-checking, and self-monitoring, under the assumption that awareness is the first step toward change. However, if thinking emerges out of lower-level functions (Edelman, 1992; Hofstadter, 1985), then trying to bring the process to an explicit, conscious level of awareness at the wrong moment in time is as likely to mess up the works as anything else. For the child with ADD there is a particular threat. This child is characterized by significant limitations to his attention/working memory system. Whenever thinking can be done in an implicit or automatic way, capacity that would otherwise be allocated to conscious, effortful processing remains available for more substantive material. Said another way, CBM techniques run the risk of *commandeering the major portion of capacity* and thus leaving the child with insufficient capacity to deal with domain-relevant information — be it social studies, reading, or math skills, or the content of a writing assignment. In this light, it is unsurprising that CBM fails to facilitate achievement (Abikoff, 1991).

In the case of those children with ADDs who also manifest language impairment, the effects of CBM are potentially detrimental. One form of language impairment typical among persons with ADDs or any other minimal brain dysfunction is difficulty with word retrieval. If self-talk or self-interrogation is to be effective at all, finding one's own language must be a critical feature. Again, it is important to recall that all "on-line" thinking is done in the attention-driven working memory store. The essence of an efficiently running attention/working memory system is the rapid juggling that allows for letting information in, processing, downloading, and returning for more, ad infinitum. When verbal mediation is required, efficiency depends on rapid access to language in order to effectively increase available capacity. One more time, the person with language-related corollaries of ADD seems to be out before he is in. Forcing the verbal mediation issue is likely to tip the delicate balance of the attention/working memory system against the child.

Social Aspects of Verbal Mediation: Self-Talk, Other Talk

The issue of outside-in vs. inside-out is a large one in the context of CBM. The adherents of CBM refer to the literature evolving out of Vygotsky's work (Wertsch, 1985) to make the point that an individual learns self-regulation in a social context — from the outside in. As part of the socialization process, in interaction with a more knowing other — a master in a master–apprentice relationship (Kaye, 1982; Rogoff, 1990) — the child learns to internalize the language needed to mediate self-regulation.

Vygotsky's is a truly benevolent and egalitarian model based firmly in the idea of apprenticeship. The child and the master/teacher work together as one integrated system. They work from the bottom up. They weave the cloth or repair the equipment or solve the problem together. At first, the master does it all. Then the apprentice takes on one step, and then another — not as in task analysis where steps are learned in isolation, but practicing each step within the context of the entire operation. In this model, everything is holistic, and each step is always practiced in total context. Once the apprentice can perform most of the steps, it is time for the master to simply talk and to pass on the role of regulating the process to the apprentice.

Ideally, then, self-talk is self-generated and evolves out of well-practiced, well-learned domain-specific knowledge. It is difficult to imagine that Vygotsky would have us believe that a well-trained weaver could "generalize" the experience to farming or industry through self-talk at the metaprocedural level. CBM, however, works from the top down. It offers the child/learner/apprentice the techniques for regulation to be applied downward to an infinite number of content areas.

Furthermore, learning in the original apprenticeship formulation was charged affectively by the master-apprentice relationship. Kaye (1982) extends this thinking to the mother-child relationship, calls it apprenticeship, and suggests that it is "inter-subjectivity" which makes possible both the transmission of information and the affective charge that drives the process. In contrast, CBM opts for contingency systems. We contend that any program intending to change the way another person thinks will need to be more intimate than that.

SCHOOL INTERVENTIONS

An effective school intervention would be designed to respond in a positive and supportive way to the self-regulatory efforts of the child and the self-organizing dynamics of learning. In contrast to CBM approaches, we suggest that interventions should be designed to foster learning by setting into play the appropriate dynamics at the local level. Top-down strategies would be abandoned in favor of making concepts come alive for the child in the context of her own background and frames of reference.

Since patterns emerge out of repeated experiences with correlated properties (Gibson, 1979; Rosch, 1977), teachers would need to be clear about what is at the essence of a concept or procedure, then select examples and activities that highlight those essential characteristics or relationships. For example, in teaching the long-division algorithm, the estimation procedures on which the algorithm is based might be brought to the child's full attention by having her solve the following sequence of problems.

These examples, of course, presume that the child has mastered and *understood* all preceding skills and concepts.

1. $10\overline{)10}$
2. $10\overline{)100}$
3. $10\overline{)1000}$
4. $10\overline{)10000}$

At this point it would be possible to point out that each answer is a derivation of the first, that in each case the process can be broken down into 10/10 as the initial step. The next sequence might be designed to force the estimation process a little further:

5. $20\overline{)200}$
6. $20\overline{)400}$
7. $30\overline{)600}$
8. $40\overline{)800}$
9. $21\overline{)400}$
10. $31\overline{)600}$
11. $41\overline{)800}$

Now the child is prepared to recognize that the problem can be subdivided into smaller units of the dividend and divisor in order to make the estimation process easier. Once the first subdivision has been made, the rest of the algorithm is set in motion; the subdivision facilitates the rest of the algorithm. When the child has progressed to this awareness, she is ready to be shown the formal procedure and to practice it. Individual children might need more or less of this assistance, or might need a different form of presentation altogether. The essence of individualized instruction is for the teacher to perceive those needs and make those adjustments.

Whenever the child *acts* on the material, she is far more likely both to attend fully and to uncover what is essential to it. For example, to facilitate a sound and insight-driven understanding of number concept in a child who was having extreme difficulty with this, instruction was based in the idea that concepts emerge out of patterned neural firings. The patterns are much richer when they are based in the dynamic, reciprocal interactions among data from multiple senses (Edelman, 1992; Thelen & Smith, 1994). The child in question carried sets of 1, 2, 3, 4, 5, and 6 bricks to specified locations (not all of these amounts were used during the first presentation). In the end, she was able to more accurately estimate the number of bricks in a stack and make more accurate and more immediate more/less judgments.

A similar pairing of action and perception has been recommended by Thelen and Smith (1994), who propose that learning letter recognition is enhanced through doing while seeing. They provide evidence of differences between what is learned with and without action. The emergent concept depends on the reentrant mapping (Edelman, 1992) that takes place between the percept (in this case, what is seen) and the action itself. The samplings from each, extended across multiple exemplars, trace a series of pathways. The repetitions allow the pattern to emerge. In turn, the pattern serves as a stable attractor to which future experiences are drawn. Perhaps this is the essence of automaticity. The child comes to a given lesson with already established reentrant mappings which comprise stable attractors. Sometimes these are facilitative and can be used as reference points from which growth can proceed. At other times they generate counterproductive expectations. One such counterproductive pattern is found in some children's approach to "decoding" words in print by guessing at them through context or using some imprecise sampling of their letter composition. This approach not only fails to produce any reasonable percentage of accuracy, but also *prevents* the careful examination of letters which would make learning the code possible.

Whether or not these preexisting conditions are facilitative, individualized instruction will need to take them into account. When they are facilitative, the teacher can start with them, embed instruction in that context, and allow the existent relationships to bring meaning to the lesson. When they are counterproductive, they cannot be ignored. Some procedure will need to be developed to inhibit their invocation. In the reading example above, the child can be asked to read isolated words, out of context, as a form of skill instruction.

In a similar vein, skills might be taught in the context of areas that are of strong interest to the child. At one level it could be said that the child is "motivated to pursue his interests" (see chapter 5), but this is a gross oversimplification. The material that interests a child is that material for which he has rich reference points, rich reentrant mappings that form stable attractors for him. No direction of causality is implied. If the child is interested in animals, for instance, or team sports, or cars, or fishing, then reading, math, and writing can all use that interest as a reference point. Again, these are important considerations in formulating an *individualized* program.

Supporting Efforts at Self-Regulation

Since the system will self-organize in a way that optimizes both growth and stability (Thelen & Smith, 1994), teachers need to assume that all behaviors are a reflection of this process. At times behaviors may seem maladaptive, *but they would not exist if they did not serve some function within the goals of the child's system.* The problem becomes one of determining what function an undesirable behavior might serve and shaping that function into a more adaptive goal.

Children say NO in various ways. The gaze aversion of an infant may serve the same function as the passive resistance of a child in middle school or the bravado of a teenager. All would be ways of preserving the integrity of the system and avoiding a kind and/or degree of stimulation that appears threatening. Asking a high school student to write out all of the steps in an algebra procedure can be threatening if he has found his solution through successive estimations and does not know the procedure at all. It is embarrassing for him and threatens his sense of success. Asking a middle school student to read aloud when she cannot decode is similarly threatening to the well-being of her system. The solution is not to set a behavioral objective to enforce compliance through contingency systems. An actual solution would help at the level of self-regulation by allowing the student to reorganize his processes from the point where he is experiencing the problem. In the examples above, an instructional solution would involve teaching algebraic procedure in a way that would be meaningful to the high school student, or teaching the child to read.

There are issues of self-organization at biological and temperamental levels as well. Some students need breaks because the effort necessary for focusing attention is draining for them. Others need frequent switches of activity in order to maintain optimal arousal and avoid frustration. Some need help in establishing a slow enough pace to work methodically or to allow for their rate of processing.

Ironically, many students with ADDs who do not finish their work on time are probably working too fast. Their impulsive runs at the material end in repeated failure and frustration. Time is spent in repetitions and ultimately sitting there in defeat. These students may need some help in the temporal regulation of their work. Here the Blue Bear metaphor is relevant. The teacher can sit with the student and model a solution along with its pace. She can point to a spot on the child's paper and say, "Do the first step here." Once this is completed, she can set the rhythm by pointing at the right time to the next place on the paper saying, "Now here ...."

The idea of all of this is to get on the same side of the problem as the child — to help the child with the regulatory efforts she *is* making and therefore *can* make. The alternative is to insist on another level of behavior. If, in its current status, the child's system sees this as nonproductive, it will — and probably should — resist.

The Apprentice Relationship

The teacher–child relationship has been compared to that of the master and apprentice. A master enculturates the apprentice into his role through successive repetitions of the task. They work together. The apprentice always sees the task in its entirety, even though he begins by performing just a small number of the steps on his own. The master has the executive function of organizing, regulating, and monitoring the process as a whole. It is through the joint effects of repeated action and intersubjectivity that apprentices internalize the actions of the other, "making these actions their own, and adopting the other's actions as self-regulatory routines" (Foley et al., 1993, p. 374). This seems an ideal intervention for children with ADDs whose essential difficulty is one of self-regulation. The pedagogy here, however, is different from simply overlearning, or what CBM has to offer. The essential elements are the *relationship*, the *action*, and the opportunity for *recursive repetitions*.

It has been established that the child truly internalizes dyadic activity as his or her own. In a series of well-designed studies, Foley et al. (1993) have shown that children aged 4–6 quite literally appropriate the actions of an adult partner as their own. They will say, "I did it," when shown a piece of work actually performed by their partner.

In school, the more complex the task, the more likely it is that a child with ADD will need the advantage of this kind of model. Writing is one example of such a complex task (see chapter 10). The model has an infinite number of applications. What is essential is the bottom-up nature of the process — that the instruction start with the child and take place within the child's own self-regulatory efforts, that there be repeated and recursive action, and that there be a relationship from which the child can draw regulatory support.

5

Motivation:
An Emergent
Property

The process of diagnosing ADDs has become entangled with the question of motivation, especially in schools. A debate can ensue concerning whether a child is having difficulty in school because she has an ADD or because she is unmotivated. Or, a slightly more sophisticated debate might involve whether her ADD is causing motivation problems or her motivation problems are causing loss of attention. Of course, from a systems perspective, these are meaningless debates: since everything is connected, everything is cause and everything is effect. From the perspective of self-organizing systems, a higher-order function such as motivation is of necessity an emergent property arising out of lower-level functions.

There are some unexpressed assumptions embedded in the concept of motivation that warrant clear articulation. In schools, *motivation* has come to mean volition or will. The belief is that the child is in charge of her motivation: she need only *will herself* to focus and persist in pursuing the goal. *If she wanted to, she could*. Given this view of motivation, one is forced to ask, what is the site of this will, this volitional center? What is the mechanism by which a person can take charge of herself? Perhaps there are answers to these questions, but they are not simple ones, and motivation is certainly not an issue of "I will." We shall try to examine the aspects of motivation most relevant to attention from the bottom up, to demonstrate how fundamental and below the level of consciousness many aspects of motivation are. We shall show that motivation is itself a part of a complex system requiring regulation, a system that overlaps attention in many respects. Finally, we shall suggest that motivation is an emergent property, a higher-level function that is created out of dynamics operating at a far lower level.

Motivation as Arousal or Interest

The right-hemispheric, norepinephrine-driven component of the attention system has been associated with affect and mood regulation (McGuiness & Pribram, 1980; Trexler & Zappala, 1988) and with orienting to events external to the self. Impairment often results in depressed mood as well as depressed motivation for attention (Mesulam, 1981) and, in the ADD population, mood swings. It is underlying emotion that gives personal charge to general arousal (Damasio, 1994; McGuiness & Pribram, 1980; Mesulam, 1981) and approach to a stimulus situation or, conversely, to failure to orient as a result of either avoidance or lack of interest. Interest in this case is part of the essence of arousal and bound up with the sense of what is relevant and within grasp (Mesulam, 1981).

Lack of interest in the pursuit of a goal can manifest as learned helplessness and depression. Both are often found in children with ADD. The child with ADD is frequently described as "unmotivated," or at least not motivated to orient toward external, other-determined, and often anxiety-provoking goals. Among professionals there is a common assumption that the helplessness is *learned* as a result of repeated failure and frustration. Perhaps more pejoratively, lack of interest is sometimes conceived as the result of a lack of character, a failure to adopt the values of hard work and persistence. From the neuropsychological view, however, failure to orient and direct behavior toward a goal is as much a part of the original cortical and subcortical network of attention centers as it is a secondary outcome of discouragement.

In animals, depression is known to manifest itself as learned helplessness (Robbins, 1984). If an animal is repeatedly shocked, it will become inactive and cease to make efforts to escape. Both depression and learned helplessness are related to low levels of norepinephrine (NE). NE depletion may simultaneously, but through different mechanisms, affect both the hypoactivity and the disruptions of learning and memory associated with depression/learned helplessness. The subtype of ADD without hyperactivity and with social withdrawal, anxiety, and depression has long been recognized. Children with this subtype are often described as passive. It is interesting to question whether the depression and learned helplessness are comorbidities or, as in our view, two different parts of the essential disorder.

Just as original biochemical imbalances can manifest as learned helplessness, so can repeated failure to find gratification manifest as an imbalance in norepinephrine levels (Derryberry & Reed, 1996). Again, it doesn't really matter what comes first. In the end, the entire system is disrupted.

Norepinephrine (NE) pathways further influence motivation by directing attention to novel perceptual events. The role of those pathways enervated by NE, then, is to keep the animal orienting to a broad environmental field. The survival aspect is clear. There is a constant scan for life-threatening (predators) and life-enhancing (food, mates) events. Tucker and Williamson (1984) refer to this as "loose" regulation; "rather than being restricted to given semantic or motivational content," they explain, "the animal's processing capacity is allocated to the *most novel — usually the most informative — feature of the stimulus array*" (p. 194, emphasis ours).

NE influence seems to run counter to what is perceived as motivation in the schools. It is broad, not focal. It defines curiosity and interest in terms of external events that pull attention because of their immediate, primary, perceptual meaning (Gibson, 1979). Habit, including previously laid down, temperamental patterns of attending, and stimulus novelty tend to have a stronger effect on attentional resources than the anticipation of an external reinforcer (Derryberry & Reed, 1996; Levine, 1989). Motivation, in this sense, is not an internal mechanism willing the direction of attention and behavior. It is, itself, at the mercy of environmental and personal, historical circumstances.

Motivation as Reward

The attention network spans, at minimum, the right parietal areas, the cingulate cortex, the frontal areas, and the reticular activating system (Mesulam, 1981; Mirsky et al., 1991). The network, then, allows for the link between arousal (reticular formation), perceptual (right parietal areas), and reward (frontal areas) mechanisms. Given the close proximity of the right parietal areas and the cingulate cortex to limbic structures, the attention network also allows for the emotional charge with which stimuli are or are not cathected. Given the intricacies of the network, perception is enhanced with the motivational significance of objects, while responses to insignificant or irrelevant stimuli are muted and can be more purposively inhibited (Mesulam, 1981; Price, Daffner, Stowe, & Mesulam, 1990).

It has been postulated, based on neurological, pharmacological, and behavioral evidence, that *reward dysfunction* — specifically, an elevated reward threshold — exists in ADD/hyperactive children (Haenlin & Caul, 1987). Children with ADDs do not seem to internalize contingency systems as easily as non-ADD children. Rewards must be greater, more intense, to have any effect for people with ADDs (Barkley, 1990). Elevated reward thresholds can be normalized in people with ADDs who are given Ritalin (Cantwell & Baker, 1991).

The regulation of dopamine (DA) and norepinephrine (NE) function has been viewed as essential to the mediation of reward (Tucker & Williamson, 1984; White, 1989). There is at least a dual nature of reward. First, there is the reward associated with orienting toward external events in conjunction with behavioral contingencies. This form of motivation appears to be linked to norepinephrine and its role in orientation to external events at large. There is also, and perhaps predominantly, the reward associated internally with electrical brain stimulation. "To receive brain stimulation," report Tucker and Williamson (1984), "the animal's only requirement is to emit a motor response and motor control is regulated by the DA pathways" (p.190). They conclude:

> Progress in understanding how the catecholamine pathways are important to reward ... requires moving from an unspecified association of the neurotransmitter with the behavior toward a more definite notion of how the change in neural activity mediated by the neurotransmitter may carry out the information processing and sensorimotor operations required for the behavior. (p. 190)

The strong suggestion is that reward is in the form of neurochemically based neuronal activity. Behavior, then, is not shaped by external contingencies which make the behavior expedient. *It is shaped by the neuronal dynamics associated with experience itself.* The question becomes *how* the neurological system, via its neurotransmitters, "supports the attentional components of learning" (p. 190) by augmenting arousal to rewarded events and/or augmenting persistent responding despite redundancy, repetition, or irrelevance. Derryberry and Reed (1996) point out that patterns of attending can persist *despite contingencies* if they serve a more fundamental need. Children who have experienced early abuse or painful failure in learning and social environments may be hypervigilant in regard to specific environmental cues, regardless of what is reinforced as acceptable in their classrooms.

In schools, what is valued and reinforced is sustained focus. The endurance associated with overriding a habituation bias in favor of sustained focus in the face of repetition or personal irrelevance is under the influence of dopamine pathways. Specifically, a dopamine-rich frontal cortex allows for the inhibition of preferential orientation toward novelty and stimuli of more immediate relevance:

> because of its connection with the frontal lobe and limbic system, the dopamine system is thought to be important to higher order motivational processes via sensorimotor integration (nigrostriatal dopaminergic pathways) and motivated interac-

tion with the environment (mesocortical dopamine pathways).

(Tucker & Williamson, 1984, p. 191)

Dopamine seems to facilitate "a tight control of behavior" (Tucker & Williamson, p. 192). By providing a redundancy bias, dopamine-enhanced pathways facilitate fixed, persistent behavior. In the face of motivational urgency, tight controls provide organized, sequenced, and focal behavioral repertoires that might otherwise disorganize.

This kind of motivation — tight, organized, intense — is reminiscent of what is included in the concept of motivation as it is used in school. However, the kind of tight control described here arises out of primary, internal urgency and is not superimposed by external value systems or consciously willed outcomes.

It is the regulation within the system that is critical. Norepinephrine, according to this model, facilitates attention to perceptual events and allows dopamine's facilitation of motor control, which is necessary to receive stimulation. Dopamine challenges the norepinephrine push to keep re-orienting; it helps to override natural arousal to new stimuli. Without this override, one would see a continuing tendency to respond to whatever is new and different — manifesting as distractibility, hyperactivity, and the loss of the goal. Norepinephrine "pushes" to override dopamine's "tight control," which would otherwise result in overfocusing (perhaps in the subtype of ADD sufferers known as overfocusers), stereotypies and obsessive-compulsive traits, and perseveration (Kinsbourne, 1990). Together, the NE and DA systems create a dynamic interaction of contrasting functions: one that is in need of well-tuned regulation, and one that forms the basis for the arousal/activation system which defines attention (see chapter 4). It is not surprising, then, that medications that facilitate regulation of the norepinephrine and dopamine systems are effective in treating attention deficits.

Motivation as Effort

The work required to change and maintain attentional state is integrally aligned with the concept of motivation as effort (McGuiness & Pribram, 1980). The effort that drives attention beyond its habituation bias is part of the left-hemispheric activation system we have described (see chapter 4). In this model, motivation is part of the regulatory system that maintains balance between the structural and biochemical asymmetry within the attention (arousal–activation) complex. It is *effort* that maintains focus and vigilance in service of moving from habituation-prone arousal to sustained attention for more careful and conscious analysis.

According to the McGuiness and Pribram (1980) model, effort is very closely aligned with its literal meaning of work and energy. It represents the work necessary to change state from a relatively effortless habituation bias to a more vigilant and sustained form of attention. Just as energy in the form of heat is required to change state in the transition from liquid to gas, so is effort required to change states from tonic arousal to activation. When the energy supply diminishes, steam will revert to a less-organized liquid state; similarly, focused vigilance will disorganize to more diffuse levels of arousal. It is important to remember, however, that energy in the form of effort must be well modulated. Too much effort — perhaps based in the desire to achieve or gain a reward, or in the increased arousal associated with anxiety — is disorganizing in its own right (Hockey, 1984; Robbins, 1984). Urging a child to try harder is frequently nonproductive and even counterproductive.

The effort needed to activate and control incoming information is exerted as part of the working memory function — once again accentuating the attention/working memory connection. While one maintains information in working memory, a great deal of effort is required to override fading attention for the mundane and trivial purpose of simply keeping information active. Effort, then, is required to deal with low-level processes. It is not until these demands are met, until data are collected and kept alive in the temporary store, that more interesting, arousing, and personally gratifying thought can take place. In our work, we have found this need to expend extraordinary effort on trivia to be extremely irritating for competent people with ADDs.

The relationship between effort, volition, and attention has been appreciated as early as the origins of psychology itself (James, 1902). In *The Principles of Psychology*, James spends some time in his chapter on attention debating whether the focus of attention is something willed or merely an effect of circumstances. James clearly sees all attention as volitional and argues that even followers of the nonvolitional school will be persuaded to recognize the "spontaneous power" (p. 457) of the effort to attend. Ordinarily, argues James, the effort (will, volition) to attend goes unnoticed, since attention is propelled by the natural flow of thought of which it becomes a part. It is only when this flow (Csikszentmihalyi & Larson, 1984) is absent, where no organic interest exists or where conflicting interests are in competition for attention, that effort raises itself to the conscious level. In James' (1902) words:

> Effort is felt only where there is a conflict of interests in the mind ... such inhibition [of the preferred object of thought] is a partial neutralization of the brain energy which would otherwise be available for fluent thought. But what is lost for thought is converted into feeling, in this case into the peculiar feeling of effort, difficulty or strain. (p. 451)

We, like many others, have found much in these few words. It is quite provocative to consider the relationship between limited conscious intellective capacity and feeling. It is possible — and seems quite probable — that those objects that appeal to, but cannot fit into, the limited capacity of attention get converted to feeling, where the subconscious capacity for processing remains unlimited. There is a cost to inhibition of prepotent responses, paid at the level of feelings — perhaps frustration, dissatisfaction, lack of enthusiasm, confusion, or even a false feeling of clarity.

The more limited one's attentional capacity — as in attention dysfunction — the more content must be allocated to the subconscious, feeling state. We have found that children with ADDs, when questioned about a topic, say they feel as if they might know about it but are not sure. They can tell you *that* they know, but not *what* they know. These are the youngsters who never know how they have performed on a test. Or, worse, they think they have done well only to find out later that they have earned a low grade. These are also the youngsters who process a good deal at the level of affect and might seem highly reactive or even labile.

As James suggests, the feeling of effort is often associated with "difficulty" or "strain." In the context of ADDs, these attributes take on particular relevance. Children with ADDs are often described as "lazy" or "unmotivated," as expending insufficient effort. The observers who use these descriptors are apparently themselves subject to the effects of limited attention, spending theirs on the outward manifestations of effort. In school, effort means work production, eyes on the page, pencil in motion. The effort that James (1902) appreciates, that which goes into coping with insufficient attention, is not readily observable. In addition — or perhaps essentially — children with particularly limited attention have a heightened awareness of their efforts in James' sense of "thought ... converted into feeling." The adage that says children with ADDs have poor tolerance for frustration is, in our opinion, false. It would be more to the point to say that children with ADDs have more frustration to tolerate.

Motivation: The Drive Toward Homeostasis

A system is driven by the need to stay functioning. Motivation, when well modulated, keeps an individual's neuropsychological system optimally aroused — not too much, not too little. In fact, in a well-regulated system, the amount of effort and incentive seems to be out of the individual's voluntary control, determined instead by the intrinsic demands of the task — which in turn are determined by the internal, memory capacity of the observer/performer (Gibson, 1979). In Kahneman's words:

The tentative conclusion, then, is that the performance of any activity is associated with the allocation of a certain amount of effort. This standard allocation *does not yield errorless performance.* Allocating less effort than the standard probably will cause a deterioration of performance. Allocating more than the standard seems to be beyond our ability. (p. 15, emphasis ours)

What does seem to be under motivational control is the decision to stop or start. If the task demands are so great that they exceed capacity limitations, coping can take the form of simply saying *no.* This is akin to infant gaze aversion (Sroufe, 1990; Zeskind & Marshall, 1991) and to the "unmotivated" school-age child's refusal to even get started or try (Cherkes-Julkowski & Stolzenberg, 1992). Both responses are highly motivated to maintain homeostasis, an optimal level of functioning, self-regulation, *self.*

When homeostasis is threatened by prevailing stimuli (be they internal or external; thought, somatic, or sensory), emotions occur (James, 1902; Meldman, 1970). The turning off and the turning on of attention can serve to maintain homeostasis by preventing excess stimulation from invading the system (Zeskind & Marshall, 1991). Through arousal and selectivity, the attentional system decides which stimuli will occupy the limited capacity of working memory. If this regulation is dysfunctional — or if capacity is overloaded for some reason — homeostasis will be disrupted, and disorganization will occur. For example, if a task appears overwhelming, the homeostatic function would shut down attention to preserve optimal levels of arousal (Karmel, Gardner, & Magnano, 1991; Zeskind & Marshall, 1991). If a task is underarousing (e.g., repetitive, or perceived as being irrelevant or "ungraspable"), homeostatic function will promote the seeking out of other, more arousing forms of stimulation. In school, this need could be satisfied by a more challenging level of instruction, or with novel materials — or alternatively by nudging a nearby classmate, or "acting out" in any number of other ways.

In our view the child/adult is driven unconsciously, biologically and cognitively, to maintain homeostasis. This condition creates primary motivation and delivers the most primary form of pleasurable feedback. Novelty will always have a greater draw than redundancy (James, 1902; Tucker & Williamson, 1984). Behavior that confirms self-worth will always dominate over behaviors that serve to make one question one's competence (Sullivan, 1953). As a result, *not trying* is a highly motivated response when effort is likely to result in failure (Dweck, 1987; Robbins, 1984). In fact, Leventhal (1990) purports that learned helplessness can become a permanent, biological change. In the case of animals, when it becomes evident that negative stimulation (shocks) cannot be avoided, waiting for a shock is no longer associated with heightened levels of anxiety. The animal has learned to cope, at the neurophysiological level.

Responses that maintain one's sense of balance will dominate over those which threaten to disorganize (Karmel et al., 1991; Thoman, 1987). As both Lois Murphy (1962) and Virginia Satir (1988) point out, all behaviors are an individual's motivated, best efforts at adaptation, i.e., coping — regardless of how maladaptive those behaviors might appear to others. The process of socialization is the process of overriding natural forms of motivation to comply with those having to do with the good of the group: delaying gratification, denying personal interest, and taking the perspective of others (Kaye, 1982). The problem, then, becomes one of finding a harmony among internally and externally driven regulatory forces. This is not a simple learning or contingency-appreciation issue. Furthermore, it requires a well-tuned executive function, something that does not develop easily in children with ADDs.

Motivation, then, is a drive to preserve homeostasis, not necessarily a response to an external reinforcer. External reinforcers *may* affect behavior, especially if they serve to arouse an underaroused system. But attention behavior is influenced by habit (see chapter 4), novelty, and the drive to maintain homeostasis of optimal levels of arousal. Only the individual has the resources to mobilize in the face of any of these influences. Therefore, and most importantly, the teacher or practitioner is *not* providing the reinforcement. Rather, the individual provides her own reinforcement through her recovery of homeostasis or, through reorganization at a more advanced level, *homeorhesis* (Sameroff, 1982).

When viewed as a dynamic, nonhierarchic, self-organizing system, motivation depends upon the interplay among many internal and external factors. It serves to maintain some degree of stability and homeostasis while promoting the inherent drive of all open systems to reach increased levels of organization and complexity (Gell-Mann, 1994). The term *homeorhesis* captures this process of evolution through higher stages of development by seeking dynamic stability at successive rest points, where the system can again oscillate and find homeostasis at a comfort level requiring the least energy expenditure. The system gets into an in-phase, smooth level of function at which each oscillation promotes the next with minimal effort (as with pendulum oscillations). The internal and external constraints that influence stability at such a level constitute *attractors* for that phase.

All systems, then, including children with ADDs, are internally driven to develop to the next stage of complexity. Motivation propels them to reach higher levels of organization by using field resources for the energy to do so. Until stability is found at the most recently achieved level of organization, the system remains vulnerable. If there is insufficient energy to maintain that level, there can be a regression to the previous one. This regression maintains some integrity and balance within the system.

Effort: A Point of Diminishing Returns

The curvilinear relationship between arousal and performance (see chapter 4) is well known (Eysenck, 1982; Hockey, 1984; Robbins, 1984; Yerkes & Dodson, 1908). Simply put, increased energizing of the arousal system (effort) will improve performance up to a point. Beyond this, more effort becomes disorganizing. It disrupts the regulation among processes. Once regulation is disrupted, the entire system becomes compromised, and otherwise functional coping mechanisms might cease to be effective. We have observed this in a number of highly (overly?) motivated students. In their efforts to cope, when understanding is elusive due to attention dysfunction, they "pump up" the effort system. The frequent result is extreme activation directed toward repetitive focus (overfocus) on small, manageable, but often trivial data points. The overfocus often leads to cognitive rigidity and anxiety. When this strategy fails to be effective, their solution is to try harder — further disrupting the balance between the "forest and the trees," the self-regulatory potential of the system; this makes it impossible for the rest of the attentional, cognitive, and affective systems to stay in balance.

It makes sense that the issue of motivation should arise as part of the complex of attention (Barkley, 1990). Attentional resources are limited. Attention must work in harmony with the rest of the cognitive system, which in turn must remain in synchrony with all other intrapersonal and interpersonal systems. When resources are limited, decisions — however subconscious — have to be made. Demands are made in the attentional/arousal system to maintain an optimal amount of arousal for taking in information about the world, but at the same time regulating a homeostatic state both autonomically (Thoman, 1987) and cognitively (Kahneman, 1973; Navon & Gopher, 1979). In a well-regulated system, the child can balance and trade off between the demands of homeostasis and intense, goal-directed attention. This is not possible for more vulnerable systems.

Motivation as Response to Contingent Reinforcement

Lack of motivation has been seen as both an effect and a cause of attention dysfunction. An early position of Barkley's (1990) was that motivation, rather than attention, is at the heart of ADD. He saw persons with ADDs as dysfunctional in "the manner in which behavior is regulated by its consequences" (p. 46). His theory holds that the inability to regulate behavior according to social consequences is, in effect, an inability to self-govern or to comply with rules.

In order to benefit from external contingencies (i.e., consequences), a person must maintain awareness of the goal upon which the consequence is contingent. Executive function deficiencies make this difficult for most individuals with ADDs. Dopamine depletion in the prefrontal cortex diminishes the ability to maintain the on-line awareness necessary to delay response and keep the goal in sight while progressing through the intermediate stages (Diamond, Zola-Morgan, & Squire, 1989; Goldman-Rakic, 1992). In this light, what has otherwise been identified as *dysfunctional regulation by consequences* might seem to be a distorted reflection of what is essential to the problem, i.e., executive dysfunction that dismantles the ability to maintain and pursue a goal that is not immediately attainable.

The exercise of subdividing or splitting the attentional system in this way is not fruitful. It is particularly problematic when applied in some diagnosis and treatment models. Child study teams can spend long hours debating whether *attention* or *motivation* is the problem. Ironically, regardless of how the debate is resolved, the treatment is nearly always the same: place the child on a more systematic, more concrete, more intense, and more refined reinforcement schedule. These elaborate, individual behavior management programs do nothing more than restate the original situation: *do this, or else!*

The strong behaviorist tradition in psychology and education promotes the interpretation that behavior is driven by learned associations between behavior and its consequences. Motivation, then, is determined by reinforcement schedules. Behavioral theory purports, further, that if a behavior is rewarded adequately and intermittently, it will persist even in the face of unrewarded events — at least for a while, and at least as long as some intermittent reinforcement is still forthcoming. Eventually, according to this view, the underlying rule system that governs behavior and its rewards takes on a control function. Such a model makes no reference to any other internal systems that contribute to self-regulation and might be in competition to drive behavior (Levine, 1989).

Such a model also assumes that behavior is controlled lawfully, by rules handed down from a central control agency. The homunculus is invoked again. In contrast, on the view of self-organizing systems, behavior is aggregated in real time (Thelen & Smith, 1994) and organizes itself out of the dynamic aspects of function. As Zeskind and Marshall (1991) point out, one oscillation in a pendulum swing within the arousal system is the motivation for the next, opposing one. Ultimately, as with a pendulum, the system will find the most rhythmic cycle of oscillations that requires the least energy to operate smoothly.

This chapter has been in large part devoted to the thought that a person's attentional or other responses are motivated by the maintenance of homeostasis or self-regulation, and not by externally imposed contingencies. This is true at a conscious as well as a biological level. In fact, motivation and attention do not appear to be separable phenomena. Mesulam (1981) has made the point that attention is driven by an internal representation of what is relevant or within one's grasp. The effect is so strong as to create complete neglect of some aspect of the visual field if it has been rendered irrelevant. The neglect effect can be generated by lesion but can also be generated simply by restraining a (monkey's) arm so that objects ordinarily in its grasp would also be rendered irrelevant (see chapter 4, p. 58). The internal forces determining motivation can be far more persuasive than the force of a reinforcement schedule.

Motivation as a Response to Novelty and Redundancy

It is important to remember that neither attention nor motivation is a single, homogeneous entity. Recall that Tucker and Williamson (1984) have established at least two distinct driving forces behind (i.e., motivators of) attention. The first, invoked by novelty and holistic processing, is associated with norepinephrine-rich, right-hemisphere pathways. The second requires dopamine-facilitated activation in the form of redundancy and repetitive, focused cognitive action.

When the context is familiar and the action already practiced, then controlled, focused attention is not in high demand. The child can be led by what is, at that moment, arousing. Situations of this kind do not require highly organized, controlled attention, as would the learning of arbitrary associations — which in turn would create the need for repetition to achieve mastery. They do not require meeting a set of performance criteria set by another and quite possibly viewed by the child as arbitrary, not arising out of context or meaning.

In contrast, school learning hardly ever calls upon the child to attend solely on the basis of novelty and inherent meaning. A good deal of the curriculum, especially during the elementary years, is based in symbol learning. Learning symbols is the epitome of rehearsal-based, repetitive, arbitrary associations. To teach the symbol system efficiently, a good deal of the curriculum in math or reading classes is dedicated to repetition. And the repetition is supposed to be done independently by each child. This is a situation designed to disorganize and frustrate any child whose dysfunction involves those aspects of attention related to forced and sustained activation without the enhancement of novelty/arousal.

When learning is viewed in this way, a concern about whether or not ADD symptoms are situational seems irrelevant. Historically, diagnosis of ADDs has insisted that attention dysfunction be pervasive, not situational. However, attention functioning is *always* situational. Some contribution to attention is always made by novelty and familiarity, by the need for repetitive focus, and by domain-specific knowledge.

In fact, it can be argued that situational effects are *stronger* for children and adults with ADDs. They are more dependent on external enhancement of attention. They have less internal control. The typical ADD child who gets identified and treated lacks controlled focus and the ability to invoke repetitive cognitive action in non-novel situations.

The continual interaction and seeking of a balance between novelty and familiarity is a powerful determinant of attentional behavior, one that overrides reinforcing contingency systems. Self-regulation is not a top-down phenomenon; rather, it emerges out of local properties as elemental as cell associations. There are certain novel stimuli (a sudden loud noise, for example) that cannot be avoided, regardless of the attractiveness of reward. Likewise, there are strong habitual modes of responding that result from previously established and repeatedly practiced cell associations (Derryberry & Reed, 1996; Hebb, 1949; Penrose, 1990) and that compete, in effect, with reinforcement programs. What entrained these associations in the first place is left to discussion. Even if a purely behavioral, contingency-based explanation were assumed, it would be naively optimistic to believe that a new contingency system could change behavior as if the pre-existing set of internalized motivators had no influence.

The Importance of Active Involvement

The effect of feedback is extremely sensitive to the conditions under which behavior is executed. If a child (Thoman, 1987) or other animal (Mesulam, 1981) selects his own focus of attention and generates his own response, the feedback is qualitatively different from what results if the same behaviors are induced by an experimenter manipulating the child's/animal's body. This fact has been established through electrophysiological studies that reveal different cortical glucose production patterns for identical self-generated and other-generated behaviors (Porrino et al., 1984).

There is a feedback loop that provides information back to the individual *as a result of* the individual's actions, and that impacts on the next action (be it motor, cognitive, whatever). This is a *spiral*, not a linear progression. Information generated as feedback from environmental stimuli as a result of active participation is more usable than information that is externally imposed. A purely common-sense perspective reinforces this notion: unless a child generates his own response, the context for interpreting reinforcement is simply not meaningful. Studies of "everyday cognition" have established that performance based on in-context, self-generated thinking far exceeds performance in an out-of-context condition, such as school, where others determine the focus (Lave, 1988; Rogoff, 1990). This point is especially relevant to the ADD population. It is a nearly universally recommended intervention to provide

ADD children with a highly structured environment, where they receive tightly constructed, consistent external regulation and rapid, direct feedback about appropriate vs. inappropriate behaviors. Such an approach places the child in a situation where she seldom has the opportunity to structure her own experience, generate her own behavior, and interpret feedback within that context. Ironically, it has been our experience that under conditions of *self-selected attention,* children with ADD manifest far fewer problem behaviors.

The fact that children with ADDs fail to internalize a self-regulatory representation of how "behavior is regulated by its consequences" (Barkley, 1990, p. 46) might, in some part, be due to the fact that regulatory systems are often imposed on them in a nonfacilitative, directive fashion — one that is arbitrary from the perspective of the child. Children who develop in a more typical fashion have more opportunity for self-generated, personally relevant experimentation. The accepted practice of giving rapid feedback and offering clear contingencies for behavior is apt to check the worst of behavior, at least while the intervention is in process, but it is also likely to interfere with the child's own efforts to achieve or maintain self-regulation. And then generalization never happens because *learning* never happens.

Motivation as Volition

The debate about motivation vs. attention comes up frequently in the context of "volitional" behavior. The overtold story runs something like this: "But he can attend when he's doing something he likes, Lego playing, TV watching, fishing ... *If he wanted to, he could.*" Many children with ADDs are able to function at an optimal level some of the time, but fail to perform at that level at other times. To teachers and parents this appears to be evidence of a problem of will: he did it before, therefore *he could do it now if he wanted to.* It is likely, however, that conditions were more facilitative the last time. Maybe some subtle form of support (energy) was available earlier that is now missing. Perhaps the child was better rested; perhaps he had taken medication at a more opportune time ... These *are* issues of motivation, but they emerge out of the conditions of the situation, not out of volition. Even well-regulated, nonimpaired individuals experience natural fluctuations. Not every day is a good day. No one expects a baseball player to get a hit every time.

The question of volition is a problematic one. To assume volition, that an individual has a will, is to assume a central mechanism that can take charge and give orders to the rest of the system — a homunculus that stands above all other operations and wills what should happen next. But postulating one homunculus leads to an infinite regress (Edelman, 1992), like Hofstadter's (1979) metagenies. After all, who or what is telling that homunculus what to do, then *that* one ... ?

Certainly no one would dispute that individuals appear to want to do some things and not others. This is part of what builds the sense of a personality, a self. The question is whether the cohesion we call a self is a top-down mechanism or an outcome of "natural drift" (Varela, Thompson, & Rosch, 1993) which takes on a pattern emerging out of the lower-level processes we have described here.

The top-down theory is becoming increasingly untenable (Dennett, 1991; Edelman, 1992; Hofstadter, 1985; Penrose, 1990). Once one homunculus, or one center for will and control, is postulated, there is an immediate need for another. There is no way out of the series. Will — which is essentially the self, since "I will" implies an essence whose will it is — must emerge out of the local properties we have discussed as aspects of motivation: neurochemistry, cell associations, self-regulatory, and self-organizing functions, and the immediate, local properties of context.

To demonstrate how higher-order functions or entities such as motivation and self emerge out of lower-level ones takes some explanation indeed. The phenomenon can be observed in inanimate systems as patterns emerge out of self-organizing dynamics. Grains of sand dropped from a fixed point will consistently form a symmetrical shape as they pile up (Ruthen, 1993). It has become increasingly clear that dynamic, chaotic activity at the microscopic level self-organizes into macroscopic, ordered patterns and rhythms (Nicolis & Prigogine, 1989).

Order, however, requires energy to create and maintain itself. In an equilibrium state, where all parts of the system are homogeneous, a physical system can maintain stability with minimal energy supply. As the system is perturbed through energy infusion, it begins to "behave" — to organize itself into patterned, increasingly complex states. The global entity represents a highly ordered state that is not recognizable at a more microscopic level (Nicolis & Prigogine, 1989).

Higher-level, more organized cognitive states can emerge out of very basic, chaotic, elemental ones. Edelman (1992) proposes that this takes place through a series of recursive, reentrant circuits that he likens to "bootstrapping." As in the metaphor of a man who lifts himself out of a viscous medium by holding on to his boot laces and propels himself by creating a cycle with repeated rotations, higher-level mental activity can emerge out of fundamental recursive brain activity.

This is admittedly difficult to conceptualize, but it is far more believable than an infinite regress of homunculi. However, if one accepts the view offered by self-organizing theory, one is forced to accept that *no one is in charge here*. Attributions of lack of will or lack of motivation as the simple *cause* of behavior no longer are possible. Applying this view of motivation in schools would translate into a nearly complete paradigm shift. Motivation would be understood as an emergent property, fundamentally connected to the individual's place and time. Rather than exhort the child to get her motivational act together, teachers would provide support at lower levels to help her system self-organize so that higher-level forms of self-regulation and motivation could emerge. This approach means giving up manipulating the "volitional center" through contingency systems and joining the student at the level of her internal struggle to promote optimal outcomes.

Summary

Motivation is a complex phenomenon, much of which is embedded in the biochemistry of attention, and much of which is below the level of consciousness — certainly beyond what might be thought of as will. It is argued that motivation is driven by the forces of novelty, emotion, the nature of the situation, expectations built by experience, and the need to preserve homeostasis. Motivation is not easily susceptible to modification through external reinforcement (i.e., behavior modification approaches).

Arousal serves the primary function of rapid habituation — orientation to intense or novel stimuli — and thus creates a continual scan of the environment. *Activation* constitutes a counter-force and serves to create a more focal, sustained organization of behavior. Both arousal and activation are part of the attention system. Both are driven by the biochemistry of attention. As a result, interest, focus, and task commitment emerge out of the dynamic regulation of attentional processes.

An individual's motivation is first and foremost to achieve and maintain stability, or *homeostasis,* a comfort level emerging out of a system in dynamic balance. In the effort to maintain stability at the most complex level of organization possible, external reinforcers can be denied or ignored. In fact, *no one is in charge here.* Teachers cannot motivate a child without consideration for the complexity of her system. The child cannot motivate herself independently of the dynamic, self-organizing properties of her attention system.

6

Medication Effects on the Regulation of Cognition

Pharmacological interventions are the most common means by which ADDs are managed. Despite the sensation created in the popular media, there is very little scientific debate concerning the effectiveness of medication in treating ADDs. Furthermore, many of the suspected risks of stimulant medications now appear to be unfounded. Growth deficits have been found to be temporary and slight, and growth tends to normalize during adolescence (Spencer et al., 1996). Perhaps the greatest concern in using stimulant medication has been the risk of triggering tics associated with Tourette's Syndrome (TS). Even this concern, however, has been attenuated by the possibility that ADDs and TS exist on a continuum. Tics might, therefore, be associated with the underlying disorders and not necessarily related to the medication used.

The scientific debate centers on valid identification of ADDs. Once an ADD is identified, the questions about pharmacological treatment concern how much, what kind(s), and according to what schedule. The doubters have charged that too many children have been identified and conclude that, therefore, some are falsely identified. They cite the increasing incidence of identified cases as proof that overidentification is taking place. However, there are certainly other possible explanations for the rising numbers, such as:

- Better identification procedures mean that children who would formerly have gone undiagnosed are able to be identified today.
- Greater awareness in the community has resulted in a greater number of referrals to professionals who themselves have a heightened awareness of the possibility of the disorder.
- Evidence of the strong genetic component of ADDs suggests that an increase in incidence from generation to generation should be *expected*. ADDs, learning disabilities, and other mild genetic disorders do not extinguish themselves like more severe disorders (such as autism) which may cause death prior to the age of reproduction or result in social traits that reduce the probability of social relationships and childbearing. The latter kind of disorder would remain at a stable rate of incidence across generations.

Neither popular nor scientific discussion has concerned itself much with the cognitive effects of medication. Because ADDs have been considered to be and are classified as behavioral disorders, the debates about medication effects have centered on improvements in behavior. It is common practice, for example, for practitioners to adjust levels of medication based on teacher, parent, and sometimes self-ratings on a behavioral checklist such as the Connor's scale. Since this and other similar scales emphasize issues of hyperactivity, behavioral impulsivity, and mood, they provide little if any direct information about the effects of pharmacological treatment on those cognitive processes affecting learning and thinking in school.

In fact, there has been the belief that any cognitive benefits derived from medication would be the indirect outcome of improved behavioral control (Richardson, Kupietz, Winsberg, Maitinsky, & Mendell, 1988). The suggestion is that if a child can sit still longer, she will be able to learn more in school. A recent expression of this belief appeared in an interview with John Werry, M.D. (*Attention!*, 1995):

> And it [stimulant treatment] does not, of course, enhance learning in any substantive way. What it does ... is first of all, enhance performance of what the child already knows, and second of all, shape a child's prelearning skills ... [i.e.,] the kinds of things you need in order to learn, of which motivation and concentration are the two main things. (p. 7)

Barkley (1990) advocates a similar view — that any apparent deficit in information processing in children with ADDs is better explained by their inability to enforce the effort necessary to drive processing.

It appears that in actuality, both the attention system and the biochemical systems that drive it are more complex than this view might allow. The neurotransmitter systems thought to be most directly involved in attention are dopamine and norepinephrine (see the discussion in chapter 4). However, the systems are quite complex, since these two neurotransmitters are interdependent in their regulation, and both are subject to regulatory interactions with serotonin (Rogeness et al., 1992; Spoont, 1992). The goal of pharmacological intervention is to effect a propitious balance among these and other neurotransmitters to bring function to an optimal level.

DETERMINING A MEDICATION REGIMEN

The Options

Depending upon the precise presentation of the disorder, one (or more) of a number of classes of drugs might be prescribed. Ideally, behavioral and cognitive characteristics would reveal the nature of the biochemical imbalance and, thus, suggest which line and magnitude of medication would be most effective. In reality, it is still not possible to make this determination.

There are three major classes of drugs that have been used to treat attention deficit disorders: *stimulants*, various forms of *antidepressants*, and *serotonin enhancers*. Despite a developing knowledge base about the general behavioral and cognitive effects of various medications, it is still not possible to predict which medication, at which dosage, will be most efficacious for a given individual (Greenhill et al., 1996). Most physicians will begin with small dosages of methylphenidate (a stimulant, also known as Ritalin) and increase dosage gradually until the child, parents, and teachers register satisfaction. Comorbidities, family history, or poor reaction to Ritalin might lead to a trial of other medications.

Out of the drugs prescribed for ADDs, Ritalin has been the most frequently studied. Findings suggest that children with low anxiety, low severity of the disorder, and relatively high IQ tend to benefit most from Ritalin therapy (Buitelaar, Gaag, Swaab-Barneveld, & Kuiper, 1995). Yet even this finding fails to identify those factors that would contraindicate its use or suggest an even better line of medication. Furthermore, neither empirical findings nor clinical practice shed much light on how to determine initial dosage or subsequent increments of the medication. The standard practice of calculating dosage as a function of weight has not proven to be the method of choice. In addition, there are no established criteria for determining what are considered adequate behavioral or cognitive outcomes of medication interventions (Greenhill et al., 1996).

It is not clear what is the precise mechanism for change with each of the drugs used. The stimulants are thought to increase levels of dopamine directly. Antidepressants are aimed directly at norepinephrine. Selective serotonin reuptake inhibitors (SSRIs), of course, target levels of serotonin (Rogeness et al., 1992). Appendix A (p. 256) offers an outline, albeit simplified, of the suspected neurotransmitter and behavioral effects of these three classes of drugs. Chapter 4 discusses these aspects of neurochemistry, and the associated behavioral and cognitive effects, in more detail. Table 6.1 (below) provides more specific information concerning individual medications and their effects on neurotransmitter enhancement.

The main effect of ADD medications seems to be to increase levels of dopamine and norepinephrine at the synaptic cleft, thereby stimulating receptors (Hobson, 1994; Shenker, 1992). What is unclear is which of the stimulated receptor sites yield beneficial outcomes and which may promote undesired side effects (Shenker, 1992).

Pliszka et al. (1996) suggest that the effectiveness of drugs for ADDs is mediated by levels of central norepinephrine and peripheral epinephrine. The peripheral sympathetic nervous system and the locus ceruleus (which is comprised largely of neurons related to norepinephrine) can be stimulated simultaneously. Both systems contribute to the response to stimuli and to "preparing the cortex to process information" (p. 265). Both Ritalin and d–amphetamine (another stimulant, known commercially as Dexedrine) increase urinary peripheral epinephrine, and they have been found to share no further biochemical effect. Also, the salutary effects of clonidine (an antihypertensive) on ADDs may be due to its activation of norepinephrine presynap-

Table 6.1
Relative Effects of Medications on Neurotransmitter Release

	Norepinephrine (NE)	Dopamine (DA)	Serotonin (5-HT)
methylphenidate/Ritalin (stim)	+	+	+
imipramine (TCA)	+	0	+
amitriptyline (TCA)	+	0	+
nortriptyline (TCA)	+	0	+/0
desipramine (TCA)	+	0	+/0
buproprion/Welbutrin (non-TCA)	+	+	0
fluoxetine/Prozac (SSRI)	0	0	+
clonidine (antihypertensive)	−	0	+

tic receptors and its inhibition of the locus ceruleus — resulting in lowered arousal, motor activity, and aggression.

Development of the medication regimen begins with determining the nature of the presentation of the ADD, i.e., whether the individual does or does not demonstrate hyperactivity/impulsivity, overfocusing, anxiety, or aggressive behavior. Stimulants are most often prescribed to improve vigilance, sustained attention, and behavior control. Tricyclic antidepressants (TCAs) and selective serotonin reuptake inhibitors (SSRIs) target anxiety and perhaps overfocusing; also, because of their long-acting nature, they contribute to a steady state of functioning (Huessey & Wright, 1970). Clonidine might be prescribed for aggressive behavior and a possibly accompanying conduct disorder. Ultimately, medication type and level are refined through continuous monitoring of behavioral and sometimes cognitive outcomes.

Of all the medications prescribed for ADDs, stimulants are the most widely used and are most often the first line of intervention (Rapport, Carlson, Kelly, & Pataki, 1993). Of the stimulant medications, Ritalin has been most widely used and studied. Dexedrine (d–amphetamine) is used next most frequently. Cylert (pemoline) is also used, but less frequently than the other two stimulants. In our data (Cherkes-Julkowski, Stolzenberg, Hatzes, & Madaus, 1995), 80% of children taking a single medication take either Ritalin or Dexedrine. Sixty-nine percent of the total sample were treated with Ritalin alone. An additional 3% were treated with both Ritalin and desipramine. It is important to note that each of the stimulants has a different mechanism for affecting function (Shenker, 1992) and each, therefore, could affect a given child differently. When one stimulant medication does not work, it is generally well worth trying another.

Tricyclic antidepressants (TCAs) are used to affect mood and reduce the effects of anxiety. As mentioned above, their long-acting nature helps maintain a steady state of functioning. Prescription of antidepressants has generally been the second line of treatment. There are now a number of TCAs that have been prescribed: imipramine, amiptriptyline, nortriptyline, and desipramine. However, all of these, especially desipramine, are prescribed less frequently these days because of concerns about a few reported cases of sudden death (Popper & Elliott, 1990).

Welbutrin (buproprion) is a non-TCA antidepressant that has been used in the treatment of ADDs. Welbutrin and Ritalin were found to have similar effects on three cognitive measures: Kagan's Matching Familiar Figures, the Continuous Performance Test, and the Rey-Auditory-Verbal Learning Test (Barrickman et al., 1995). In practice, Welbutrin is often prescribed in combination with Ritalin.

The third line of intervention has been the SSRIs: medications that block the reuptake of serotonin, thus increasing the level of serotonin at the synaptic cleft.

Most frequently used are Prozac (fluoxetine) and Zoloft (sertraline). TCAs and SSRIs can be prescribed in isolation or in combination with a stimulant. Clonidine is believed to enhance serotonin levels and is also sometimes prescribed, particularly if there is a good deal of aggression or reactivity accompanying the attention symptomatology.

There is an increasing number of new medications being applied in the treatment of ADDs, although there has yet to develop a literature concerning their cognitive effects. For instance, carbamazepine (an anticonvulsant and analgesic) has had positive effects on the behavior of children and adolescents with ADDs, but data on cognitive outcomes of its use are unavailable (Silva, Munoz, & Alpert, 1996). Pharmacological treatment remains an inexact science, dependent on clinical judgment and careful monitoring of outcomes.

Co-occurring Conditions

Mood and behavior symptoms often occur concurrently with ADDs and must be considered in pharmacological treatment. As mentioned earlier, behavioral symptoms are often taken into account in the process of prescribing medications. There is sparse information, however, concerning medication effects on ADDs with comorbid cognitive disorders such as learning disabilities and language impairment.

In one study, Tannock, Ickowicz, and Schachar (1995) found a distinct difference in response to Ritalin in children with ADHD with and without co-occurring anxiety. Although overt behavior was affected similarly in both groups, Ritalin failed to produce beneficial effects on a working memory task in subjects with accompanying anxiety. It did not seem to produce adverse cognitive effects, however. Arousal (as measured by radial pulse) increased over baseline for the ADHD with anxiety group, but not for the ADHD group. The presence or absence of learning disability did not appear to influence drug effects.

Our research suggests that children with language impairments may benefit less or even suffer a detriment to language functions when taking medications[1] (Cherkes-Julkowski, Stolzenberg, Hatzes, & Madaus, 1995). Other functions, such as working memory and extended information processing, improved with medication. Medication was described as optimal with 80% taking stimulants alone, 3% taking Ritalin

---

[1] It is important to note that the study in question compared medicated ADD children with language impairments to other unmedicated ADD children with language impairment. It is not clear, therefore, how the same individuals taking medication might have done in an unmedicated condition. Yet there is some suggestion that the observed decline in the medication group reflects a true phenomenon. There has been a reported curvilinear effect of increased stimulant dosages specifically on language functions (Nigg, Swanson, & Hinshaw, 1993). That is, language functions will improve with increased dosage only up to a certain point. Dosages exceeding that point would result in a decrement in language functioning. Those children with already impaired language would be expected to suffer most from such a decrement.

and desipramine, and the remainder taking a single TCA.

The following discussion summarizes research findings concerning the cognitive effects of each of the medication types. Table 6.2 (below) provides an overview of these findings.

STIMULANTS

As indicated in Table 6.2, stimulant medications appear to promote vigilance, sustained attention, and concentration. Ritalin has been found to enhance selective attention. According to current thinking, they do so by enhancing dopamine effects (see chapter 4, Appendix A, and Table 6.1). Overall, the stimulants have clear and positive effects on both classroom behavior and academic performance (Tannock, Schachar, Carr, & Logan, 1989). Ritalin has been shown to have a positive effect on information processing, regardless of the presence or absence of comorbid aggression (Klorman et al., 1990). Ritalin brings clear improvement in working memory functions, such as those required by paired-associate learning (PAL), an extended, relatively difficult learning-over-time task (Swanson, Cantwell, Lerner, McBurnett, & Hanna, 1991). There is also evidence of improved performance on complex information processing tasks. Children with ADDs who are taking stimulants rely less on external prompts to solve the complex patterns on the Raven Standard Progressive Matrices

Table 6.2
Summary of Empirically Derived Cognitive Effects of Medications

	Stim	TCA	Stim + TCA	SSRI	Stim + SSRI	Welbutrin
academic performance	+				+	
attentional shift	-/+					
sustained attention	+	+		0		
paired-associate learning/ working memory	+	0				+
vigilance	+	-/0	-			+
selective attention	+					
complex information processing	+	+	+			+
inhibition		+	+	+		
steadiness of state		+		+		

than children with ADDs who are not taking these medications (Cherkes-Julkowski, Stolzenberg, & Segal, 1991).

As stated earlier, stimulants increase dopamine levels in the brain. Animal studies support the role of dopamine in learning. Learned, conditioned responses and memory show improvements with increased dopamine levels (Shenker, 1992). Selective inhibition of norepinephrine uptake — the effect achieved most directly with TCAs — does not seem to bring animals to optimal levels of function. Thus, the direct enhancement of dopamine may be necessary for full therapeutic value. Shenker (1992) goes on to suggest that the value of stimulants could well be their underselectivity for target sites.

Stimulant medications do not appear to normalize functions, however. Despite having intelligence equivalent to that of a normal group, ADD children medicated with either Ritalin (N=8) or Dexedrine (N=2) performed with significant maturational delays on the Bender Visual-Motor Gestalt Test and the Benton Visual Retention Test (Risser & Bowers, 1993). Although these children had no identified learning disabilities, EEG findings established persistent "problems in cognitive processing for ADHD children on tasks requiring motor and visual analysis, even under stimulant medication" (p. 1029).

There also seem to be interactional effects between dosage levels and information load. Sprague and Sleator (1977) described a U-shaped dose–response relationship when information load was high, and a linear relationship when information load was low. That is, with reduced amounts of information, performance improves *steadily* with dosage increases. When there are greater amounts of information, performance improves with increased dosage *to a point*, and then begins to decline. This phenomenon may explain the U-shaped relationship of stimulant dosage to language functioning (see note to p. 102), in light of the information-intensive nature of language processing. A similar U-shaped function is suggested in the study of Ritalin and desipramine in combination (Rapport et al., 1993); dosage increases reached a point of diminishing returns at which further increases produced decrements in cognitive performance.

There is substantial evidence that optimal cognitive effects are reached at lower levels of stimulant dosages than optimal behavioral effects. Furthermore, there has been some suspicion that when stimulant dosages are high enough to improve behavior, cognition can be adversely affected, resulting in decreased ability to shift attention (Swanson & Kinsbourne, 1978). Tannock and Schachar (1992) found that even at low levels (0.3 mg/kg) of Ritalin, there was some evidence of initial increase in perseveration on the Wisconsin Card Sorting Task. Although perseverative errors decreased upon a second administration, the findings suggest at least a temporary decrease in cognitive flexibility even at low dosages. Although the difference between lower and higher (1 mg/kg) doses was not significant, there was a tendency for greater perseveration at higher levels.

While they may impair cognitive flexibility, higher dosages of Ritalin (1 mg/kg) have been found to improve sustained attention (Dyme, Sahakian, Golinko, & Rabe, 1982). Increased cognitive performance in general and increased cognitive flexibility in particular have been documented with dosages of Ritalin up to 1 mg/kg (Douglas, Barr, Desilets, & Sherman, 1995; Solanto & Wender, 1989). These findings establish a positive, linear relationship between increased dosage and cognitive improvements.

The dosage level that appears to bring about optimal cognitive function — at least as defined by performance on an extended paired-associate learning (PAL) task — appears to be 10 mg of Ritalin *regardless of the child's weight or age* (Swanson et al., 1991). In the Swanson et al. (1991) study, 10 mg of Ritalin was equivalent to 0.3–0.45 mg/kg of weight. They found, further, that in children who weighed more, the actual mg/kg dosage reached optimal cognitive effects at lower levels. At higher dosages, cognitive performance has been found to decline (Douglas, Barr, O'Neill, & Britton, 1988; Rapport, Stoner, DuPaul, Birmingham, & Tucker, 1985).

Rapport, Denney, DuPaul, and Gardner (1994) have been able to refine one question of differential dosage effects on academic versus behavioral performance. Most of their 6- to 11-year-old ADDH subjects improved in on-task attention, classroom behavior, and academic performance with increased dosages of Ritalin through 20 mg. However, they also found a group of children whose response to stimulant medication was more specific. Although 94% of the group demonstrated behavioral improvements under at least one Ritalin dosage (5, 10, 15, or 20 mg), only 53% manifested improvement in academic functioning. Those who failed to benefit academically did improve behaviorally and, to a lesser degree, on the on-task measure. For this subgroup, academic efficiency reached a plateau at 10 mg. Rapport et al. (1994) conclude that there are at least two distinct groups of medication responders: those who improve increasingly and proportionately (at least through 20 mg) in all three measured areas, and those who will do better behaviorally without realizing appreciable gains in attention or academic performance, particularly at doses beyond 10 mg. They conclude, further, that the existence of these differential effects on behavior and academic performance *refutes the hypothesis that academic gains are a result of improved behavior.*

Given the finding that optimal cognitive and behavioral effects are achieved at different dosage levels, and that at least some aspects of cognition risk impairment at dosages high enough to improve behavior adequately, there are clearly choices to be made. At least in the school environment, cognitive improvements cannot afford to be considered secondary or irrelevant goals of pharmacological intervention. The question arises whether medication levels that are well titrated to improved cognition might eventually be able to improve behavior as well, through the mechanisms of improved social judgment (i.e., less cognitive impulsivity, better social perception based in sustained attention, and heightened vigilance) and generally improved inhibitory control (Kinsbourne, 1990; Rapport et al., 1993; Rogeness et al., 1992).

In addition to the chance that relatively large stimulant doses might impair cognitive abilities, stimulant treatment may have a number of other drawbacks. It is not effective in all children with ADDs. Biederman and Jellinek (1984) report that 3% of their ADD sample did not respond to stimulant treatment. There are also risks of appetite suppression, irritability and dysphoria, inadequate mood control, and lack of steady state due to the short half-life of stimulant medications (Gammon & Brown, 1993).

Tricyclic Antidepressants (TCAs)

As mentioned earlier, the TCAs have often been the second line of medication utilized to treat ADDs. They are ordinarily prescribed to improve mood and decrease hyperactivity (Gammon & Brown, 1993). However, they fail to improve vigilance, sustained attention, or working memory adequately (Biederman, Baldessarini, Wright, Knee, & Harmatz, 1989; Rapport et al., 1985).

One antidepressant, desipramine, does appear to yield cognitive benefits when taken in conjunction with Ritalin (Rapport et al., 1993). Rapport and colleagues found that children's performance on the Matching Familiar Figures Test improved over baseline when they took either Ritalin or desipramine alone. There was, however, an even greater improvement when both drugs were taken together. Ritalin in combination with desipramine was superior to desipramine alone in improving performance on the PAL. And on tasks requiring inhibition and complex information processing, adding desipramine to Ritalin brought improvements in performance over Ritalin alone. The researchers suggested that tasks requiring inhibition were more sensitive to desipramine, a conclusion supported by Kinsbourne (1990).

Alone, desipramine does not improve vigilance, and it may even block the vigilance ordinarily gained with Ritalin when they are taken in combination. It is possible, however, that what is lost in vigilance is gained in extended cognitive availability. Shenker (1992) found that medicating with either TCAs or Dexedrine had similar positive effects on continuous calculations.

Risks of TCAs include sedation and cardiovascular side effects, which have proven lethal in a small number of preadolescent children (Popper & Elliott, 1990). Furthermore, when TCAs are taken in conjunction with Ritalin, there is the possibility that Ritalin can elevate their concentration in the bloodstream (Greenhill, 1992).

SELECTIVE SEROTONIN REUPTAKE INHIBITORS

Like the tricyclics, selective serotonin reuptake inhibitors are beginning to be used in combination with Ritalin to achieve optimal cognitive/attentional effects, improved mood, reactivity (Spoont, 1992), and steadiness of state. Prozac (fluoxetine) alone seems to have a positive effect on both the behavioral and affective symptomatology of ADDs. As with TCAs, it has been found to be less effective than the stimulants in facilitating sustained attention (Barrickman, Noyes, Kuperman, Schumacher, & Verda, 1991). Gammon and Brown (1993) found that Prozac and Ritalin together significantly improved grade point averages in children from ages 9 to 17. The most improvement occurred in the most severe cases. The researchers propose that Prozac may intensify Ritalin action by increasing responsiveness to dopamine; this interpretation is supported by Spoont (1992). Prozac appears to have further direct benefits in terms of inhibition and risk avoidance (Gammon & Brown, 1993).

Manipulation of serotonin levels can have effects on a number of the behavioral presentations of concern in ADD children (Spoont, 1992). Low levels of serotonin can influence failure to suppress punished behavior, decrease the inhibitory function of dopamine, and increase aggression. In proper balance, serotonin constrains information flow and sensitization to stimuli, thereby mitigating against reactions of being overwhelmed. This would have clear effects on purely academic as well as social information processing.

CONCLUDING THOUGHTS

As we have discussed, the goal of medication for ADDs is to achieve the proper balance among neurotransmitters, those of primary concern being dopamine, norepinephrine, and serotonin. The system, however, is extremely complex; for instance, the same behavioral symptoms, reflecting the same neurotransmitter imbalance, may be caused by different underlying neurotransmitter problems. For example, the same lack of impulse control could hypothetically be driven by "absolute" low levels of serotonin *or* by typical levels of serotonin in conjunction with high levels of norepinephrine and dopamine (Rogeness et al., 1992). It is the balance among neurotransmitters that affects behavioral state. The strong suggestion is that there will be idiosyncratic differences among children with ADDs that cannot be captured by attempts at any form of subtyping. Since there is at present no direct way to measure neu-

rotransmitter levels or the balance among them, prescription of appropriate medication regimens requires the art of clinical judgment and readjustment. Teacher observation of cognitive functions will be critical in this process.

7

Social and Emotional Aspects of the Attentional Network

Much has been said about the social difficulties of children and adults with attention deficit disorders. Social functions impaired by attention-related problems may include peer relationships, compliance with authority figures and rules of conduct, and the perception of nonverbal emotional cues. The wide range of concerns about the social and emotional difficulties of children with ADDs reflects the complexity of the attention network.

The nature of the social difficulty is likely to reflect the nature of the underlying attentional difficulty. For example, conduct problems involving social judgment and inhibition are attributed to frontal lobe dysfunction (Price et al., 1990; Shapiro, Hughes, August, & Bloomquist, 1993). Problems with the perception of emotional cues, as expressed through facial expression, prosody, or gesture, are often associated with right-hemisphere-based difficulties that also affect the deployment of attention (Denckla, 1991; Mesulam, 1981; Rourke, 1987; Semrud-Clikeman & Hynd, 1990). Since both of these functions are part of the attention network, they can influence each other as well as other aspects of the attention system.

Much has been made of the high incidence of behavioral and adjustment problems among people with ADDs. Social adaptive skills in this population, as measured by the Vineland Social Adaptive Scale, have been found to be significantly discrepant with average IQ scores, and this gap increases with age (Stein, Szumowski, & Blondis, 1995).

Children with ADDs have been found to be more negative, more disruptive, and less compliant than their peers (Barkley, 1981), as well as less able to benefit from the consequences of their actions or to internalize social rules (Barkley, 1991). There is a high prevalence of dysfunction in peer and family relationships among ADD children (Biederman, Faraone, & Chen, 1993). ADD children tend to elicit undesirable behaviors from those around them (Mash & Johnston, 1983).

ADD children are likely to be more aggressive than other children (Hinshaw, 1987). They initiate approximately the same number of interpersonal interactions, but they are involved in a disproportionate number of disruptive or negative episodes (Abikoff, Gittelman, & Klein, 1980; Campbell & Cluss, 1982; Schleifer et al., 1975; Whalen, Henker, & Finck, 1981). Even when they join a new play group (and thus do not have the disadvantage of a negative reputation), they are not able to employ positive interactions, and their unpopularity is reestablished by the end of the first meeting (Pelham & Bender, 1982). These difficulties have been attributed to disruptions in frontal-area functions such as inhibition, social judgment, and self-monitoring. Treatment ordinarily includes medication, some kind of social skills training, firm contingency systems, and possibly group or individual therapy. However, it is hard to escape the irony of treating a problem that is defined by the inability to benefit from the consequences of behavior with an intervention based on the consequences of behavior.

A higher-than-expected proportion of children with ADDs also manifest Conduct Disorder or Oppositional Defiant Disorder. These comorbidities greatly increase the risk for poor social relationships with peers, siblings, and parents (Biederman et al., 1993). However, even without the co-occurrence of Conduct Disorder, ADDs with and without hyperactivity are strongly associated with peer rejection — that is, low likability and high dislikability on sociometric measures (Carlson, Lahey, Frame, Walker, & Hynd, 1987).

Less has been said about social problems that are of a less aggressive kind and less evident in behavioral manifestations. These include the right-hemisphere functions of mood regulation (Mesulam, 1981) and possible depression, social withdrawal, and/or emotional lability. This is true despite the fact that a subtype of ADD without hyperactivity but with social withdrawal, anxiety, and possibly depression has long been recognized (Borden, Brown, Jenkins, & Clingerman, 1987; Shaywitz & Shaywitz, 1988).

Shapiro et al. (1993) raise the important question of where the source of the social difficulty might lie. They suggest that the two most likely sources are issues of comportment, associated with frontal areas, and the perception and processing of social cues, based in right-hemisphere areas. However, there are other issues that need to be considered as affecting social and emotional functioning. Populations with attention difficulties exhibit difficulties with disinhibition, working memory, information processing more generally, communication, arousal-seeking, inattention, hyperactivity, hypersensitivity, reactivity, and verbal fluency — difficulties that must be considered in any discussion of social difficulties for those with attention dysfunction. It seems logical that the nature of the treatment would vary significantly depending upon the nature of the breakdown; therefore, we believe, it is important to understand the sources of dysfunction for each individual child, prior to designing intervention.

Moreover, the impact of these issues on individuals changes as they grow older. For example, older persons with ADD are more likely to attribute their achievements — as well as their failures — to external causes, suggesting that one long-term effect of academic and social difficulties is a sense of having little personal control over achievement events (Borden et al., 1987). This inclination to "blame" persons and events external to the self promotes a failure to take responsibility for one's behavior. Under these conditions, it is difficult to imagine how a person with ADD might become the agent for her own change.

Distractibility and Neglect

The seemingly simple act of paying attention during social interactions is really a compilation of various kinds of attentional skills.

- *Divided attention* is required when one must attend to two or more things at once. In a social situation, the participants must attend to the conversation as well as to conditions around them; when another student approaches the group, or when there is a signal to change activities, they must be aware of it. Social situations are complex, involving verbal, nonverbal, contextual, and historical cues with direct and indirect messages. The dimensions increase exponentially with each new participant.
- *Selective attention* is necessary when one must focus on one task and ignore irrelevant or less important stimuli. The individual must prioritize what is important to attend to and filter out everything else. The student who is able to focus on the teacher's voice or attend to a conversational partner, while ignoring the other interesting sights and sounds around him, is using selective attention.
- *Sustained attention*, or persistence, is needed when one must complete a

lengthy task. Lengthier or more complex tasks require more sustained attention. The independent work students complete at their desks in many classrooms places heavy demands on sustained attention. So too do many social interaction activities, such as games or group projects.

- *Vigilance* is needed when one must wait for some event before responding. Right fielders in baseball games often must wait for many minutes before they are called upon to catch a fly ball, but they had better be ready when it happens! Turn-taking in conversation and in games also requires vigilance, as does the detection of subtle but important social messages.

In order for a positive social interaction to occur, the individuals involved must be actively engaged. Interactions require a commitment of attention from both parties. Conversations require both individuals to contribute, and ideally they must share the same topic. ADD students tend to be poor conversational partners. They have difficulty staying with a topic and do not respond well to requests for more information. Since they do not follow what others are saying, they may ask for repetitions to an annoying degree. They tend to dominate interactions or monopolize the conversation (this may help them keep their attention on the conversation, but it doesn't accommodate the social requirements of the situation). They may misinterpret what others are saying, either because their inattention causes them to miss an important word or point, or because of difficulties deploying attention to absorb the subtleties of communication. This deficit in the ability to focus on specific environmental cues and to respond appropriately to them is a form of neglect (Mirsky et al., 1991). As the speaker, a person with ADD can be hard to follow; her thoughts may be incompletely expressed and followed by new ones that are sometimes only tangentially related to the first topic, and are often introduced without obvious transition between thoughts.

Similarly, the ADD student's attention may wander during a game or other goal-directed activity. If other students are going to be held accountable for the group's performance (winning the game, for instance, or turning in a group project), they may resent the constant need to refocus the attention of the ADD student. As one fourth-grade student told us, "I don't want him on my team because it's like giving the other team an extra player." Sandler et al. (1993) found that inattention and distractibility were disruptive to peer interactions, above and beyond the effects of hyperactivity.

Pelham et al. (1990) investigated the effects of medication on attention within a common social situation: a children's baseball game. They did not find any effect of Ritalin on baseball skills *per se* (e.g., hitting or catching), but subjects taking Ritalin did improve on measures of attention to the game (e.g., remaining in the ready-position on the field or correctly answering game-awareness questions). The researchers suggest that medication may help individuals in such situations to make fewer of the inattention-based errors that result in poor performance and, thus, social ostracism.

Another component essential to communication — and ultimately to the ability to find intimacy with a social partner — is *joint attention*. At the superficial level, joint attention involves eye contact, gesture, and contextual reference. These serve the essential purpose of finding a common, shared ground as the basis for interaction. When severe enough, breakdowns in joint attention can manifest as the extreme social dysfunction seen in children with autism. The ability to establish joint attention is essential (although certainly not sufficient) for the development of meaningful social exchanges, and is often associated with the ability to formulate attachment relationships (Mahler, 1979). This would be as true for early parent-child relationships as for strong and intimate relationships with peers throughout development.

Prerequisite to the ability to formulate a joint topic of attention is the ability to regulate one's own attention. The establishment of joint attention requires that one or both communication partners subordinate their individual interests to the joint topic. As we discussed earlier, this comes under the control of inhibitory processes mediated by an integrated neural network comprised of frontal cortical and mid-brain structures (Bachevalier, 1994). Furthermore, it is important that the participants have adequate ability to detect the frame of reference of another. Youngsters with ADDs are deficient in the ability to take the perspective of the other (Landau & Milich, 1988), even though they presumably have an adequate "theory of mind" (Baron-Cohen, Tager-Flusberg, & Cohen, 1993). They appear to experience a breakdown in the flexible and well-regulated deployment of attention, as well as in the adequacy of the attention resources themselves.

Joint attention dysfunction has been described as a secondary disturbance, one that is rooted in a primary disruption of executive functions (Mundy, 1995). The prefrontal executive function system helps facilitate the regulation of affect and approach/avoidance behavior (Dawson, Klinger, Panagiotides, Hill, & Spieker, 1992). In the absence of positive mood and the desire to approach, there would be little motivation for establishing joint attention. Disruptions can contribute to disjointed social styles that present as withdrawn or overly intrusive and interfere with the balance necessary for establishing a shared plane of interaction.

Infants are dependent upon a regulated interpersonal system with a responsive caregiver who is sensitive to the infant's needs for levels and kinds of stimulation. The caregiver serves as a pacesetter (Thoman, 1987), helping to regulate the intensity of stimulation as well as the child's focus of attention. ADD children are poorly equipped to participate in this process, since their own dysregulation provides unclear patterns of behavior for teachers and caregivers to build upon.

The ADD child's social style also exerts a reciprocal effect on others. Landau and Milich (1988) created a talk show simulation task, with subjects adopting the roles of guest and host. The ADD boys, in comparison with normal controls, requested feedback less often, communicated less efficiently, dominated more when in the host role and less when in the guest role, and were less competent at shifting communication patterns in response to changes in their roles. These boys seemed to become locked into a particular response strategy, and were not able to shift. Furthermore, the ADD style affected their non-ADD partners, who increased their level of controlling behaviors. This negative, reciprocal influence has been noted in interactions with mothers (Cunningham & Barkley, 1979), teachers (Whalen, Henker, & Dotemoto, 1981), and peers (Clark, Cheyne, Cunningham, & Siegel, 1988; Cunningham, Siegel, & Offord, 1985).

Disinhibition

A good deal of the social difficulty experienced by people with ADDs seems due to their inability to inhibit responses. The effects of uninhibited impulses can range in severity from interrupting another speaker to acts of verbal or physical aggression, or even to criminal behavior in the form of theft or injury to property or to others.

In its extreme form, disinhibition can take on aspects of Tourette's Syndrome, where there is difficulty controlling verbal impulses. Aspects of disinhibited overfocus can either simulate or co-occur with obsessive-compulsive disorder and other forms of perseveration or overfocus. The relationship between ADDs and Tourette Syndrome is now well established (Comings & Comings, 1990; Pauls, Leckman, & Cohen, 1993), even if the exact genetic link between the two remains a matter of debate. Extreme disinhibition can also simulate psychoses; disinhibition has in fact been proposed as the basis for such aspects of schizophrenia as thought intrusions, hallucinations, and confusing, unmonitored speech (Breslin & Weinberger, 1991; Hobson, 1994).

To illustrate this degree of disinhibition, we present the story of a child whom we shall call David, who was referred for evaluation at age 6 and had already been placed in a special transitional classroom prior to a first-grade program. He had been identified at age 4½ as having ADD. His development during the preschool years was characterized by extreme rigidity, repetitive question asking, some proneness to tics, and frequent and extreme flights into fantasy (more than would be expected for his age). In kindergarten, there were concerns about his rigidity, his unprovoked biting, kicking, and shouting, and his refusal to follow directions. He was noted to make up words when he did not know one. Transitions were difficult; he had a compulsive need to finish anything he had started. Social interactions with peers and adults were extremely problematic. He was identified by his school as having social and emotional maladjustment.

David was referred for educational, psychiatric, and neuropsychological evaluation. Evaluators agreed that disinhibition was central to his social and cognitive difficulties. David had many thoughts and interests that he could not easily check. Difficulty with inhibition seemed to be at the root of his difficulty shifting attention during social interaction and conversation, his difficulty complying with classroom routines or requests, and his tendency in conversation to become stuck on a question or idea. Inappropriate, excessive talking is a common problem among people with ADDs and one that is a strong predictor of peer problems (Sandler et al., 1993). David's difficulty with inhibition seemed to contribute to a sense of oppositionality or need for control, since he did not seem able to inhibit his need to pursue his course.

Disinhibition, in conjunction with a narrowed field of attention, also contributed to David's other social difficulties, such as wanting to finish a task despite a shift in group activity, pursuing his own frame of reference while neglecting that of others, and failing to notice whether another child was prepared for his advances or might need a more gradual shift to David's focus of attention. All of this contributed to the sense of rigidity that was noticed by all of his teachers and specialists.

Disinhibition and concomitant cognitive inflexibility comprise a large part of social impairment and have been found in other disorders that involve frontal areas (Grattan, Eslinger, Damasio, & Damasio, 1989). Behaviorally, these problems manifest as difficulty with shifts in conversation and irritation when a course of action or topic of attention is disrupted (Ackerly, 1950).

Although David had many positive social intentions, he was seen as aggressive in an unprovoked way. He was capable of real empathy and seemed to desire positive social contact. He simply did not have the control over his interests and impulses or the general self-control to be a responsive social partner.

In another case, a 20-year-old man experienced major problems with distraction and disinhibition in his attempts to communicate with others, both casually and more formally in writing. In his words, "Things go through my mind so fast" that his original thoughts became fragmented and were never fully expressed. He had not been successful in inhibiting the rush of his ideas so that he could manage coherent self-expression. This problem was especially upsetting to this young man, who was extremely intelligent and could imagine much more than he could say. His communication difficulties were aggravated by notable word finding problems, which are common in people with ADDs or other forms of minimal brain dysfunction. This slows the process still further and makes it that much more vulnerable to disruption.

Ironically, extreme verbal fluency can *also* be associated with social interaction problems among people with ADDs. In combination with disinhibition, verbal fluency allows things to be said impulsively that can create significant social difficulties. In fact, Sandler et al. (1993) found verbal fluency to be the strongest correlate of peer problems among children with ADDs. It is important to note that Sandler et al.'s study employed measures of verbal fluency that reflected rate of language *production* rather than language *content*. They hypothesized that children with attention deficit disorders who manifest frontal lobe dysfunction may have intact lexical access and retrieval, but have deficits in the executive functions of planning, editing, and self-monitoring, often involving language processing. There can also be problems with fully attending to what others express; again, rapid and prepotent associations tend to take charge.

There appears to be a deep cognitive underpinning to the process of inhibition that has the potential to permeate a good deal of information processing, even as it might affect personal and social functions. The inability to inhibit preferential, prepotent responses creates particular difficulty for a person who must update his learned expectations to incorporate new, relevant information — an essential capacity if he is to remain attuned to others and the social dynamic at large. In this way social functions are firmly rooted in cognitive processes. A purely cognitive task that illustrates the problems associated with disinhibition is Piaget's *A not B* test of object permanence. In this task, the solver confronts two screens. At first, an object is hidden consistently under one screen (A). Eventually, there is a switch: the object is hidden under the second screen (B). At this point, children younger than 12 months tend to search for the object under A but not under B. It would appear that there is a contribution made by memory function to performance on this task. However, young children who present the *A not B* error pattern are quite competent with other, more stripped-down object permanence tasks that are dependent on memory alone. One interpretation is that they cannot inhibit their earlier preference (Diamond et al., 1989).

People with ADDs appear to have a combined difficulty with inhibition and integration of information over a span of temporal separation. Delays require controlled, well-synchronized processing. Since the prefrontal cortex plays a role in controlled information management/integration and in inhibition of prepotent responses (Diamond, 1985; Luria, 1966, in Diamond et al., 1989), studies of lesions to this region have yielded some relevant findings. Monkeys with dorsolateral prefrontal lesions perform similarly to young children from 7½ to 9 months of age on the *A not B* problems at delays (Diamond et al., 1989). However, monkeys with bilateral lesions on the hippocampus, an area that influences memory more directly, are not impaired on the delayed *A not B* task. The same pattern appears when a non-memory task requiring inhibition of prepotent responses is introduced.

It has also been found that the *A not B* task is related to the ability of a child and her caretaker to establish joint attention (McEvoy, Rogers, & Pennington, 1993). In order to establish joint attention, it is necessary to subordinate current, prepotent interests to a jointly determined topic. This process calls upon the executive functions of behavioral and attentional inhibition, as well as the flexible deployment of attention (Mundy, 1995).

Another Piagetian developmental task involving inhibition is the object retrieval task (Uzgiris & Hunt, 1987), which requires the solver to use indirect means to solve a problem. Specifically, the solver needs to avoid a transparent shield by reaching around it to grasp a desired object. The challenge is to inhibit the perceptually-driven tendency to reach directly for the clearly visible object. Again, monkeys with prefrontal lesions are impaired. Diamond et al. (1989) interpret this to mean that the challenge is based less in delay *per se* than in the need to integrate information over a "temporal or spatial separation" (p. 535) and the need to inhibit responses to prepotent stimuli.

When viewed from the perspective outlined above, disinhibition is a good deal more than the lack of behavioral control. It is a very basic cognitive function that affects one's perception of a situation and alters behavioral responding at that level. Thus, it is not true that the child with ADDs affecting prefrontal functions perceives what is happening and what an appropriate response might be, but simply cannot or does not execute the appropriate response. Rather, without support, he simply cannot make use of a good deal of the cognitive material that would yield an adequate perception in the first place. Certainly an effective intervention would have to be directed at the level of perception itself.

Impulsivity

Impulsivity is closely related to disinhibition. The urge to do something overrides any thoughts of consequences before acting. As a result, the student often breaks rules for conduct. The impulsive student says what she thinks, before filtering or evaluating the content for appropriateness and logic. She acts without regard to consequences. The resulting frequency of rule violations places ADD students in trouble with both their teachers and their peers.

As students grow and develop, they become increasingly concerned with conformity. In the elementary grades, conformity to adult expectations is paramount, but in adolescence, conformity to expectations of the peer group prevails. The impulsive student's behavior is often at odds with his peers' expectations and quite possibly with his own. After all, impulsivity is driven by momentary energy; it can exist despite consciousness of and respect for the rules or standards of the community.

There are considerable consequences that follow from these impulsive behaviors:

- The impulsive student receives a significant amount of negative feedback from his teachers. When he breaks minor rules in school, his name is usually called out, followed by some corrective feedback. When he breaks more serious safety rules, there are trips to the principal's office and telephone calls to his parents.
- The presence of an ADD student in a classroom significantly decreases the teacher's tolerance of behavior and increases the amount of negative interactions between the teacher and all of her students (Whalen, Henker, & Dotemoto, 1981). Discipline and punishment begin to transform the classroom from a place of learning and discovery to one where behavioral conformity is the goal.
- Impulsive behaviors can disrupt an ongoing activity, thereby annoying or angering other students who value the goal of the activity.

The resulting negative atmosphere interferes with the types of experiences that improve self-confidence and positive social interactions. It would be naive to imagine that the other students are not aware at some level that the unfortunate atmosphere in the classroom is related to the performance of the "problem child." Furthermore, children with ADDs, used to being criticized, can become "kindled" or primed for a defensive response to even innocuous, well-meant, constructive criticism. (For further discussion of the effects of impulsivity in classroom settings, see chapter 8.)

Arousal Seeking

We spent some time in chapter 3 discussing the habituation bias of the right hemisphere and its cognitive implications for people with ADDs. The behavioral issues are similar. There is a high incidence of risk-taking behavior among children and adults with ADDs. Speeding, whether in cars or on bikes, is not uncommon. Gambling and shopping addictions have been documented among adults with ADDs; the attraction of these activities has been attributed to the increased arousal they bring about

(Hallowell & Ratey, 1994). The ADD child's tendency toward provocation and teasing may be due to several factors (for instance, the child's repertoire may lack more positive ways to initiate a peer interaction), but certainly these behaviors are consistent with an interpretation of arousal seeking.

There may also be a neurological "bias for novelty." As touched on in chapter 4, Tucker and Williamson (1984) have postulated a neurological system that may explain learning behavior. The right hemisphere, which is rich in the neurotransmitter norepinephrine, seems to be especially sensitive to any new or novel stimulus, while the left hemisphere, rich in dopamine, is specialized for more thoughtful analysis and repetitive motor activity. ADD sufferers seem to be wired to detect novelty; in fact, they are "novelty junkies." Given any situation, the ADD individual will attend to the novel. Once a stimulus is no longer new and interesting (often within seconds), the individual will once again search for something that is novel.

In a classroom, as one can imagine, this bias for novelty can be deadly. After one or two subtraction problems, the rest of the page loses its allure, and something taking place in the hallway steals the student's attention. Once that event is no longer novel, the pencil's eraser suddenly seems interesting. And when nothing in the environment is interesting, the average ADD child will engage his imagination and free association of thoughts. When events and materials are routine, too easy, or too difficult, they are perceived as boring and do not hold the attention of the ADD student. Under these conditions, the student with ADD is likely to find herself out of sync with the ongoing activities in the classroom. She seems, and is, egocentric; when all options for novelty are exhausted, it becomes instrumental for her to *provoke* enough activity to reach a satisfying level of arousal — subverting the structure of the classroom to meet the demands of her own system.

Tactile Defensiveness and Perceived Threat

Some ADD students are especially sensitive to touches. One parent reported that her child would only wear highly specific clothing: one shirt that was old and soft and tolerable, no turtlenecks or elastic waistbands, and one pair of very old sneakers. This supersensitivity, or tactile defensiveness, is often reported by parents as one of the "soft signs" of attention deficit disorders. Supersensitive children have particular difficulty waiting in line or working near other students. They perceive the most innocent bumps as serious aggression, and may respond to a perceived offense with anger or distress. Social interactions usually require some degree of proximity, so tactually defensive students are bound to experience difficulty in such situations.

Processing of Complex Social Information

Social situations are among the most complex stimulus fields encountered. One must attend to many cues, including facial expression, gesture, prosody, paralinguistic aspects of reference, and indirect references. True social interaction requires a partnership in which a give and take occurs. Neither partner is in control, yet both are in charge.

Price et al. (1990) have demonstrated a clear association between the ability to formulate complex social judgments and competence in more purely cognitive complex reasoning tasks. In their case studies of adults who suffered early developmental frontal lobe damage, they documented both extreme difficulty in learning social relationships, despite a history of negative feedback (including arrests and physical assault), and inability to perform adequately on a Piagetian task requiring formal operational thought. The ability to take the perspective of another on a map-reading task was also impaired. The authors conclude,

> The prefrontal cortex provides a template for the convergence of limbic outputs with extensively processed associative information [Mesulam, 1990]. This part of the brain is likely to provide one of the most important components of a neural network underlying the integrations of thought with emotion. (Price et al., 1990, p. 1391)

They stress the almost purely biological roots of this disorder, documenting the lack of typical risk factors in the social backgrounds of the subjects' parents. Furthermore, it appears that early bilateral frontal lesions do not benefit from the capacity for reorganization that is available to other early brain injuries. Rather, this condition seems to lead to progressively greater disturbances of behavior.

Information Processing Load Deficits

Like any cognitive activity, social interactions require orienting toward the future, editing, and self-monitoring — all attention-driven acts. Failure to invoke these processes will result in losing the thread of a conversation, missing an important piece of information, misinterpreting the speaker, saying something inappropriate, or committing some other social *faux pas*. Since social situations carry the complexity of a large and multifaceted information load, they are susceptible to breakdowns that result from an inability to manage that load, i.e., that are due to insufficient attention capacity.

It has been found that illogical thinking correlates with a narrow span of apprehension (Caplan, Foy, Asarnow, & Sherman, 1990). Caplan et al. also found that illogical thinking correlated negatively and significantly with the ability to accomplish a Piagetian conservation task (i.e., the ability to recognize the greater of two quantities despite the fact that the lesser set occupies more space). Although these researchers studied children with schizophrenia, the issue of a relationship between the amount of information apprehended and the ability to achieve logical thought is highly pertinent to any group characterized by breakdowns in attention. The degree to which thoughts are communicated clearly and logically affects the ease with which the listener can follow, and thus the satisfaction she will find in the interaction.

Johnson-Laird (1985) has also suggested a relationship between logical thinking and span of apprehension or attention/working memory capacity. The challenge to working memory is to manage information points on-line (Shankweiler & Crain, 1986) well enough and long enough to create an integrated mental model that provides cohesion and meaning to the stimuli. Separation of events over time or the need to rearrange information points to find meaning are extreme challenges to the on-line working memory system. Again, capacity and overload are very much at issue.

Carpenter and Just (1989) have pointed out that the tasks of working memory go beyond what we commonly think of as memory function. Working memory deals with more than just retention of information that is no longer present. It deals with pieces of information that must be maintained in an on-line holding area while information management or integration takes place. This includes information drawn up from previous experience. It is the role of the executive function aspect of working memory, situated in frontal cortical regions, "to update inner models of reality" (Goldman-Rakic, 1992, p. 117). When this function is disrupted, the person experiences fragmentation and partial representation of relevant information. On a larger scale, social maturation will be delayed if experience cannot be easily integrated with current developmental status.

Shapiro et al. (1993) found that ADD children aged 6¼ to 11 years were able to process and respond to emotional cues such as facial expression, language, and speech prosody, although younger ADD children had difficulty decoding facial affective stimuli. Significant differences were found, though, when the tasks required complex auditory processing and working memory: children with attention deficits had much more difficulty on these tasks than the normal control group. This would be complicated enough if social interactions and language content were straightforward. Real social situations, though, are far more complex, even at the sandbox. Speakers use irony, metaphor, negation, double-entendre, etc. in their language constructs, and all of these place increasing demands on working memory.

Any social situation increases in complexity exponentially with the number of people and issues involved. Furthermore, there is little predictability in social events. A person will behave differently given a slight change in the situation or a different group composition. Social situations require efficient on-line processing of a good deal of information. This is, in part, an executive function issue involving the prefrontal cortex (Grattan & Eslinger, 1991; Lezak, 1983), an area that has been established as part of the attention network (Mesulam, 1981).

Many language problems that characterize children with ADDs appear to be related to difficulties with attention and information processing. Globally disorganized speech has been conceived as a difficulty with inhibiting uninformative, irrelevant information, rather than a problem with the semantic network *per se* (Cohen, 1978). Loose associations can be thought of as sudden topic shifts based in the combined effects of distractibility/disinhibition and of difficulty with the information-processing function of monitoring expression and communication (Caplan et al., 1990). In fact, Caplan et al. (1990) have established that loose associations correlate with the WISC-R distractibility factor. Distractibility disrupts the control processes that are necessary to mediate language processes.

Many ADD students also experience difficulties in cognition that make problem solving difficult. They have difficulty thinking about long-term consequences: their behavior is "managed by the moment" (B. Busch, personal communication, February, 1993). They have trouble perceiving a situation from someone else's point of view. ADD students may do or say something that pleases or upsets someone, yet not understand the connection between the action and the reaction. Since social competence requires an awareness of such connections, ADD students are disadvantaged. Whalen, Henker, Collins, McAuliffe, and Vaux (1979) created a "space flight" game that simulated a social situation. The ADD boys were "role appropriate" when playing Mission Control (the message sender), but they were overly intrusive and argumentative when playing the Astronaut (the message receiver). They requested feedback less often and communicated less efficiently, yet showed no awareness of the effect their communication style had on their partners. Others have noted a similar lack of awareness, reflected in ADD subjects' relatively infrequent visual observation of their partners' behaviors and relatively frequent violation of no-talking rules (Cunningham et al., 1985). Interestingly, ADD children may be able to accurately judge appropriate and inappropriate social behaviors in others (Whalen, Henker, & Granger, 1990), but unable to monitor their own behavior while engaged in an active social situation.

ADD students' attention may not be sufficient to carry them through the process of problem solving: they forget the problem, they settle on the first solution they think of (regardless of its viability), or they terminate the problem-solving process prematurely. Since much of social competence involves ongoing problem solving, ADD students' chances for positive social interactions are diminished.

Hyperactivity and Disorganization

Not all students with ADDs exhibit hyperactivity, and even those that do may experience it to differing degrees: some are just slightly active and fidgety under specific circumstances, while others constantly have such a high activity level that they wear out anyone around them. However, hyperactivity is one of the symptoms mentioned most frequently when parents and teachers discuss the challenges of ADDs. The child who never sits still is not only failing to get his work done, but also preventing other students from doing their jobs. Clearly, the hyperactive student is noticed by his peers even more than the inattentive student.

One of the side effects of hyperactivity is the preference for large muscle movements over fine muscle movements (Zentall & Smith, 1993). Jungle gyms and playground running take priority over pencils and scissors. Given a choice, the attention-deficient child will often choose activities that are less structured and therefore more tolerant of movement, such as racing around the playground, climbing, playing with mobile toys such as bicycles and tire swings, or even building with blocks. The ADD child often avoids fine motor activities, such as cutting, drawing, writing, or tracing, with their demand for precision and controlled movement; he therefore does not have the opportunity for practice that leads to mastery of fine motor skills. Schools favor order and quiet over chaotic and rambunctious activities, and they emphasize fine motor skills over gross motor skills. The more constraints on movement, the more difficulty children with attention deficits will experience.

Some ADD students are blessed with athletic skills that tap their hyperactivity and channel it into successful performance. The ADD student who can't play Monopoly or work with Legos, but can score touchdowns or win races, may have enough success to become resilient to his weaknesses. The majority of ADD students, however, have to cope with hyperactivity without the bolstering success of sports. Furthermore, poor perception of team dynamics, overaggressive behavior, and impulsivity can overwhelm even the most gifted athlete's talents and render them subordinate, or even irrelevant.

When the high activity level interferes with turn taking, cooperation, and goal-directed action, the ADD student's peers may resent the behaviors and reject the student. In one kindergarten classroom, it was clear that during free play time a very active student was segregated from the building-block area. When asked, two little boys said, quite matter-of-factly, "Jimmy always knocks them [referring to their constructions] down. He runs too close." Their solution was to exclude Jimmy, but just for that activity. Older students, with more at stake than castles and bridges built from blocks, may reject the ADD student altogether.

ADD students are frequently disorganized. Their management of space and time is so poor that the phrase "marches to the beat of a different drummer" barely begins to cover their behavior. Parents and teachers of children with ADDs are often frustrated by this very prevalent characteristic. ADD students misplace or lose their belongings, toys, and schoolwork. They have difficulty handling materials that have lots of pieces (e.g., board games or boxes of crayons), and their work and play spaces are messy. They have difficulty planning their time for activities that involve multiple steps. Long-term projects such as science projects or book reports are unwieldy and overwhelming to the ADD student. He may procrastinate until the last minute; this may make the situation worse, or in some cases, he may be able to do his best work only under such intense time pressure. Individuals differ. Group projects can be a disaster, unless the rest of the group is able to manage the organization and assign a specific and structured part to the ADD student. In one classroom, two fifth-grade boys were upset and angry because the ADD student, who had been in charge of the maps for the social studies project, had lost them somehow, and the project was due the next day.

SUMMARY

Problems in social and emotional functioning are intimately connected with the attentional network. Distractibility, disinhibition, impulsivity, arousal seeking, tactile defensiveness, and hyperactivity interrupt and disrupt the regulation of attention needed for the complex information processing involved in social interactions. A strong executive function is required to actively process and sort through information from a variety of sources, edit, plan, and monitor one's responses, all on-line, in sometimes emotionally charged (and sometimes terribly nonstimulating) situations. Deficits in language processing complicate the situation further. Since the problems in social functioning are as much cognitive as behavioral, interventions would need to occur at a cognitive level. Social perception and social judgment training is at least as important as social skills training. Intervention at the level of behavior targets events too late in the chain.

8

Classrooms and Attention Deficit Disorders

The school environment places tremendous demands on students to regulate their attention. The school community presents students with expectations of conformity to many rules (some explicit, others less clear) and has little tolerance for those who do not conform. As students progress through the grades, these expectations escalate in at least two ways: the demands become more complex, and the level of support is decreased. Every area is affected; as academic progress, social skills, and independent behaviors become more and more intertwined, weakness in any area impacts upon the others. The student who has disordered attention is vulnerable to attack from any, and ultimately many, fronts.

An inspection of a typical elementary school report card illustrates the mismatch between school expectations and the effects of attention deficit disorders. In addition to evaluations of progress in academic areas, nearly every report card includes comments regarding the student's compliance, independent work habits, self-control, motivation, and social-emotional development. Many include a category specifically labeled "attention." Table 8.1 lists the behaviors frequently associated with these categories. Taken together, these behaviors could serve as a diagnostic protocol for attention deficit disorders. Any deficiency in attention regulation will almost certainly earn the student a negative comment in any or all of these areas.

Early supports are withdrawn as students progress through the grades. Those who cannot "make it" without the supports are penalized. Supports are often withheld, intentionally, in a misguided effort to "motivate" the student to "stand on his own." This is a clear example of an attempt at operational conditioning of independence/ motivation when the desired response is simply not within the individual's repertoire. Sometimes this is a sink-or-swim theory; at other times it seems to be an expression of the teacher's anger at the inconvenience. Dependence on prosthetic devices such as extra reminders of directions, closer supervision, modifications of assignments, etc., is interpreted as weakness. (You still need those eyeglasses to see? You've had them for years.)

During the early elementary grades, teachers are often willing to provide supports that cue students' attention, behavior, and learning. However, these supports seem to

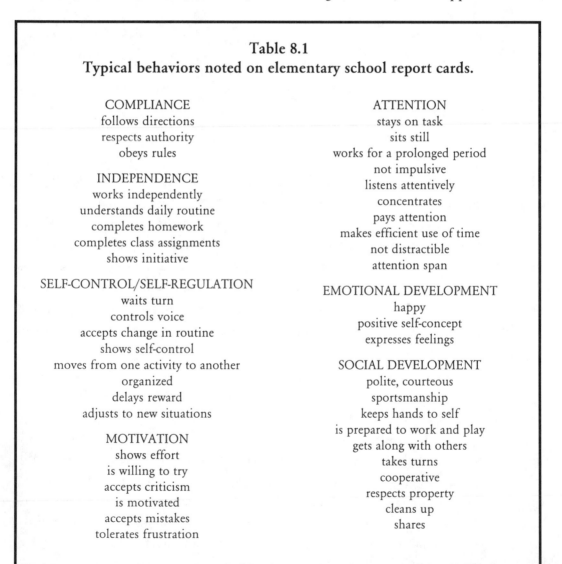

Table 8.1
Typical behaviors noted on elementary school report cards.

COMPLIANCE
follows directions
respects authority
obeys rules

INDEPENDENCE
works independently
understands daily routine
completes homework
completes class assignments
shows initiative

SELF-CONTROL/SELF-REGULATION
waits turn
controls voice
accepts change in routine
shows self-control
moves from one activity to another
organized
delays reward
adjusts to new situations

MOTIVATION
shows effort
is willing to try
accepts criticism
is motivated
accepts mistakes
tolerates frustration

ATTENTION
stays on task
sits still
works for a prolonged period
not impulsive
listens attentively
concentrates
pays attention
makes efficient use of time
not distractible
attention span

EMOTIONAL DEVELOPMENT
happy
positive self-concept
expresses feelings

SOCIAL DEVELOPMENT
polite, courteous
sportsmanship
keeps hands to self
is prepared to work and play
gets along with others
takes turns
cooperative
respects property
cleans up
shares

have implicit expiration dates. After a certain period of time, students are expected to have the knowledge base, skill levels, and/or self-control to replace these external supports.

The following sections discuss some of the demands on, and the difficulties experienced by, the attention-deficient student.

LANGUAGE DEMANDS

Language is the commerce of the classroom, and words are indeed mightier than the sword. The vast majority of instruction in academic areas is structured with words — from the teacher, other students, or audio-visual materials — or around print — in texts or trade books, on the blackboard, on worksheets, on charts, and so on.

The amount of oral language in the classroom can be daunting. New concepts are introduced and described with words, discussed with words, linked with previously learned material, and related to upcoming topics. Vocabulary words for these new concepts are also defined orally — language upon language upon language. Expectations for conduct are expressed verbally, as well.

The teacher's oral language, especially during instruction, is presented at a pace at which *the teacher* feels comfortable. Some students may need a faster presentation in order to maintain their arousal, while others may need a much slower presentation, or one with a different vocabulary or complexity level. A student who has difficulty with language processing may become lost in the tangle of words. Attempts to slow the flow of information, such as requests for clarification or repetition, may be misinterpreted as misbehavior. They are certainly *not* encouraged.

Spoken language, especially in a continuous stream, places excessive demands on limited attention and working memory resources. As information comes in it must be rapidly processed, understood, and stored. Lapses in attention increase the processing burden, since missing information has to be constructed out of current context and previous knowledge, both of which may be deficient. If notes are to be taken on the lecture or discussion, the challenge to juggle all these demands within the limitations of attention/working memory capacity is that much greater.

To provide support for students with attention deficit disorders, in this context, it might be helpful simply to pause periodically in the lecture or discussion. During the pauses, the individual with attention deficits would have the opportunity to process information more fully and perhaps to access his own language to paraphrase well enough to take meaningful notes. When used with learning disabled students at the college level, the simple pause intervention was effective in increasing free recall of lecture information. Simply pausing was *more* effective than providing an outline *or* an outline in combination with pausing. The intervention provided three two-minute pauses during a 22-minute lecture. No further cues or supports were provided (Ruhl & Suritsky, 1995).

It is an important finding that pause time alone is superior to pauses in combination with teacher-made outlines of the material. It seems that students benefit from the opportunity to self-organize, to find their own pace with the material, rather than use an externally determined structure. Although this finding may fly in the face of conventional wisdom that advises that teachers provide structure for youngsters with ADDs (Barkley, 1990; Hallowell & Ratey, 1994), it makes a good deal of sense. Any time an individual has an opportunity to actively process information in her own language — based in her own, personalized perspective — learning will be more meaningful and easier to generalize as it becomes organized and integrated into the learner's knowledge base (Ausubel & Fitzgerald, 1962; Chi, 1985). Moreover, the pause intervention allows the learner to self- pace and self-regulate, which is the way in which the longed-for independence is most likely to develop.

Certain kinds of language are especially taxing of working memory resources and thus are difficult for children with ADDs to process (Shankweiler & Crain, 1986). The more information that needs to be held on-line until meaning is found, the more essential are adequate working memory resources. Sentences that begin with a subordinate clause require holding all of the initial information on-line until the main point is presented. Similarly, relative or embedded clauses, negations, and ambiguities increase the need for forward and backward processing, and thus increase information processing demands. This is an issue for both spoken and printed language (see chapter 9 for further discussion of this topic and suggestions for addressing it).

Language skills facilitate the management of attention. As we discussed in chapter 4, language can help mediate focus, facilitate executive functions, and enhance active engagement. Self-talk is a way to maintain arousal as well as focus. It is particularly helpful when the language is self-generated rather than prescribed. For children with attention deficits, as for developmentally younger children, self-talk on a particular task may begin aloud and move inward through progressive decreases in volume (Vygotsky, 1962). Audible self-talk is certainly a potential disruption in the classroom — but according to Vygotsky's formulation, it is a necessary precursor to internal verbal mediation. Teachers might provide a separate work area for those who need to talk aloud so that they don't disturb others.

Cooperative learning situations can also provide opportunities for using language to help facilitate attention. Group learning situations encourage self-expression and provide a good deal of modeling of the explicit use of language to formulate and develop ideas. The key, however, would be to establish a compatible group with a pace suitable for each child.

Dealing with print is also required in the classroom. During the early elementary years, the job is *learning to read* — to decode the puzzle of the orthography and combine that with language comprehension to make meaning from print. After the first few years, "learning to read" is replaced with *reading to learn.* Reading and writing are essential in acquiring new information and communicating understanding of content. The special challenges of reading and writing for individuals with attention disorders are discussed in later chapters.

Students are also expected, at some level, to connect the new information they are learning to previously learned information. This requires a solid knowledge base, as well as a strong attentional mechanism that can shuttle between reception of new information, short-term memory, and long-term memory. Working memory, with executive function, is vulnerable whenever the knowledge base is weak, or when new information is presented too quickly or with too much complexity. Too many times,

Table 8.2 Language		
TYPICAL CLASSROOM DEMANDS	**PROBLEM FOR CHILDREN WITH ADDs**	**REMEDY**
process large amounts of language	processing load	• use simple, direct statements • pair statements with demonstrations
keep up with rapid delivery	difficulty shifting attention; inefficient processing	• slow down pace • pause periodically
make sense of complex language	limited working memory capacity	• use subject-verb constructions • present main clause first • use unambiguous statements
paraphrase	slow lexical access; trouble managing dual tasks of listening & paraphrasing	• pause periodically • slow down pace • provide key words
engage in self-talk	difficulty with rapid lexical access; need to talk aloud	• provide space to speak aloud • create cooperative learning groups
read efficiently	decoding & comprehension problems	• provide individualized reading instruction • use bypass-strategies
produce written language efficiently	difficulty with spelling; graphomotor problems affect fluency/legibility	• provide individualized written language instruction • use bypass-strategies

teachers believe they have taught something and it is the ADD student who hasn't held up his part of the deal. But as Ann Welch reminds us, "telling isn't teaching and told isn't taught" (Welch, 1993).

Table 8.2 (p. 129) summarizes the deficits ADD students are likely to experience with regard to the language demands of the classroom, with suggested interventions that will help promote the student's self-regulation efforts.

ATTENDING AND FOLLOWING DIRECTIONS

Teachers expect students to "look" like they are paying attention. This includes looking at the teacher during lessons, especially when she is speaking or demonstrating something. Students are also expected to listen when others are speaking. The assumption that one must both look *and* listen is rather silly, but is often accepted as axiomatic. The fact is that listening can sometimes be facilitated when one does not look at the speaker (especially if the speaker is exhibiting distracting stimuli), and not-looking is absolutely required if one is trying to take notes. Still, it is remarkable how often we hear "look at me" as a demand for proof of attending.

Students are also expected to listen carefully and quietly, even if they don't understand the content. This presents a double bind to many who cope with attention disorders. Asking too many questions tends to get you into trouble, at best; at worst it will lower your position in the knowledge hierarchy of the classroom, and maybe even in the social hierarchy. Yet asking too few questions will impede your ability to follow the lesson and to complete the usual follow-up assignment. And if you truly do not have a clue about the lesson, you are likely to become bored and place yourself at the mercy of your distractibility and restlessness.

Following directions is a central activity in the classroom. Students are expected to attend to, understand, remember, and follow spoken and written directions. Although many directions are signaled as such immediately prior to the assignments, teachers also give directions in the middle of assignments. For example, if the classroom is becoming too noisy, the teacher may interrupt students while they are working with a reminder about noise rules. If the teacher perceives that a number of students are confused about an aspect of the assignment, he may give clarification directions. And teachers frequently give directions to students to signal upcoming transition times.

Following directions places demands on many aspects of attention control. The ability to divide attention among sources of stimulation allows students to simultaneously look at the assignment and listen to the teacher's directions, or to follow along in their books as someone reads. Vigilance, or the ability to maintain readiness to receive information, is especially necessary in the classroom. The individual maintains a kind of on-line attention scanner, ready to engage whenever an important source of stimulation (e.g., the teacher's voice) presents itself. Once the student perceives the important stimulation, he must be able to shift attention away from the task on which he was working to this new, higher-priority source of information. Of course, this requirement calls into play the entire span of attention dysfunction: initiate, sustain, inhibit, shift [ISIS] (Denckla, 1996).

Table 8.3, below, summarizes the problems ADD students are likely to experience with regard to attending and following directions in the classroom, and recommended interventions for alleviating the problems.

Table 8.3
Attending & Following Directions

TYPICAL CLASSROOM DEMANDS	PROBLEM FOR CHILDREN WITH ADDs	REMEDY
look/listen to speaker	difficulty initiating, sustaining, inhibiting, & shifting attention [ISIS]	• allow non-disruptive motor activity • use demonstrations that allow ADD child to participate • use manipulatives, visuals • call on ADD child with forewarning
attend to, remember, and follow directions	difficulty initiating, sustaining, inhibiting, & shifting attention [ISIS]	• use standard routines • provide written/picture clues • highlight directions on paper • use color cues to note shift
don't interrupt	disinhibition	• teach delay for purposes of planning • let student know you are aware of them (signal, etc.) • limit wait time (use timer)
remember what you want to say	difficulty sustaining attention	• teach delay for purposes of planning
make connections between new info and previously learned info	executive function deficits; limited working memory capacity	• provide time & support for student to construct firm knowledge base • highlight initial structure of info when .teaching

WORKING WITHIN GROUPS

The school environment is structured around groups of various types, sizes, and purposes. While the organization of groups is helpful pragmatically (fewer teachers can reach more students), and even defensible realistically (most humans will function within groups throughout their lives), it creates problems for the student with attention deficits. The group experience makes substantial demands on this student's attentional network because she must not only regulate herself, but also work in synchrony with the other group members.

A great deal of instruction involves discussion, and with that comes a host of implicit and explicit expectations. Of course, students must be able to contribute to the discussion, but more precisely they must be able to stay on the topic and make remarks that are *relevant* to the discussion. If the ADD student's attention wanders, the likelihood of his staying on the topic or following the thread of the discussion is diminished. If he cannot inhibit highly associative, prepotent responses, he will make off-topic comments. Students are expected to take turns and not interrupt those who are speaking, a real challenge to those who are impulsive. They are expected to remember what they want to say during this waiting period, because if they forget, they risk violation of the first rule: stay on the topic!

Students are also expected to work within groups of their peers. They must share

Table 8.4
Working in Groups

TYPICAL CLASSROOM DEMANDS	PROBLEM FOR CHILDREN WITH ADDs	REMEDY
perform in front of peers	impulsivity, difficulty sustaining attention, high activity level, weak skill levels, weak social skills	• choose peer group carefully • keep group small • make goal of group explicit
share materials	impulsivity	• keep groups small • provide sufficient materials so everyone can be doing something at all times
work cooperatively	weak social skills	• teach individual roles of cooperative group members
take turns	impulsivity, limited working memory capacity	• keep groups small • encourage making notes to cue memory

materials with peers, take turns, and in general cooperate well enough to complete assignments. They often have to read aloud, express opinions, and work at the blackboard before their peers. There are substantial social and academic penalties for the student who cannot work within a group. The issue of social skills for students with attention deficit disorders is discussed further in chapter 7.

INDEPENDENT WORK

When students are not working within groups, they are nearly always expected to work independently. Without question, the skills needed to deal with independent work demands depend on a finely tuned and effective system of attention regulation.

Students must maintain a level of attentiveness to the tasks, with little supervision. They are expected to manage time allotments, devise a plan for completing the work, and monitor their progress. Assignments should be completed accurately, and the student should request assistance only when necessary (read: "when the teacher feels it's needed"). This requires the ability to selectively direct one's attention to *relevant* details, while simultaneously ignoring irrelevant or unimportant information. It requires the ability to temporarily shift attention away from a task to refer to appropriate supplementary tools (e.g., dictionaries or calculators) without losing sight of the original goal, and to reengage attention back to the task at appropriate times.

Sustained attention, or persistence, is needed to complete repetitive tasks (e.g., learning addition facts or copying spelling words) that may or may not be challenging, interesting, or understood. This situation has proven to be very problematic for the student with attention deficits. As we pointed out in chapter 7, students with ADD are biochemically wired to detect and attend to novelty. Once a stimulus is no longer new and interesting (often within seconds), the student will once again be on the search for something that is novel. When events and materials are routine, too easy, or too difficult (and therefore meaningless), they are perceived as boring and do not hold the attention of the ADD student. It is not that the student is unmotivated, but that the tasks are not motivating to him.

Persistence is also required when a task is complex or lengthy. The amount of sustained attention needed depends, of course, upon the complexity and length of a task, and it varies with the individual and the situation. For example, completing ten long-division problems requires much more sustained attention for a fourth-grader than for an adult who is fluent in the basic math operations.

A special challenge to students is the tendency for teachers to assign work that has multiple instructional objectives. For example, a typical third-grade "spelling" assignment tacitly incorporates the following skills: spelling the words correctly, writing grammatically correct sentences that show comprehension of the meanings of the words, practicing neat handwriting, and working independently for thirty minutes. Such a situation is problematic for students with learning disorders because there are so many places for the task to break down. A student may be able to handle the attention demands of spelling the words, but have insufficient resources to simultaneously generate sentences and produce polished penmanship. "Jam-packed" assign-

Table 8.5
Independent Work

TYPICAL CLASSROOM DEMANDS	PROBLEM FOR CHILDREN WITH ADDs	REMEDY
maintain on-task attentiveness	distractibility, craving for novelty, high activity level	• use nonverbal cues • use interesting tasks • use interactive formats for drill and rote tasks, e.g., computer for math facts • keep tasks brief • allow for breaks
manage time appropriately	distractibility, high activity level, impulsivity	• provide frequent feedback • use color in materials • set intermediate goals with student, using a timer if necessary
complete assignments accurately	distractibility, inattention to details, skill deficits	• make accuracy a priority • review tasks with child before she begins work • note directions, shifts, materials needed
request assistance only when necessary	disinhibition, need for stimulation	• provide opportunity for interaction with teacher
pay attention to relevant information & ignore irrelevant information	inattention to details, difficulty with shifting attention and selective attention	• preview materials • use highlighter to note critical features • teach how to "cross out" unimportant info
handle assignments that have multiple objectives	executive function deficits, skill deficits	• simplify assignments • focus on one or two priority objectives for student • make objectives clear to student
increasingly complex reading/ writing demands across content areas	skill deficits, inadequate executive function for algorithms and procedures	• individualized instruction • provide procedure sheets • provide examples

ments save time for the teacher and can be an efficient way to consolidate learning objectives for students, but they can be overwhelming to the student with inefficient or disordered attention regulation.

Furthermore, as the curriculum progresses across the grades, students must deal with ever more complex reading and writing demands, across more and more content areas. If there is a weakness in any aspect of oral or written language, it is likely to manifest as academic problems not only in literature or reading class, but also in science, social studies, art, mathematics, or any other subject that requires reading and/or writing. The increasing trend to "integrate" the curriculum, starting in kindergarten, has had powerful consequences for students with attention disorders. With reading and writing involved in every area, there is no respite for those children with learning and attention disorders.

Finally, independent work skills also involve knowing what to do when one is done. If students finish early (which seems to happen all too rarely), they are expected to manage their free time in an appropriate manner. "Appropriate" usually is defined first and foremost as *quiet* or *nondisruptive* activity, and secondly as related in some way to academic or achievement goals — e.g., taking out a book to read for pleasure, rather than engaging a classmate in conversation.

The high activity level of many students with attention deficit disorders presents yet another challenge to success in the classroom. Trips to the pencil sharpener reflect not only the rough handling of the pencil point, but also the student's need to get up and move. As we noted earlier in chapter 7, one of the side effects of hyperactivity is the preference for large muscle movements over fine muscle movements (Zentall & Smith, 1993). Classrooms emphasize controlled, quiet activities over noisy and tumultuous activities, and as such, they emphasize fine motor skills over gross motor activity. The more constraints on movement, the more necessary movement seems to become, and the more difficulty the ADD student experiences. Teachers who can tolerate *some* degree of movement will have an easier time than those who insist on running an in-your-seat, closed-mouth, no-breaks classroom.

ORGANIZATION

Disorganization is one of the hallmarks of attention disorders, and it interferes at many levels in the classroom. The management of space, time, and self does not appear in any reading or mathematics curriculum that we know of (although there are some organization-skills curricula published now), but the assumption of fundamental organizational abilities pervades every aspect of classroom functioning.

Students are expected to locate places in printed materials quickly (turning to a specific page, finding a word in the glossary, following along when others read, etc.). They must manage their supplies — remember where materials are kept, retrieve all the necessary materials/supplies for assignments, and keep their workspaces tidy. A look at the typical ADD student's desk is enough to make any compulsive person weep; it's likely to be littered with bits and pieces of papers, writing supplies, crayons, unidentified objects, and who knows what else. The only thing *unlikely* to be found on the ADD student's desk is completed work!

This brings up another problem area. Students are expected to complete work and hand it in to the teacher for evaluation. Besides the obvious academic skills, this requires a number of organizational skills:

- remembering the teacher(s)' requirements and standards for papers
- attacking long-term or complex assignments, including setting intermediate goals
- keeping track of one's place on all assignments
- handling multiple steps in algorithms (e.g., long division or addition of mixed numbers) or procedures (e.g., writing an essay)
- remembering to turn in completed assignments

The ADD student's penchant for procrastination does not help. The recipe is this: take a complex task, add a little anxiety, and try to finish the entire process in a fraction of the allotted time. Projects and reports, which are assigned with increasing frequency as the student progresses through the grades, are among the most difficult tasks for any student because they require long-term planning. As coping behavior, procrastination works well in the short term because it avoids emotional turmoil. But it makes the situation harder than it should have been initially; it is dysfunctional for the long term.

The disorganization of the ADD student is rooted deeply, at the level of executive function. A direct and revealing measure of disorganization can be taken with the Rey-Osterrieth complex figure test. Figure 8.1 (on the next page) displays the stimulus figure that the child is to copy. Figure 8.2 is a reproduction of a copy drawing done by a child in the second grade who has ADD and who is of average intelligence. The figure is wildly disorganized. Figure 8.3 presents two copy drawings done by a 13-year-old with ADD who is highly gifted intellectually. The top drawing was done without medication. The bottom drawing was done 7 weeks later while the child was taking 15 mg of Ritalin. The more disorganized approach without medication can be seen in the failure to depict the central cross or the horizontal line as an integrated unit. Some perseveration (or perhaps failure to self-monitor) is also seen in the drawing of

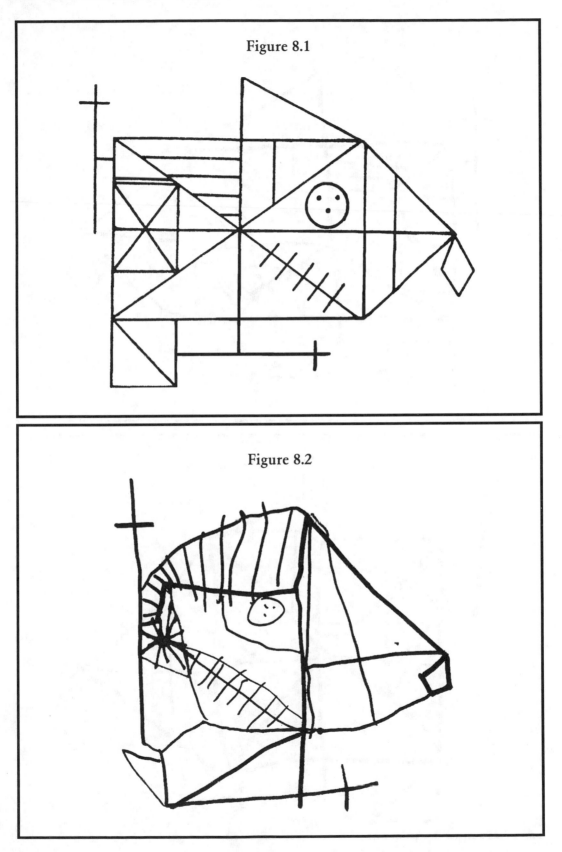

Figure 8.1

Figure 8.2

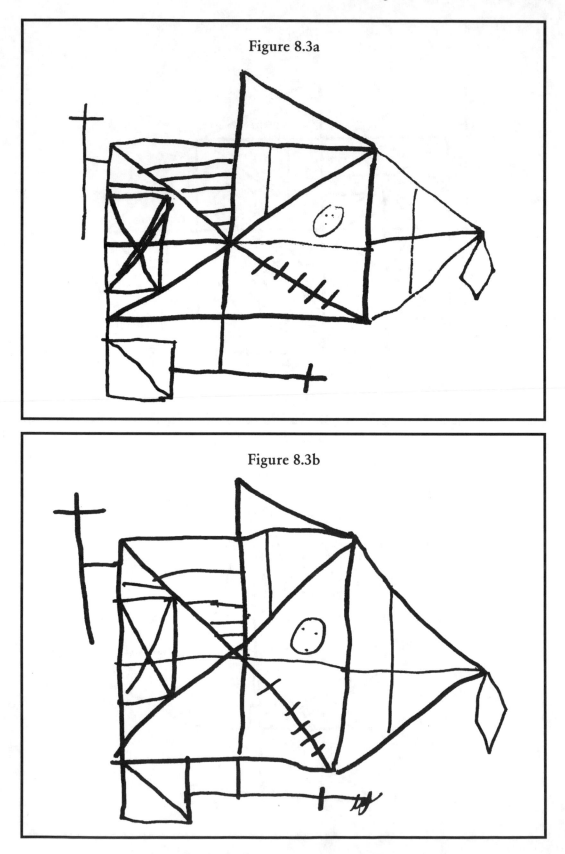

Figure 8.3a

Figure 8.3b

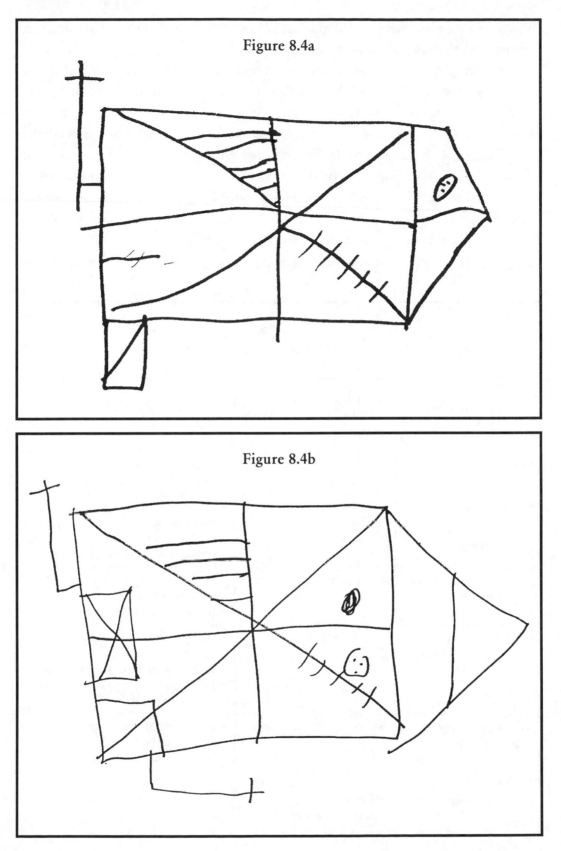

Figure 8.4a

Figure 8.4b

five vs. four parallel lines (top left quadrant of figure). With medication, these organizational units are produced more meaningfully.

Interestingly, the end products in both cases look at least adequate. It is the *process* that is disorganized. The cost of the disorganization is seen in the immediate recall condition. Figure 8.4 shows the two recall figures. The top figure was drawn immediately after the copy with no medication. The bottom one was drawn immediately after the copy with medication. In the unmedicated condition, the cost of disorganization at intake is seen far more vividly in the impoverishment and disjointedness of the recall drawing. This is a striking display of what happens to information when it is poorly organized upon intake. Despite the appearance of an adequate job (the completed copy drawing), the process has been fragmented. The lack of initial structure leaves the child without an adequate means of consolidating information and

Table 8.6
Organization

TYPICAL CLASSROOM DEMANDS	PROBLEM FOR CHILDREN WITH ADDs	REMEDY
locate place in printed materials quickly	distractibility, fine motor weaknesses, trouble shifting attention	• teach how to use concrete aids, e.g., bookmarks, binder clips • provide time or advance notice
retrieve all necessary materials	distractibility, trouble shifting attention and coordinating multiple demands	• provide adequate storage space for personal materials • keep class materials in routine place • provide time or advance notice
remember requirements and standards for papers	executive function deficits	• keep formats standard across teachers/settings • provide visual examples
attack long-term or complex assignments	executive function deficits	• teach how to use calendar, syllabus, schedule, etc. • teach how to set intermediate goals • help each student discover her own best study schedule
handle the multiple steps in algorithms or procedures	executive function deficits	• provide graphic organizers, procedure sheets • teach mnemonic strategies
remember to turn in completed assignments	distractibility, impulsivity, difficulty shifting/ sustaining attention	• provide explicit cues

thus with little available for recall. What *is* available is disconnected and reveals the original fragmentation. The results can be misleading to teachers who may misconstrue an adequate end product as evidence that the material has been internalized.

These drawings are meant to be viewed as analogues for how disorganization affects learning, performance, and recall *in general,* not just in a copy and immediate recall task. As such, they suggest that the disorganization to which teachers typically allude — i.e., materials are in disarray, the proper materials are not brought to class or home for homework, etc. — is only the most superficial manifestation. Underneath is a deep and essential cognitive disorganization that is bound to pervade all mental activity. Ironically, since persistence can lead to an adequate end product, compensating for a good deal of disorganization, it may lead teachers to believe that learning has taken place — i.e., that the material will be available for recall in the future, as a foundation upon which to build additional learning. Figure 8.4a makes clear that for a typical student with ADD, this is likely not to be the case.

CONDUCT

Teachers and schools place high value on conformity with regard to students' conduct. Students are expected to remain on task, steadily, throughout lessons. When the situation is a discussion or lecture format, one is expected to raise one's hand and wait to be called on. When others are talking, the correct response is to listen, and to look like a person who is listening. The concept of "engaged time" also emphasizes active responses such as writing, and makes the pauses between active responses seem suspect. After all, thinking *looks* just like daydreaming.

Fidgeting, one way to sustain arousal, is also viewed with suspicion, and simply not tolerated at all if it is noisy or if it disrupts others. At the same time, students are expected to be able to tune out any distracting actions, should they occur, from their classmates.

The rules for conduct vary from teacher to teacher and from situation to situation. Students need to remember the routines and rules associated with different activities, such as those for recess, the lunchroom, the math lesson, the science experiment, etc. Any adult who does not appreciate this complexity should try being a substitute teacher in a few different classrooms, or serving as a lunchroom monitor. What is amazing is not that children with attention disorders struggle with these multiple rules, but that so many other children handle them effortlessly.

In the classroom, students are expected not only to work quietly and to follow directions, but to do so in an environment that is more likely to point out failures than achievements. Students must be able to tolerate limited positive evaluations and accept criticism (constructive, of course) from the teacher. External rewards, such as stickers, recess, or favorite activities, are awarded *after* achievements are noted, requiring the student to accept delayed gratification. The delay is often determined by pragmatics (e.g., recess only happens at certain times, or the reward movie is always on Friday afternoon), but is nonetheless difficult for a child who needs the support to occur closer to the time of the accomplishment.

The impulsivity associated with ADDs presents another barrier to success in the classroom. The impulsive student acts first and thinks later (if at all); the urge to do something overrides any thoughts of consequences before acting. He may race around the playground and its equipment without apparent regard for the rules about playground safety. Sharing materials can be difficult, as the impulsive urge to take (or hold on to) what she wants overrides remembering unspoken rules regarding sharing. Sometimes, too, the need to do something *as a coping strategy* takes priority over observing the rules. As a result, the impulsive student blurts out answers in class without following the class rule for raising his hand, because if he waits his turn, he will forget what it was he wanted to say.

Barkley (1990) has characterized impulsivity as a difficulty with "rule-governed behavior." The more explicit and implicit rules involved, the more the ADD student will experience difficulty. Of course, school is an environment built around rules.

Table 8.7 Conduct		
TYPICAL CLASSROOM DEMANDS	**PROBLEM FOR CHILDREN WITH ADDs**	**REMEDY**
make transitions between activities, according to teacher's commands	impulsivity, difficulty shifting attention	• provide advance notice about changes or transitions
work quietly	tactile defensiveness, need for stimulation, high activity level	• keep transition time to a minimum • allow non-disruptive motor activity when students have to wait
respect others	impulsivity, drive to preserve system integrity (self-esteem)	• set class goals for behavior • build self-esteem and success
follow rules associated with different activities and different teachers	impulsivity, difficulty with social cues	• preview rules before they are needed • review rules after weekends and vacations

There are expectations for behavior in order to facilitate the learning of academic curricula, to protect students' safety, and to teach students how to conform to cultural standards. Many rules are made explicit for students, but a significant number are either implied or assumed under a more general rule (e.g., "don't hurt other people" includes "no hitting," "no pushing," "no ridicule," "no kicking," etc.).

The impulsive student has difficulty with both explicit and implicit rules. Part of the difficulty may be simply forgetting or never even realizing what the rules are, or what the consequences are likely to be. The mental representations for these expectations of behavior may be unclear, or inefficiently stored in the brain (not unlike the homework inefficiently stored in the student's desk). Usually, however, the ADD student can tell you clearly what the rules and consequences are, and that he knows his actions violated the rules. It is not the storage of the rules that is the problem, but rather the self-regulation or *accessing* of the rules at a moment when other responses compete. Busch (B. Busch, personal communication, February, 1993) has coined the term "managed by the moment" to describe the ADD student's difficulties with planning and problem solving. The expression holds true for many of the situations in which the ADD student appears impulsive.

The order insisted upon by all institutions, schools among them, can seem arbitrary and even mysterious to students who do not find themselves in the flow. In his novel *Borderliners*, Peter Høeg (1994) reveals how these students perceive such controls. The story is told from the perspective of a young adolescent who has been a "problem child," one on the borderline of acceptance.

About the rules of punishment in schools, the main character observes:

> There was a law ... that dated from antiquity. When gilding a surface it was not desirable to cover it 100 percent with gold. On the contrary, one achieved the best effect if one covered just over 60 percent. A variation of the law of the golden mean. So it was, too with the relationship between time and punishment. Of those violations that were proven, only just over half evoked punishment. Sort of a golden mean of violence. (p. 6)

Høeg's character tries to explain the rules about sitting still in school to a new student, and in so doing reveals his perception that the requirement to sit still is something of a set-up:

> We stood utterly still during assembly. That was the first thing I tried to get through to her. At a certain time every day you were let into the assembly hall, 240 people with 26 teachers and Biehl, and then the doors were shut, and you knew that from

this moment for the next quarter of an hour you had to stay completely still. The prohibition was total, giving rise to a certain tension in the room. As though the rule, by covering everything and by tolerating nothing, called for its own violation. As though the tension in the room was part of the plan. (pp. 4-5)

Høeg, through his character, tells us that questions asked in school are narrow and designed for the purpose of controlling information as well as students. In contrast, there are truly scientific questions for which the question itself is the object and there are no answers:

Maybe there are only two kinds of question in the world. The kind they ask in school, where the answer is known in advance; asked not so that anyone will be any the wiser but for the other reasons. And then the others, those in the laboratory. Where one does not know the answers, and often not even the question, before one has asked it .... That was what we meant by science. That both question and answer are tied up with uncertainty, and that they are painful. But that there is no way around them. And that you hide nothing; instead, everything is brought out into the open. (p. 19)

Time is a vital aspect of the control that exists in schools. There are bells, timed tests, and due dates — unspoken guidelines about what is an acceptable amount of time to spend on a given task. Perhaps more than anything else, the precision and arbitrariness of time represents the imposing forces of school regulations:

It was not just the classes and assembly that began on the dot. There was also a study period and the meals and the chores and voluntary sports .... It had all been allotted a stroke of the clock that was most scrupulously observed. The inaccuracy amounted to less than plus or minus two minutes. No explanation of time was ever given. But one knew that it was enormous, bigger than anything mortal or earthly. That one had to be on time was not just out of consideration for one's schoolmates and oneself and the school. It was also for the sake of time itself. For God .... When time itself was so exact, then so ought people to be, that was the idea. Accuracy was a characteristic, and perhaps the most important one of the universe. At assembly one had to be absolutely precise and absolutely still. Utter time and utter stillness. That was the goal. Achievement was there to bring us nearer to that goal. And to encourage achievement, there was punishment. (pp. 39-40)

It is only when the tight controls are relinquished that understanding truly comes:

... When one lets go of time one understands certain other things ... When something important was happening, one could let go, and achieve a rich moment, a full understanding. (p. 27)

Perhaps the most painful suggestion Høeg puts forth is that schools interfere with meaningful relationships among their students for the sake of control. Students who are "too" close should be separated because they could be disruptive, and because they may find the relationship more motivating than the sometimes feeble reward offered in exchange for following the rules.

Regardless of whether the existing controls are literally as tight as Høeg paints them, it is highly likely that the child with attention deficits *perceives* them to be so. School should be a place of learning and discovery, of joy and wonder and a growing sense of competence. This is not always the picture, however, if you have learning differences, and especially if you have a problem that manifests as a "behavioral" disorder. In other words, if you cannot follow the rules, and you are always being reminded that you have broken the rules, school can become a very hostile place. In a tragic paradox, discipline and punishment begin to transform the classroom from a learning environment to a place where behavioral conformity is the goal.

SUMMARY

Classrooms and schools place great demands on attention regulation. Students are expected to learn, remember, and follow implicit and explicit rules about complying, working independently, demonstrating self-control, and interacting with others. These require all aspects of controlled and sustained attention and inhibition of impulsive responses. Furthermore, curricula and instruction depend largely upon language, which in turn places demands on working memory resources. These cognitive demands often result in unacceptable behaviors as the student attempts to cope with the situation in the best way she knows.

As the student progresses through the grades, expectations increase, yet instructional supports are often simultaneously withdrawn. For students with attention deficit disorders, the demand for more finely tuned attentional resources and the concomitant withdrawal of external supports can result in failure. Interventions can be directed at the task level, by modifying the task so that less attentional control is required, and/or at the instructional level, by increasing the external supports available to help the student manage the attentional demands.

9

Reading and Attention

In this and the succeeding chapters on writing and mathematics, we first present the sequence and stages of acquisition of these skill areas — analyzing the tasks in terms of areas where students with ADDs will experience difficulties. In the last section of each chapter, we suggest specific instructional strategies that might help address the needs of these students.

Reading is a complex cognitive act driven by attention. It is the culmination of a process that involves, and often taxes, nearly every aspect of the cognitive system. Important among the components of reading are the phonological, orthographic, semantic, and syntactic elements of understanding print. We will describe each of these components and try to explain the dynamics that bring the parts into a unified process. Reading is, indeed, much more than the sum of its parts. Pressure is on the system to activate all these components, often simultaneously and extensively, in a coordinated manner. All the components are inextricably intertwined, and they grow — or fail to grow — together. We will show that seemingly lower-order processes such as alphabet identification or word decoding are not separate from higher-order processes such as appreciating the meaning of words, sentences, or text. Nor are the processes, in any simple way, hierarchically arranged. Because reading is so complex and requires controlled analytic processes, it is highly dependent on the attention and working memory systems. Particularly vital are those aspects of the systems that allow information to be activated long enough and held on-line well enough to enable analysis to occur. The attention and working memory systems play a critical role in both decoding print and understanding connected text.

Attention is necessary to bridge the gap between the writer's intentions and the reader's comprehension, and to make the connections between the arbitrary letter symbols and the basic conceptual units of language: words. Attention is necessary because the association between what is heard (syllables) and the units used to represent them (letters) depends on the appreciation of units of speech even smaller than what we naturally perceive (phonemes). Because none of this association is natural, or even reasonable, to the beginner, mastery of reading skills must be managed with conscious, directed, focused, and sustained attention.

The Demands of the Print System

Our print system is an alphabetic one. Our letters are totally arbitrary pairings of symbols (composed of lines and curves) with the nearly impossible-to-perceive individual phonemes of our language. What makes individual letter sounds so difficult to perceive is the frequent co-articulation of adjacent letters (Liberman & Shankweiler, 1987). For example, the letter *d* sounds different, and the sound is produced differently, in each of the words *dog* and *dig* and *drag*. Nevertheless, since the letter is the most basic unit of information in an alphabetic system, it must be confronted and learned. Appreciation for the differences in the letter shapes, as well as for the components of single syllables, demands an extraordinary amount of attention to very abstract constructs.

In the long run, an alphabetic system is an efficient way of acquiring literacy. Once the system — its symbols and the phonological entities they represent — is mastered, the individual has the key to unlock nearly every word in our language that can be represented with print. However, in the short run, the complexity and abstractness of the system places enormous stress on attentional resources. In order to conquer the system, a young reader must learn how to consolidate the mass of stimuli into conceptual chunks that are optimally sized for comprehension and management. Much of this can take place below the level of consciousness, but it is nonetheless dependent on all of the vital aspects of attention: arousal, activation, and mental effort.

In the beginning stages of learning,[1] children learn to attend to individual letter symbols as wholes. Consolidating an arrangement of lines and curves into a single entity with a label reduces the processing demands needed for letter recognition (and hence the recognition of anything that uses letters). Assigning a label to each letter is an important skill, for a number of reasons. The label facilitates the child's recog-

---

[1] The true beginnings of reading precede print and involve the development of subsyllabic aspects of speech. Most children accomplish this in the context of rhyme and alliteration.

nition of all the variations of a single letter (e.g., of different colors, sizes, textures, and contexts). It allows the child to recognize an *m* as an *m* whether it is printed large or small or fat or in yellow or purple or yarn letters. And it allows her to keep *m* reliably separate from *n* in her awareness of letters. The perception of the critical characteristics that define *m*-ness — for example, the invariants noted by the direct realists (Gibson, 1979) — creates a conceptual class of "m" and allows for flexible extension of the concept. Labels for letters are also important as children acquire knowledge of upper-case and lower-case letters, and need to remember that a *B* is fundamentally the same as a *b*.

Furthermore, letters are associated with individual sounds, and the paired-associative process of learning — learning that, for example, *m* makes an /mmm/ sound — is facilitated when the letter has an identity that is known to the reader, and to which the teacher can refer. Although there is not a perfect one-to-one relationship between letters and sounds, this complexity can best be appreciated after some firm, unambiguous associations have been established. The labels for letters are often related to their sounds (except for cases like *w* and *y*). Letter names can thus cue retrieval of the letter sounds. And, perhaps of greatest significance, efficient letter identification enables the child to identify the exact orthographic structure (i.e., spelling) of a word without struggle so that she can spend her limited attentional capacity on deciphering the relationships between *patterns* of letters and the sounds they make — a process that is referred to as "cracking the code."

Once letters can be perceived accurately, the cognitive system is prepared to attend to more complex information — that is, to the sequences of letters needed for whole words. Letter recognition must be at an automatic level, however, for this to proceed smoothly. While some reading skills are associated with the global shape of a word (e.g., the difference in length between *by* and *butterfly*), the overwhelming amount of evidence in the literature (Adams, 1990; Gough & Walsh, 1991) indicates that it is the sequence of letters that specifically informs word recognition. The fluent word recognition abilities of the skilled reader depend on her repeated experience with sequences of letters. Adams (1990) and others (e.g., Gough, Ehri, & Treiman, 1992) attribute this capability to an "Orthographic Processor" in the reader's mind.

Fluent readers are able to recognize clusters of letters automatically (Samuels, 1987), whereas poor readers have difficulty recognizing letter combinations and therefore consume large amounts of attention in the process. Studies done by Samuels and associates on the size of the processing unit in word recognition suggest that beginning readers and poor readers are locked into using smaller, less optimal units, sometimes as small as one letter. Skilled readers are more flexible; they are able to use units as large as the whole word or as small as the single letter, depending on purpose and familiarity (Samuels, LaBerge, & Bremer, 1978; Samuels, Miller, & Eisenberg, 1979; Samuels & Peterson, 1986; Terry, Samuels, & LaBerge, 1976). Perhaps they are skilled *because* they orient toward clusters of letters rather than individual ones. Sounds in words are associated not with letters in isolation, but rather with letters in groups. Try, for example, to proceed linearly, and to give the sound for *b*, then *o*; then pronounce the two together in preparation for the rest of the word. Then perceive an *a* and merge the three sounds. Finally, attach an *r*. What if, instead, after the *o* had come *u*, and then *gh?* The entire sound structure would have changed, and changed again if after *bough* came a *t*. Attacking the word letter by letter, from left to right, cannot provide the information needed to decipher the word. When children approach a word in this way, they are creating excessive attentional demands for themselves.

Recognition of letter sequences is facilitated by the redundant nature of English orthography. That is, letters tend to occur in patterns of two, three, and four symbols rather than in equal distributions of random combinations. For example, it is much more likely for *q* to be followed by *u* than by any other letter of the alphabet (exceptions include the abbreviation "qt," the country "Qatar," or the Hebrew letter "qoph"). Repeated experiences with attending to the *qu* combination will create a sort of "superletter" that is integrated in the skilled reader's mind. Any encounters with a combination like *qs* would be unexpected enough to disrupt the reader and cause her to stop and double-check that stimulus (note, though, that *sq* would be more acceptable). Recognition of combinations of letters condenses information load and thus preserves working memory and attentional capacity.

If the reader is still struggling to process single letters, she is not likely to appreciate letter sequences. While a struggling reader is processing the *u* in our example, she has forgotten the *q*; she will not be able to associate the letters into a single, consolidated unit of *qu*. In the worst case, an ironic, vicious cycle may result: since she does not recognize the *qu* combination, the next time she encounters it she will continue to process *q* and then *u*. The struggling reader now has the additional burden of having more information to attend to than the proficient reader, so she is further handicapped in the effort to notice the critical features of the code. This is not just an inconvenience to the attention system; efforts to blend the sequence *q-u* would result in an incorrect pronunciation (probably *koo* or *kyuhoo*). It is all the more important, then, for her teachers to help her attend to *qu-, -tion, the*, and other common sequences as critical, integrated units in the words she encounters. And, once again, we see the importance of learning the individual letters of the alphabet to a level of automaticity.

Attention and Phonological Processes

A second essential element of the reading process is the understanding of the relationship between sounds in the speech stream and the sequences of letter symbols used to represent them (Liberman & Shankweiler, 1987). Adams (1990) refers to this component as the "Phonological Processor," while others (e.g., Fodor, 1983; Shankweiler & Crain, 1986) include it as part of their conceptualization of a "Linguistic Module." This component is a neurologically based network involving phonemic awareness, phonologically based rapid automatic naming, and working memory. This is a modular function; it is helpful to discuss the components separately at first.

Phonemic awareness refers to the insight that letters represent a unit of sound not ordinarily discovered in the speech stream. For speech comprehension, it is an advantage to ignore information at the phonemic level and to orient toward larger, more meaningful, more condensed units of information. In fact, if these elements were processed individually, over even very brief periods of time, the ear would be unable to resolve them temporally; speech would sound like an unanalyzable buzz (Liberman, Cooper, Shankweiler, & Studdert-Kennedy, 1967). Furthermore, we do not have the attentional capacity to focus on these individual elements and still maintain a sense of the language. Because of these physical constraints, perception of the elements within words is unnatural and quite difficult. In fact, if our system were not an alphabetic one, but instead a syllabary as in Japanese or an ideography as in Chinese, we might not be provoked to discover speech at the level of the phoneme at all.

Phoneme sounds below the level of the syllable do not actually exist as individual entities. Efforts to create instruments that would represent individual letter sounds have failed to do so (Ehri & Wilce, 1983). Acknowledgment of this abstraction, or phonemic awareness, emerges through interaction with the alphabetic system. We learn about the "existence" of these elements in great part as we learn how to read. Patterns emerge. The words *pat* and *bat* share orthographic features and rimes (the rime is the part of the syllable from the vowel to the end of the syllable), and have different beginning letters and onsets (initial consonant sounds). A mental leap allows for the conclusion that /b/ and /p/ are individual and distinguishable phonemes.

Phonemic and alphabetic awareness co-evolve. The reader first becomes aware that there are sounds below the level of a syllable when he encounters the alphabet. Simultaneously, phoneme awareness accentuates the role of each letter. Readers map sounds onto the letter sequences to produce intelligible words. C-AT is /kat/, C-ATCH is /kach/, etc. This is made complicated by the intricacies of English orthography: some letters are associated with more than one sound (e.g., vowels, hard and soft consonants, the letter *y*). Some sounds are associated with more than one letter (e.g., /s/ in *city* and *sound*, the long *i* in *by* and *ice*). The sounds of some letters are determined by what other letters are in the word: a silent *e* affects other vowels, the vowel in a syllable determines whether *g* is hard or soft, and so on. The reader needs to be able to simultaneously consider all these types of clues in order to map the right sounds onto the letter sequences.

The reader must also be flexible and have a degree of tolerance for ambiguities. For example, pronouncing the individual sounds of *c-a-t* and *c-o-t* will produce only approximations of the words *cat* and *cot*. Humans talk in syllables, not in phonemes. Any attempt to pronounce the *c* — or for that matter the *t* — without the vowel is doomed to fail. The best one can do is get close and rely on the Phonological Processor to synthesize the sounds into recognizable words. A major problem for the beginning reader is that the consonant and the vowel that follows it are co-articulated. The *c* in *cat* is different from the *c* in *cot*. It is produced using different motor patterns. To appreciate the difference, one need only to get ready to say the *c* in *cat* and then do the same for *cot*. The effect of the vowel on motor production is easily perceptible and vividly makes the point that even though both are considered hard *c*'s, they have very different motor, speech, and, therefore, phonological qualities.

Phonological processing and rapid automatic naming are intertwined. Humans recognize spoken words based, in part, on the phonological information in them. Words are retrieved as we think or speak via a phonological route (Liberman & Shankweiler, 1987). Efficient, rapid access to words in the lexicon certainly contributes to fluent communicative language. Rapid automatic naming also enables one to find the inner language needed for controlled attentional and working memory strategies such as re-auditorization, rehearsal, or other forms of verbal mediation. Verbal mediation serves the functions of activating and maintaining information in working memory, as well as creating a structure that connects information in working memory more meaningfully. Rapid automatic naming, therefore, contributes significantly to the efficient use of working memory and the effective processing of printed language. An impaired ability to associate verbal labels with written symbols seriously limits memory consolidation and creates enormous impediments for working memory (Ackerman, Anhalt, & Dykman, 1986). Without phonological processing competence, words cannot be accessed quickly, and the efficiency that is critical to working memory is lost.

Phonological processing problems, then, have a way of coming back upon themselves. They are an essential impediment to developing phonemic awareness (i.e., awareness of the number and order of sounds within syllables). Via their interference with rapid automatic naming, they are likely to interfere with efficient letter naming

— which in turn constitutes a further impediment to phonemic awareness. And the analysis required for coming to terms with the alphabetic code requires manipulating information about the elements within a syllable. It is thus dependent on the working memory function of holding information in mind, on-line, so that it can be manipulated. Each of these processes is driven directly and again indirectly, in synergistic fashion, by phonological and attention/working memory processes.

Attention and Reading Comprehension

The third component of the reading system is one that attaches meaning to print through the use of semantic and syntactic information. Once the word has been identified phonologically from its orthography, the reader attaches a meaning to it. This step may need to be delayed a bit, especially if the word is ambiguous or unknown. Still, the reader could not process words one-by-one-by-one and still make meaning from the text. Meaning is created from phrases and sentences and sets of sentences within the larger context. For that purpose, a "Context Processor" (Adams, 1990) constructs an interpretation of the text, updating it as more words are read. This is an on-line process of taking in information and anticipating what might be coming next in the text. It also depends on information in the reader's *knowledge store:* knowledge acquired either earlier in the text or from general knowledge learned outside the text.

Comprehension — or consolidation of ideas — occurs at various places in the text. It is best undertaken at major syntactic boundaries, such as sentences and clauses (Kleiman, 1975). When material is more complex or contains difficult words, however, skillful readers pause more frequently to consolidate the meaning of what they are reading. Less skilled readers expend effort and substantial time at individual words. Ironically, they are less able to remember the individual words on which they have focused, and then they cannot construct meaning (Perfetti & Lesgold, 1977). Working memory would need to have been strong enough to keep a verbatim record of the words long enough for an accurate interpretation to occur. The limitations of working memory and attention make this approach futile. The shorter the word span toward which the reader orients, the more difficult it is to interpret sentences, especially lengthy ones with embedded clauses.

Although we have been discussing orthography, phonology, and meaning separately, the reality is that all three combine to form a powerful system, capable of taking those marks on a paper and communicating a persuasive opinion, directions for making a model airplane, or a recipe for lasagna. It is tempting to say that the orthographic component comes "first" and engages the rest of the system. That is true, at least in part, but it fails to acknowledge the feedback and feedforward that occurs when a particular word is anticipated from the semantic context ("The sleepy boy climbed into his _____") or the phonological context ("Hickory dickory dock, the mouse ran up the cl___"). All three components exercise and support each of the others. Word recognition will strengthen those sequences of letters in memory, word meanings will strengthen the contextual processes, and the pronunciations of the words will strengthen phonological processes.

The Role of Automaticity

The readability of text is defined by the orthography, the phonological load of the words, the meaning of the words, and the difficulty of the narrative (vocabulary, syntax, and concepts). If all four dimensions are too difficult for the reader to handle, the task will end in failure. There is some redundancy in the system, so that if one element is a bit weaker, the others may be able to compensate at least for some time. But an overreliance on one component will exact a cost from the others. For example, a young reader will often "read" more from the pictures and make guesses at difficult words from the context. He does this, most likely, because the demands on word decoding are too great for him to tackle all at once, because phonological awareness may not be accessible to him at that time, and because he *can* handle the attentional demands of using context cues. However, when letter sequences are not inspected thoughtfully, they cannot be consolidated into words. On the other hand, when readers focus on the visual information in a word, or on painstakingly sounding it out, a different cost is charged — this time to the comprehension of the sentence.

It is important to note here that it is the poor readers who continue to rely on visual cues (Adams, 1990). This reliance appears to be both a cause and an effect of their failure to develop phonemic awareness. Furthermore, children with various forms of left-hemisphere impairment tend to prefer configurational cues over those provided by the alphabetic sequence, and as a result often fail to notice critical orthographic patterns. Attention to configuration over elemental letter analysis is also attention-conserving. Children with ADD are particularly prone to be tempted to go, erroneously, down this garden path.

This discussion indicates the importance of developing fluency in word identification skills. Simple mastery without fluency is not enough. Only when knowledge of orthography and phonology and access to meaning are automatic does the reader have the attentional resources needed for comprehension. Speed of identification of single words at first grade has been found to have a potentially causal relationship to reading comprehension at grades two and three (Lesgold & Resnick, 1982). Reading is a self-organizing system: the meaning of a text depends on the meanings of the individual words, while the meanings of the words are more readily available when the text is meaningful. Meaning also helps in the interpretation of phonemic information which might otherwise be confusing (Pinker, 1994) — e.g., understanding "intensive purposes" as *intents and purposes*, or "my sorted pass" as *my sordid past.*

Ehri and Wilce (1983) propose that word recognition is a three-phase developmental process. Phase I is an *accuracy* phase, in which children actively and consciously attend to letters and sound-symbol mapping. Phase II is an *automaticity* phase, in which whole words begin to be recognized as units. Phase III is a *speed* phase, in which word recognition becomes faster and increases slowly to asymptote. At phase III, the task can be performed without any great degree of conscious attention. Downings (1979) describes the same three stages, naming them the "cognitive," "mastery," and "automaticity" stages.

For beginning readers, the effort involved in decoding individual words is necessary and functional, making available the kind of inspection and study of letter sequences necessary to imprint them on the orthographic processor. As the spellings of more and more words become more familiar, less effort — less allocation of working memory and attentional resources — will be needed. *Therefore, it is important that this type of effortful study be encouraged in early readers.* Guessing at a word from context (or picture) clues is often more expedient, but because it bypasses the careful study of letter sequences for the whole word, it steals important practice needed for the ultimate development of automaticity in decoding.

The development of automaticity, then, requires substantial amounts of repetitive practice spread over time, and practice with fine discriminations. Although this is an attention-intensive and mental-effort-intensive activity, its eventual outcome will be to enable automatic word recognition so that conscious attention is less necessary. The ADD student is asked to override her craving for novelty and deal with highly repetitive experiences. To become automatic with a skill, a person must practice well beyond the stage at which the information is new and interesting. She must practice with active attention, focusing on the task and only on the task. These conditions are very difficult for the ADD child to meet, regardless of the subject matter.

Many have attributed reading problems in large part to a lack of automaticity in naming and language skills (Denckla & Rudel, 1976; Doehring, 1976; Perfetti & Roth, 1981; Wolf, 1986). Compared to non-disabled peers, children with reading disabilities do not demonstrate fast, fluent performance on sight vocabulary recognition, alphabet production, or arithmetic operations (Ackerman et al., 1986; Ashcraft & Fierman, 1982; Berninger & Alsdorf, 1989; Berninger, Mizolawa, & Bragg, 1991; Meltzer, Fenton, Ogonowski, & Malkus, 1988). Early difficulties in automatization of these skills predict later achievement difficulties, especially in the area of reading, that persist even after automatization develops. It may be that the lost time can never be fully recovered. Or it may be that automatization is accomplished in some atypically organized way, perhaps in a way that places less demand on the child's faulty phonological system. Regardless, it is not just *lack* of automatization that interferes with later comprehension. The problems with phonology that caused the initial difficulty with automaticity will again affect working memory and attention directly when reading comprehension is an issue.

Wolf, Bally, and Morris (1986) undertook a longitudinal study of word retrieval speed in average and severely impaired readers from kindergarten through second grade, allowing study before, during, and after reading acquisition. Performance on continuous-naming tasks was compared with performance on reading tasks. Non-impaired readers performed with similar speed on all tasks in kindergarten, and improved to automaticity by first grade. Impaired readers, however, had significant original deficits in name-retrieval speed for letters, numbers, colors, and objects, with letter symbols being particularly slow. Although they, too, made significant gains by first grade, the original deficits seemed to be so severe that the later gains were still insufficient for ultimate reading achievement. These children "begin and end their early reading stages with distinct processing differences in retrieval speed" (p. 994). From kindergarten on, impaired readers remain significantly slower than normal readers on all naming tasks.

Processing speed may be a significant factor in the development of automaticity. Children diagnosed as learning disabled do seem to process information more slowly,[2] particularly rapidly changing information (Blackwell, McIntyre, & Murray, 1983; Shapiro, Ogden, & Lind-Blad, 1990; Swanson, 1981). When given unlimited time in reading, LD children adopt a more conservative response set (Swanson, 1983) and spend significantly more time on individual eye fixations than non-disabled students (Adler-Grinberg & Stark, 1978), perhaps as a strategy to compensate for their temporal processing deficits. When students read material with a high frequency of lengthy words, the cumulative effect of this strategy seriously impacts comprehension.

In addition to slower processing, impaired children are also more susceptible to distraction (Hardy, McIntyre, Brown, & North, 1989; Richards, Samuels, Turnure, & Ysseldyke, 1990). These students are more likely to notice additional information and are less able to narrow their focus to precise informational units such as letters. They seem to still be using controlled processes rather than automatic processes. When attention is deployed in a diffuse manner, too much information — much of it irrel-

---

[2] Slowed processing is often associated with diffuse, nontraumatic brain dysfunction (Lezak, 1983). As such it evokes the image of minimal brain dysfunction (MBD), the earlier conceptualization out of which the categories of learning disabilities and attention deficit disorders were born.

evant — creates noise that interferes with the consolidation of information necessary for automaticity.

The appropriate narrowing of attention is critical to successful processing of serially ordered information such as letter combinations (e.g., *-at*, *-tion*, and *-ization*). Input that is recorded randomly, without the frequency and/or thoughtfulness that might establish connections among previous and later inputs, will behave more as noise than as anchors. This is true for more concrete concepts (e.g., the class of "cats") as well as for letter sequences. Directed attention facilitates the perceptual reorganization (Adams, 1990) necessary for automaticity to develop.

Automaticity alone is not enough, however. Achieving automaticity with basic skills does not ensure success. All of the component skills need to be combined. There is order within each of the orthographic, phonological, and meaning processors, and there is order between and among them. Because they are intricately connected to each other, skilled readers can recognize the spelling, sound, and meaning of familiar words almost automatically, and therefore have their active attention available for critical or reflective thought (Adams, 1990). The strength of the connections is dependent on repeated experiences with language and print.

Working Memory and Controlled Attention

The complex process we call reading is largely dependent on working memory (Shankweiler & Crain, 1986) and thus on attention. Working memory, with its limited capacity, can only deal with so much information at a time. Attention must work in synchrony with working memory, modulating the intake of information with respect to the tolerance level of working memory. When too much attention is allocated to decoding, it cannot be allocated to comprehension, and vice versa.

Because of the role controlled attention commands in the working memory system, we expect that attention dysfunction will affect all processes that are implicated in the linguistic module. As the attention-intensive demands of phonological analysis increase, we can expect that performance will decline in those individuals with attention deficit disorders. We have found this to be true when word attack skills are measured using pseudowords (Cherkes-Julkowski & Stolzenberg, 1991).

Better decoders have less difficulty with complicated text because decoding is an automatic process for them, so it does not consume the attention/working memory resources needed for on-line language processing. Better decoders are not taxing their limited capacity with attention to word analysis, so they read quickly and fluently. This efficiency is also facilitated by the same control over attention and working memory that helped decoding become automatic in the first place. Efficient and extended processing is especially critical when reading comprehension involves difficult, elaborated sentences that use embedded phrases or otherwise require back and forth processing, or that simply threaten the immediacy of understanding. It is at this point that attentional resources need to be both available and efficiently deployed.

In the area of reading, it has been argued that comprehension and inference processes are negatively affected, and in some cases cannot be manifest at all, when lower-level decoding and word recognition skills are poorly developed (Perfetti & Lesgold, 1977, 1979). Analyses of the performance of poor readers and learning-disabled readers have shown that their verbal coding processes in general, and word decoding processes in particular, are slow and inefficient, demanding effortful attention (Perfetti & Roth, 1981; Vellutino, 1979). Johnson-Laird (1983) notes that good readers build up an integrated representation of a story in their working memories as they read; working memory is brought into play when new information is read and must be held on-line while being incorporated into the model. Poor readers never get that far, because they do not have the reserve working memory capacity left to do so. They have exhausted their working memory resources on lower-level skills such as decoding and word recognition. In fact, when reading achievement scores are predicted with a regression equation (Meltzer et al., 1988) automaticity of decoding enters first for the disabled group, while higher-level processes (verbal reasoning, cognitive flexibility, and metacognitive awareness of strategies) enter for the average readers.

The attention/working memory system plays a central role in reading comprehension as well. Language processing can place enormous burdens on working memory. By its nature, language is generated in a linear, sequential manner, and therefore resists compacting and condensing in the effort to formulate a single, unified, integrated awareness. One way of coping may be an on-line processing mechanism, described as "immediacy of interpretation" by Carpenter and Just (1989). In this model, each word is interpreted immediately, rather than held in working memory until clarification occurs later via additional content. If misinterpretation occurs, it need only be revised when and if additional relevant information is processed. Such a strategy does not overtax the capacity of working memory; because meaning is assigned to information in the working memory store, the active, attention-sapping processing required to maintain it on-line is no longer necessary. Whether or not the model correctly describes how connected text is ultimately understood, it certainly underscores the vital role of working memory in reading comprehension.

When information increases in complexity, even greater stress is placed on the cooperative functioning of attention and working memory. Sheer amounts of information create a burden on limited capacity. Longer sentences are more difficult for a person with attention deficits, as are larger paragraphs and longer passages. Certain kinds of constructions are more challenging to limited working memory resources than others. These include any sentence that begins with an element other than the subject. Consider the following:

> (1) Before you clean the garage, call the pharmacy.
> (2) Call the pharmacy before you clean the garage.

The first example requires more on-line working memory capacity in order to retain clause information until the main subject is found. In the second case, the main idea can be encountered and condensed to make room for the next cohesive unit (Shankweiler & Crain, 1986). Children with ADDs and other working memory problems will often trip over these constructions when they read and tend to avoid them in their writing.

Achieving the syntactic and semantic coherence essential for comprehension requires attention. Working memory must be available to hold words and phrases on-line long enough for the reader to ascertain the meaning of the text. Consider this complex sentence: "The reader who is able to decode difficult words with ease has enough attention to determine the subject and verb of this sentence." To ensure adequate attentional resources for parsing the sentence, word recognition must be automatic. Any struggle with the decoding will steal capacity from working memory, and may even crash the system. But as is evident in this example, automatic word recognition by itself is not enough to enable the reader to make sense of the sentence.

The facilitative role of syntax and sentence parsing can be appreciated if one tries to remember this word string:

> too   for   bus   it   to   takes   wait   long   the

Or, using the same words, this one:

> it   takes   too   long   to   wait   for   the   bus

It would also be easier to process this sentence:

> I like the red dress to the nines and have a good time.

if it were parsed in speech (or with commas, in print) as:

> I like the red, dress to the nines, and have a good time.

Syntax provides efficient access to meaning by providing a structure or frame to organize words before the entire message has ended (Carpenter & Just, 1989). When syntactic competence allows the sentence to be parsed meaningfully, working memory demands are reduced, and resources are available for other processes. In cyclic fashion, however, a good deal of syntactic processing relies on phonologically mediated working memory. Function words that carry critical syntactic information lack semantic value in their own right (e.g., *and, therefore, the, is,* etc.). Since there is no immediate meaning, function words must be held on-line in working memory until the preceding and subsequent words can be processed with them. Furthermore, function words, as well as syntactically informative morphological endings (e.g., *-ing, -s, -ed,* etc.), are unstressed in speech and therefore lack acoustic saliency, making them that much harder to manage phonologically. Little wonder that these are the forms misread, misspelled, omitted, and misused by children with ADDs and language-based learning disabilities.

Constructions with embedded phrases or negation also require extra processing. Embedded phrases require the reader to hold the semi-completed main phrase in mind while processing the embedded one:

The red dress, which I have saved forever to buy, is perfect for the occasion.

Similarly, negation can create the need for additional processing steps:

Pick an apple, not the red one.

John is happy or he is not old.

Indirect allusions can likewise create an increased attention/working memory load. All of what is mentioned must be held on-line until the inference is discovered. Of course, a highly effective metaphor can circumvent the cumbersome aspects of working memory processing altogether by evoking an immediate reference or image.

These are examples of difficulty at the sentence level. Paragraph and chapter constructions present their own processing demands, which create additional stress for the attention/working memory system. It is much easier on the attentional system when the main idea of a paragraph is presented in the first sentence, or even in the last sentence. Students with ADDs often struggle to identify main ideas when they are placed in the middle of paragraphs, and may not identify them at all if the main idea must be inferred or constructed by integrating all the discrete information contained in a paragraph.

Teaching Reading: Instructional Approaches Helpful to the Student with ADD

When teaching the attention-deficient child how to read, it is critical to remember what the reading process is, and how it can interact with attention dysfunction. If the diagnosis is made before the child has encountered any reading difficulties, intervention can start with good instruction, planning for the potentially troublesome areas and hopefully averting major problems. If the child is already having difficulties, and developing idiosyncratic ways of coping with them, intervention will need to be more artfully designed with that particular child in mind.

Decoding

Since attention and working memory capacity is especially limited in students with attention dysfunction, it is critical to provide instruction that condenses information into the most compact, integrated form to reduce the load created by discrete bits of information. Happily, this need fits neatly with the reality of speech perception: that the most basic unit of sound is the syllable. For children with ADDs, the best strategy is to present patterns of syllable sounds. This approach uses "word families" to highlight the regularities among words. The child learns to read lists of words such as *cat, fat, sat, zat* — pseudowords are fine since the concern is decoding and not finding meaning. This approach, known as *linguistic reading,* is distinct from other code-based approaches in a number of ways.

The purpose of linguistic reading is to highlight a word pattern in order to condense information and reduce the need for well-managed attention. To achieve this goal, it is necessary to keep the pattern intact. The word, then, cannot be sounded or approached from left to right, one letter at a time. The child must orient first toward the pattern, and then toward the initial part of the word. In all cases, as the child progresses through syllable types — i.e., from the *-at* family to the *-an,* and ultimately through *-ough* and other configurations — it is critical that she be able to divide the syllable into the rime (the part that begins with the vowel and goes to the end of the syllable) and the onset (the initial consonant[s] that precedes the vowel).

While pattern recognition provides direct attentional advantages, it also facilitates the decoding process indirectly, by narrowing the field of possible pronunciations. As we have pointed out before, a left-to-right approach leaves one with a nearly infinite number of possibilities for letter sounds. It is impossible to determine the sound of an initial letter *c* until the next letter is known. If it is *h,* there are more decisions to be made. If it is *o* — well, that would be different from *a,* but still not certain, because what if the *o* were followed by an *a* or possibly a *u*? Individual letters, especially consonants, do not make sounds; patterns of letters do.

If the child is not ready for linguistic reading, the teacher must plan for some work with phonological speech processing, in the absence of print. Any activity that prepares a child to be aware of rime and onset would be appropriate. The standard ones are games or nursery rhymes involving rhyme and alliteration. There are also phoneme deletion activities, in which the teacher might instruct, "Say *cat*. Now say it again but don't say the /k/" (Rosner & Simon, 1971). For further activities of this kind, we refer the reader to Rebecca Treiman's work (Treiman & Zukowski, 1991), or to Stone, Merritt, and Cherkes-Julkowski (in press).

Of course, children with ADDs are impulsive and want to get on and get through with whatever task is presented. Given typical whole-language instruction, or other forms of instruction that do not insist on using the cipher to determine what the word on the page is, they are unlikely to weed systematically through the morass of information on a page of connected text to discover the code. Instead, they will use a picture to determine that the *ch-* word should be *children*, not *chicken*. They will use their background knowledge to determine that the word that starts with *z* in the story about the tiger is likely to be *zoo*. And, since careful and methodical analysis is not the hallmark of ADD functioning, they are unlikely to return to the printed word and discover *why* these letters make *zoo* or *children* or anything else. What is unfortunate about this situation is that these children can experience a great deal of "success" using this approach during the early stages of reading, with no reason to suspect that they have hit upon a strategy that is anything but sound, effective, and quick. In fact, most often the teachers and tutors in non-code-based programs will encourage students to use these kinds of contextual clues.[3] The false sense of security created by this situation comes back to haunt the learner as "learning to read" is replaced by "reading to learn" in the upper grades.

The guess-the-word approach will "work" as a way to guess meaning as long as the child is reading material whose content she already knows about or can deduce from pictures. But this is not the purpose of reading as she gets older. Reading ultimately serves the purpose of finding out about things that are new, as a way to learn additional information. Approaches based on context or pictures will no longer work, since the important words are probably not in the child's lexicon in the first place (Adams, 1990). For example, imagine guessing "photosynthesis" from an illustration of a plant and sun.

---

[3] Iverson and Tunmer (1993) have established that code-based instruction is *far more effective* than whole-language approaches for all children who have any difficulty with reading. Children will learn to read with fewer hours of instruction, experience less failure, and cost the school system less money.

If the child has already developed a whole-word guess strategy rather than one that attacks the composition of the printed word, that predisposition will have to be taken into consideration when instruction is designed. The teacher then has the additional problem of trying to prevent the child from using a strategy which, in her view, has worked quite nicely up to now and certainly brings a more immediate return. It may be necessary to remove context completely so that it cannot be used as a way of guessing. It might even be important to use just pseudowords so that a child cannot use vocabulary to refine the word. These are extreme measures and might need to be considered only if the child has developed a truly resistant maladaptive whole-word or context strategy.

Because automaticity is critical if decoding is to form the basis for comprehension, it is important for children with ADDs to practice until they are fluent with each syllable type. Of course, the craving for novelty with which ADD children must cope interferes with sustaining their attention to repeated presentations of information. Thus, anything that can be done to increase arousal will help:

- Colorful computer games are indicated, as long as they use a linguistically controlled vocabulary (word families), and as long as color is applied to the word itself, not to surrounding pictures.
- It might help catch the ADD child's attention if the teacher were to read and make errors. The child's role would be to play teacher and to discover the errors made.
- Some reading programs include fluency drills. Most ADD children would need to work on these with an adult or another student, in order to use interaction to enhance attention during such drills.

Once the child has developed an effective way to attack a word (e.g., dividing it into syllables and finding the rime, then the onset), it is far more likely that she will be able to discover new rules of orthography on her own. At the beginning stages of reading, the strategy itself is as important as what is actually learned about the cipher. This is likely to mean relatively slow progress in the beginning, but the benefit is in establishing the correct form of word attack and mastery, as well as fluency with each successive syllable type.

Comprehension

Passages. If decoding is not a problem, other sources of difficulty with reading comprehension are most likely to come from the processing demands made by the length of, and kinds of language used in, the passage. Longer passages are more difficult because there is more information to manage. This kind of assignment is likely to become an issue at late middle school, and certainly by high school.

We have collected some data (Cherkes-Julkowski et al., 1995) demonstrating both the effects of long passages on youngsters with ADDs and the effects of medication. These data represent reading comprehension of short passages on the Woodcock-Johnson passage comprehension test and comprehension scores for longer passages on the Gray Oral Reading Test. Two groups were studied. One group was assessed prior to having medication prescribed. The other group had already been taking medication at a level determined to be optimal. Table 9.1 below demonstrates the drop in performance from short (2 or 3 sentences) to long passages (7 or 8 sentences) for both groups, as well as the generally superior performance of those children already taking medication.

In the unmedicated condition, there is a drop of more than ⅔ standard deviation as the child moves to longer passages. In the medicated condition, there is a drop of a full standard deviation. It is important to bear in mind that the length increase from the Woodcock-Johnson to the Gray is only five or six sentences. If the drop continued proportionately, a page of reading would be nearly impossible to comprehend. In interpreting these data, it is important to consider that there are differences in the two scales besides the passage length. Nevertheless, if there is any cohesion to the concept of reading comprehension at all, it is most likely that the length of the passages accounts for a major proportion of the decline in performance.

When passages are longer, it is helpful to subdivide them into conceptually meaningful segments, each to be read as a smaller unit. Notes can be taken on each part, and then some time can be spent on integrating the subsections. This also helps define clear breaks in the assignment so that the child does not feel that he is facing

Table 9.1
Effects of Medication on Reading Comprehension Scores

	mean (standard deviation)	
	ADD/No Meds	ADD/Meds
short passages (WJ)*	110.16 (7.72)	128.00 (15.26)
long passages (GORT)**	9.83 (2.08)	13.20 (2.85)

* These scores have a mean of 100, standard deviation of 15.
** These scores have a mean of 10, standard deviation of 3.

a 4-hour, nonstop study session. The use of a content- or trade book-notebook for recording new vocabulary and/or characters, and for keeping a running record of main ideas and key events, has been successful with children who have reading comprehension difficulties.

Repeated readings are sometimes necessary, since a youngster is likely to pick up only some of the information with his limited attention system during the first pass through. Multiple passes are more manageable if the reading is subdivided, but this can turn into an overwhelming task with high school assignments of typical length. Another approach might be to encourage the student to use books on tape. This does not take less time, but the student can listen to a tape while driving in a car or cleaning his room. Using the tape, then, means that a student need not carve out additional time for just sitting and studying. It also means that there can be some attention-arousing motor activity while listening.

If repeated or subdivided reading is necessary, it will also be necessary to give the student advance notice of assignments so that she can pace herself, work with smaller units of information, and still complete the work in time for class discussion. The provision of a syllabus, just like those provided to college students, is enormously helpful to students (and their tutors) in planning time for reading and writing assignments.

Sentences. Difficulty with comprehension at the sentence level is likely to pose a larger threat to comprehension and a larger challenge to instruction. The most direct way to help a child cope with the syntactic demands of complex sentences is to teach explicit ways of parsing a sentence. This need not be highly refined, but a student should be able to decide which words hang together in a phrase and what the function of each word is.

Once the student begins to have a more explicit appreciation for how sentences are naturally parsed in speech, it should be far more obvious how punctuation helps to mark off the naturally occurring segments; punctuation can be learned as what emerges from the way one phrases as one speaks, rather than as a formalized rule system. The latter strategy is painfully difficult for people with ADD and is probably ineffective in any case.

There is likely to be a particular need for instruction in words of conjunction, one form of the abstract function words with which ADD/LD children have distinct difficulty. Since conjunctions give expression to the clear relationship between thoughts, they are critical to the cohesion of a passage. It would be particularly helpful for a teacher to work collaboratively with a student to discuss the choice of conjunctions and consider the effects on meaning of alternative choices. There should be a follow-up in writing as well, in which the student's choice of conjunctions could be refined. Conjunctions would be developed as a means of making transitions between ideas, sentences, and passages. In all cases, any construct emphasized in reading comprehension will need to be developed in writing as well. The two processes co-evolve and can be used to support and enhance each other.

MEDICATION AND READING

Some literature has claimed that attention deficit disorder has little effect on reading and that therefore medication does little to enhance reading skill (Forness, Cantwell, Swanson, Hanna, & Yonpa, 1991). We have found the opposite to be true. We have studied some individual children and young adults to assess their reading with and without medications as well as on varying dosages. Two of these case studies are reported below.

Case 1: Fifth-grade male

The purpose of testing was to evaluate the effect of a range of medication dosages on reading. Measures were taken under four conditions. At test period I, the child was taking no medication. Test period II occurred one year later and assessed performance at 10, 15, and 20 mg of Dexedrine.

Table 9.2 illustrates the increase in comprehension score at 15 mg and 20 mg. Rate and accuracy are minimally affected on this test. In actual applications, however, improved comprehension is likely to improve the rate of reading, since repeated

Table 9.2
Effects of medication on reading ability of a fifth-grade male with ADD

		Test Period I (1992)	Test Period II (1993)		
		no meds	*10 mg*	*15mg*	*20mg*
GORT-3*	comprehension	11	10	13	14
	rate	8	9	9	
	accuracy	11	9	8	
Word Attack (WJ-R)**		103	108		118

* Mean for GORT-3 scores is 10, standard deviation of 3.
** Mean for WJ-R is 100, standard deviation of 15.

readings would be less necessary. This child had been making decoding errors with words in isolation, which he no longer made while taking medication (as evidenced by the drastic improvement in his word attack scores).

Case 2: 20-year-old female, college sophomore

The purpose of testing was again to evaluate the effect of a range of medication dosages on reading and general cognitive performance. The following is the schedule of medication dosages:

June 19–22		10 mg Prozac
June 23–24		no Prozac
June 24	*9:30 am*	10 mg Ritalin
	10:15 am	5 mg Ritalin
		Testing began at 10:15 and lasted until 1:00

A major concern at this evaluation was the effect of the two dosages of Ritalin (in combination with whatever Prozac was still active in the young woman's system) on reading comprehension.

The change in GORT-3 performance is extreme. With 10 mg of Ritalin there is slight improvement, 0.67 standard deviation, from the below-average to low-average range. However, an additional 5 mg of Ritalin elevates her score to the superior range. With 15 mg of Ritalin, she performed consistently well on higher-level passages. Her difficulty seemed contained to her unfamiliarity with a good deal of the vocabulary. This is as much a result of development in the context of ADD as anything else. This student has not had access to the refined attention or analytic approach that would have allowed her to infer the definition of new words while reading in context.

On the WJ-R passage comprehension test, this student worked slowly and very

---

Table 9.3
Effects of medication on reading ability of a 20-year-old female with ADD

	December 1993	June 1994	
	no meds	*10 mg*	*15mg*
GORT-3 comprehension	6—Form A	8—Form A	14—Form B
WJ-R passage comprehension	99		106

carefully through the short passages of the test. She was able to read correctly many of the items that she had missed at the last testing in December 1993. She avoided the errors on the easier items that had characterized her performance when unmedicated. However, she made errors on some of the more advanced items that she had answered correctly at the December 1993 testing. One possible explanation for this is that she had expended more energy/concentration during the earlier items. Another possibility is that she is still not optimally medicated for this task.

At the December 1993 testing, this student had a specific difficulty with comprehension of idioms; this difficulty was not at all evident at the June 1994 evaluation. With medication, she seemed to appreciate the indirect language with no difficulty and could answer these items correctly.

CONCLUSION

Teachers can expect their ADD students to have difficulty with decoding and comprehension. The difficulties are not simply or even mainly due to behavioral issues of inattention or off-task activity. They are essentially bound up with the cognitive aspects of attention, particularly in its intricate connection with working memory. Instructional and pharmacological interventions can be extremely beneficial.

10
Attention and Written Language

The academic domain of written language presents an enormous challenge to students with attention deficit disorders. While most published studies on writing disorders focus on children with learning disabilities (LD), many of these children have concomitant attention deficit disorders. In a recent study, more than 50% of the sample had co-occurring ADDs and learning disabilities (Berninger, Abbott, Whitaker, Sylvester, & Nolen, 1995). Some estimate that as many as 25% of students with ADDs also meet the diagnostic criteria for specific learning disabilities in written language (Barkley, 1990). No doubt there is a much greater proportion of ADD students who don't meet the technical definition of LD, but still experience very significant problems with written language. There is evidence for a common genetic influence on both hyperactivity and spelling disabilities (Stevenson, Pennington, Gilger, DeFries, & Gillis, 1993). In our own practices, we have found that nearly all students with ADDs experience difficulty with one or more aspects of the writing process. An informal inspection of our files of ADD students referred for evaluations over the past few years revealed that, of the most recent 100 referrals, 92 were found to have significant written language disabilities.

Why does written language pose such a problem for those with ADDs? Perhaps more than any other academic domain, the production of written language entails an intricate interweaving of many processes. These include lower-order processes such as the use of a pencil to form a letter symbol, higher-order processes such as sensitivity to the text requirements of a genre, and the many processes in between. Competence in written language requires skills in spelling, grammar, and syntax, use of conventions in capitalization and punctuation, facility in word usage, and idea generation, along with the even more mechanical aspects of text production, such as handwriting or word processing. And those are just the lower, more concrete elements of writing! Additionally, good writers are able to create a text — a piece of writing — that is cohesive in language and tone. Such a text presents enough content and detail to tell the story or explain the concept or express the point of view, but does not include irrelevant or distracting information. The text is also appropriate to the audience for which it is intended. The attentional resources of the writer must be adequate to allow allocation to the lower-level and higher-level processes as needed.

Competence in written language is extremely important. Proficiency in written language becomes increasingly essential as students progress through the grades: "learning to write" is replaced by "writing to learn" and to "show what you know" in the upper grades. Written language becomes the mediator for other academic areas and is the main method through which teachers evaluate students' learning (Poplin, Gray, Larsen, Banikowski, & Mehring, 1980). Content area teachers often assume students' competence in written language, and judge content mastery through projects and examinations that require writing.[1]

Such a complex process is vulnerable to breakdown at many levels. Research on the written language skills of students with writing disabilities, including learning disabilities and attention deficit disorders, has documented deficiencies that substantiate the existence of many such breakdowns. The compositions of writing-disabled students are shorter than those of nondisabled students (Barenbaum, Newcomer, & Nodine, 1987; Graham & Harris, 1989a; Newcomer, Barenbaum, & Nodine, 1988) and tend to include less varied word types (Morris & Crump, 1982) and fewer mature words (defined as those not found on the undistinguished word list, which includes the very common words frequently used in written language; Deno, Marston, & Mirkin, 1982). Their written language is plagued with mechanical errors, including spelling errors (Deno et al., 1982; Moran, 1981; Poplin et al., 1980; Wong, Wong, & Blenkinsop, 1989) and capitalization and punctuation errors (Anderson, 1982; Houck & Billingsley, 1989; Poplin et al., 1980; Poteet, 1978; Tindal & Hasbrouck, 1991). Writing-disabled students also commit more grammatical errors and errors of omission than their nondisabled peers (Anderson, 1982; Johnson & Grant, 1989).

Additionally, many students with attention deficit disorders are highly resistant to writing and have developed negative attitudes about writing and about themselves

[1] Research indicates that teachers are strongly influenced by handwriting and spelling when determining grades, even when content is good (Markham, 1976). For students with discrepant skills in spelling, handwriting, and/ or language generation, teachers might consider awarding separate grades for the different elements. That way, for example, spelling competence can be appreciated separately from competence in content, and strengths are not obscured by weaknesses.

as writers. Coping strategies are varied: they range from out-and-out refusal to use a pencil or pen for any writing, to producing truncated answers and very short stories, to using simple vocabulary words rather than more mature words (words that are longer and/or more difficult to spell). The presence of such resistance to writing is diagnostic: the teacher's job is to determine *why* the process of writing is so unpleasant to the student.

THE NEED FOR CONTROLLED ATTENTION

In any cognitive act, the amount of available attention is important to success (LaBerge & Samuels, 1974). In a process as complex as writing, an enormous demand is placed on the cognitive processes to be functioning at their most highly tuned, efficient, and powerful best. Writing places enormous burdens on working memory, because ideas are recorded word by word (actually, letter by letter), while higher-level goals (e.g., text structure, story grammar, audience) must be maintained on-line and referred to throughout the writing process. Information is retrieved from long-term memory and held in working memory while the writer is planning, generating sentences, and revising (Berninger et al., 1995).

The act of writing is an act of managing multiple demands. The writer first establishes a goal or set of goals (Hayes & Flower, 1980). Higher-level goals (e.g., purpose, audience, voice) lead to the creation of subgoals as the writer moves from planning to producing the draft to revising. The subgoals can pile up, taxing working memory. Since it is impossible to focus on everything at once, the writer must be able to temporarily set aside certain goals (but still hold on to them at some level) as she attends to a more immediate goal. Higher-level goals must be temporarily abandoned as the writer searches for content or deals with lower-level goals such as word choice, syntax, and spelling. Subprocesses are activated and postponed as needed by the writer (Applebee, 1984; Flower & Hayes, 1980; Graves, 1983).

The process of writing is not linear but recursive: planning, drafting, and revising steps interweave with and overlap each other (Berninger et al., 1995; Flower & Hayes, 1980). While working, the writer moves back and forth, in and out of these three stages. During the planning stage, the writer decides the purpose for writing, collects ideas, classifies and manipulates the ideas, and makes decisions regarding the organization and presentation of his text. In the drafting stage, the writer generates sentences. He translates his ideas into oral language, uses words as signals to connect ideas and make his text cohesive, and refers to his knowledge of text structures to ensure that he includes the right types of information (e.g., details to support main ideas). He transcribes his ideas from oral language to written language, using orthographic symbols to spell words. During the revision and editing stage, he judges the success of his draft in meeting the goals decided upon during planning. If necessary, he modifies the information in his draft, or he modifies his goals, so there is a good fit between them. He also considers the needs of his audience; if it is for himself, the courtesies of spelling, capitalization, punctuation, grammar, and neatness can be handled less strictly than if the text is intended for others.

Again, this process is not unidirectional or linear. As the writer is drafting, he may realize that his original plan is inadequate, and therefore return to the planning stage. Revising may mean returning to the planning stage, or to the drafting stage, or it may be the final stage. The successful writer is able to move freely among and between the stages as needed. Central to this process is a complex organization of goals (Hayes & Flower, 1986). The writer moves among global goals — such as the overall purpose for the composition — and local goals, such as choosing just the right word for his audience, or placing quotation marks correctly, or a myriad of other goals relevant to the audience, the content, and the context of the writer's piece. Flower and Hayes (1980) characterize the writing process as a "juggling act." The writer retrieves topic knowledge from long-term memory, uses linguistic conventions, considers his audience, executes motor skills, and, remarkably, creates a text. The writer must be both producer and critic, regulating the process by himself (Flower & Hayes, 1981). It is clear that the process of writing depends on a strong dancer with a dynamic sense of choreography.

PRIOR KNOWLEDGE AND CONCEPTUAL CONNECTIONS

Accessing the knowledge store for information is a critical step in the writing process. Competent writers are able to generate ideas with relatively little effort, drawing on their background knowledge and using "metamemorial" searches to retrieve ideas and groups of related ideas, which can then be evaluated and edited to fit into their plans (Englert & Raphael, 1988; Scardamalia & Bereiter, 1986). A familiar topic, with its richly connected knowledge store, is easily accessed. Unfamiliar topics are more difficult. The writer's working memory capacity can be exhausted as the writer struggles to find some relevant information to use in his composition.

There is evidence that ADD students have excessive difficulty accessing their knowledge stores. Students with attention deficit disorders have far more difficulty than nondisabled students with producing informative or instructional text, designed to communicate with the reader or have an emotional impact. They are more likely to include personally interesting tidbits that are only tangentially related to the topic, perhaps because they have such difficulty accessing relevant information. Research findings showing that significant improvement in quality of information results from prompting by a knowledgeable source (a teacher, a cue card) suggest that these students have the knowledge, but either it is stored in a disorganized or inefficient form (Graham, 1989), or their accessing mechanism is faulty (Graham, Harris, MacArthur, & Schwartz, 1991). Graham (1989) also found that a simple prompt to "write more" has doubled or even tripled the output of students with writing disabilities.

When facts have been retrieved from the knowledge store, writers can either process them separately and keep them isolated or combine them into a larger, conceptually linked whole. There is evidence that writing-disabled students have difficulty making the conceptual connections that their nondisabled peers do, thereby increasing the burden on working memory resources (Hayes-Roth, 1977, discussed in Englert, Raphael, Anderson, Gregg, & Anthony, 1989). Englert and her colleagues (Englert, Raphael, Fear, & Anderson, 1988; Gregg, Raphael, & Englert, 1987) report that writing-disabled students had significantly greater difficulty than their nondisabled peers with categorizing ideas into sets of related ideas and providing conceptual or superordinate labels for these ideas. For example, when planning to include information about animals, the nondisabled subjects generated categories such as "where it lives" and "what it eats." The writing-disabled subjects were more likely to include isolated facts with a personally associative meaning (e.g., "cats eat fish. They like it too."). Without a conceptual framework or a way to represent relationships among ideas, each piece of information must be stored as a unique entity, isolated from other pieces. Imagine trying to find the staples and the stapler among all the stuff in a cluttered desk drawer, thrown together willy-nilly. It may take so long to find them that you forget what you needed them for, or simply give up and settle for a lesser-quality solution, such as a paper clip.

Difficulty in knowledge access and conceptual linking may be reflected in various ways in student writing. When the accessing mechanism is weak, the ADD writer is even more susceptible than usual to disinhibited, associative, off-track thinking. Such weakness can lead the writer in many directions that are hard for the reader to follow. For example, the compositions of students with ADDs often seem to be direct transcriptions of their inner thoughts, serving their own interests rather than the reader's. Figure 10.1, a writing sample from an 8-year-old girl with ADD, illustrates this tendency: two of her four sentences are personal statements ("I like the moon, do you? I like to be up on the moon").

Figure 10.2, a writing sample from a 10-year-old boy with ADD, hyperactivity, and learning disabilities, shows another egocentric tendency: the use of elliptical phrases and abbreviated forms. A word or phrase that is rich in meaning for the writer might need substantial elaboration for others to understand it. In this story, Joshua writes "my raisins came out of the box dancing and singing I heard it through the grape vine," recollecting a television commercial that was popular at the time that he wrote this, but the context of which would be foreign to most readers by now. Joshua also uses the colloquial phrase "No way Jose" in his writing; he was fond of saying this orally as well.

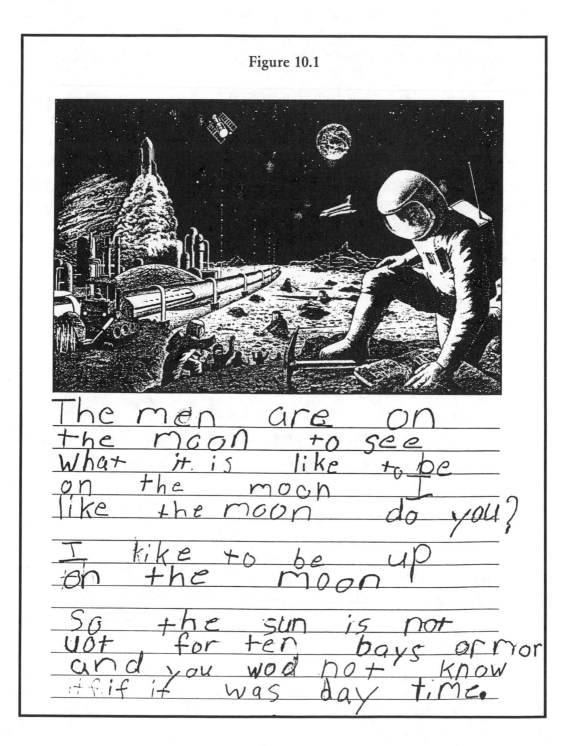

Figure 10.1

The men are on the moon to see what it is like to be on the moon I like the moon do you? I like to be up on the moon So the sun is not uot for ten bays or mor and you wod not know if it was day time.

Many writers use dialogue in their compositions. Jason, a 15-year-old boy with ADD and nonverbal learning disabilities, carries this to an extreme. He produces a "story" (Figure 10.3) that is almost entirely dialogue, to the exclusion of any plot or theme development. Jason was a big fan of the *Star Trek: Voyager* television series, and he seems to have pulled that association from his long-term memory when he considered the space scene depicted. Many of the phrases he uses in his writing are commonly used in the television show. By depending upon dialogue, especially co-opted dialogue, the writer exempts himself from making connections and offering explicit explanations.

Another example of writing that is extraordinarily difficult to follow is shown in Figure 10.4. The writer, a 10½-year-old boy with ADD and Tourette's Syndrome, is vulnerable to the intrusions of his tics even when he is writing. Note the overuse of interjections ("WHOOSH!!! Ahhhh! BOOM CRASH!! THUD!! WHACK!"). The extra letters in "Ahhhh" and double and triple exclamation marks may also be symptoms of Tourette's disinhibited, perseverative behavior, similar to the heavy overstrikes and scribbled-out words (O. Sacks, personal communication, 1996).

Figure 10.2

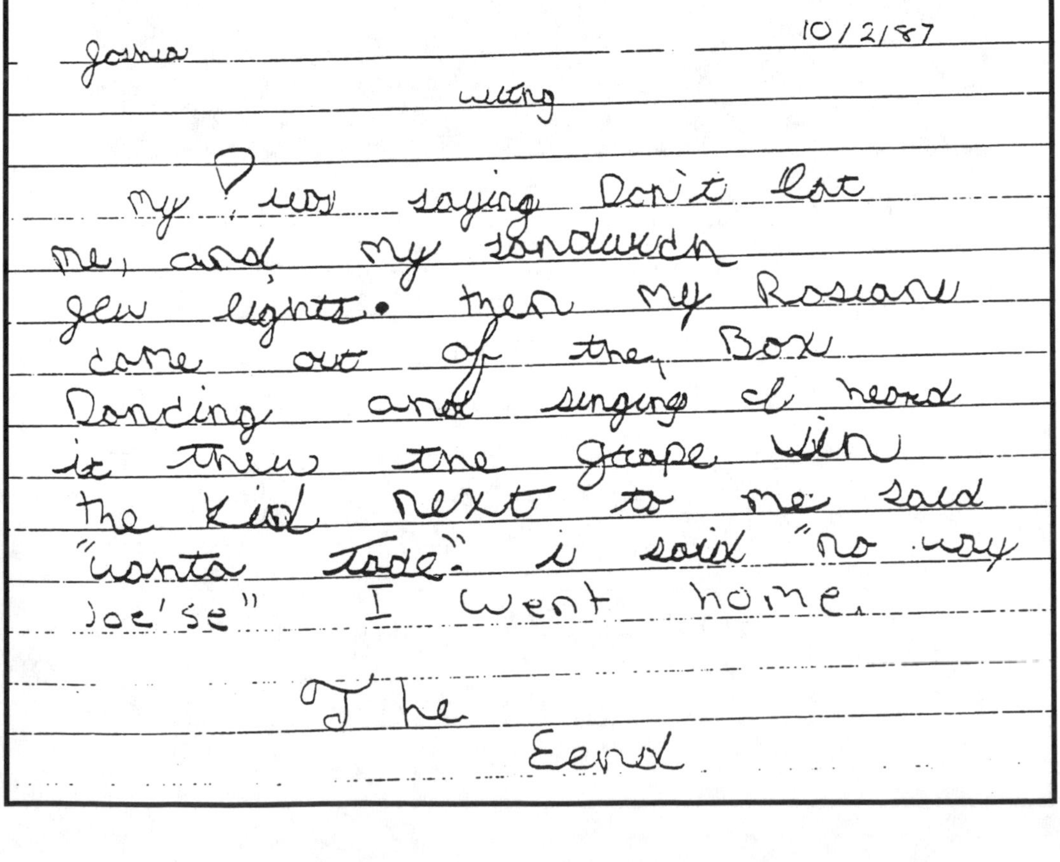
Joshua 10/2/87

writing

My ? was saying Don't eat me, and my sandwich flew lights. then my Rosiane came out of the Box Dancing and singing I heard it threw the grape win the kid next to me said "wanta trade" i said "no way Joe'se" I went home.

The Eend

Figure 10.3

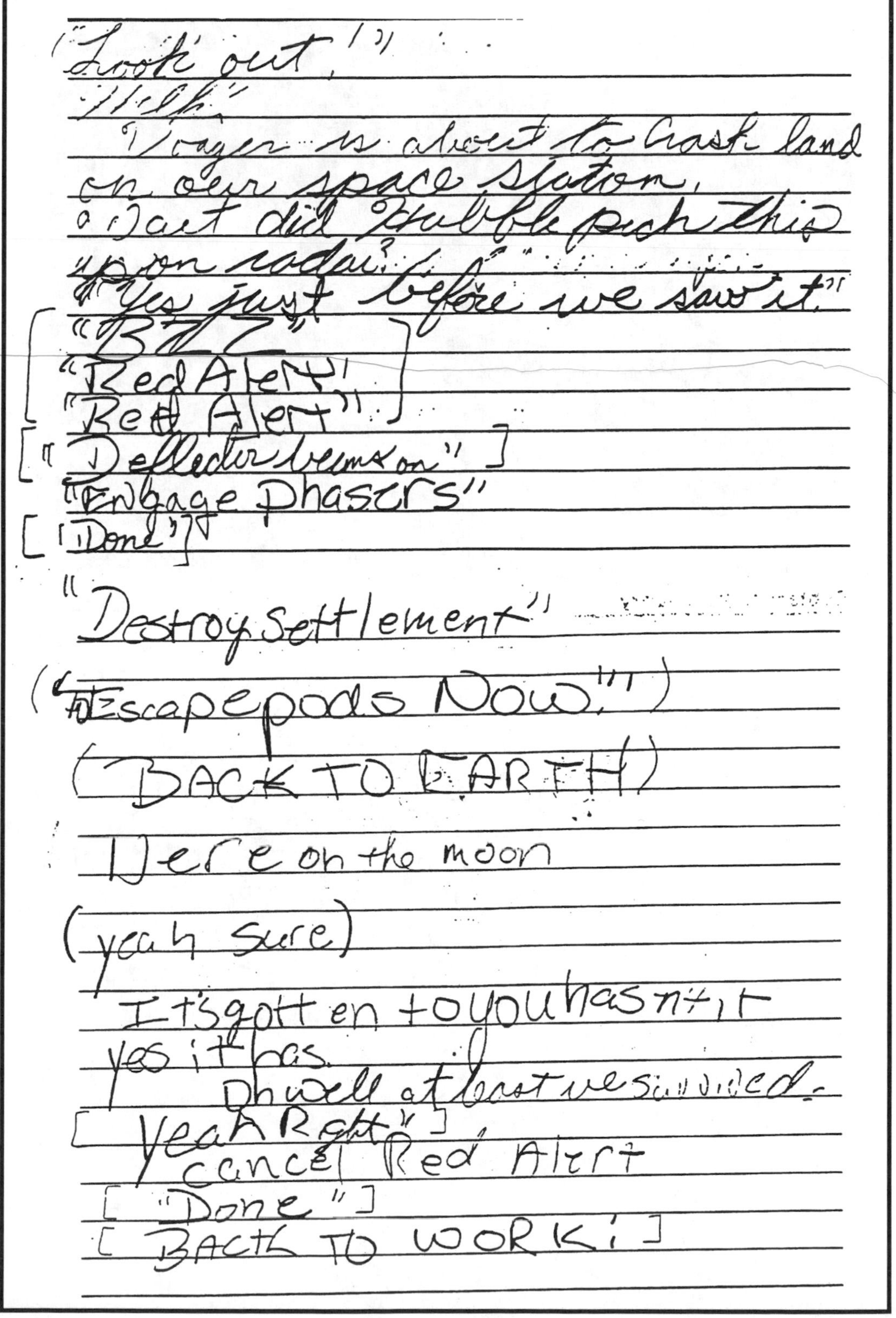

"Look out!"

"Help"

"Voyager is about to crash land on our space station.

"Wait did Hubble pick this up on radar?"

"Yes just before we saw it."

["BZZ

"Red Alert!"

"Red Alert"]

["Deflector beams on"]

"Engage Phasers"

["Done"]

"Destroy settlement"

("Escape pods Now!")

(BACK TO EARTH)

Here on the moon

(yeah sure)

It's gotten to you hasn't it

yes it has.

Oh well at least we survived.

[Yeah Right"]

cancel Red Alrrt

["Done"]

[BACK TO WORK!]

Figure 10.4

We need food. I know let's go hunt.
I want ~~ev~~ evrey hunter ~~in~~ this
town or I'll eat you ~~████~~ hair
later.~~████~~

WHOOSH!!! Got 'em in the chest
but he's still not dead! WHACK!
Ahhhh! a man falls, the clear water
is now an ugly red. Make sure
the women and children are safe!
BOOM CRASH!! THUD!! one down
Two ta go. 2 hours later. ~~████████~~

2

Facilitating the Process

There are a number of instructional interventions that can provide support for the systematic accessing of prior knowledge. *Scaffolding* can be provided through an interactive dialogue between the teacher and the student. In such a dialogue, the teacher asks questions, makes comments, and uses cues to frame, focus, and provide feedback to the student (Nelson, 1995). The interaction is individualized and cannot be prescripted (Englert, 1992), although the teacher certainly may have some specific instructional goals or content that she hopes to include. Englert and Palincsar (1991) properly note that an "important part of the teaching equation is teachers' moment-to-moment responsiveness to their students, and their abilities to make bridges between what their students know and need to know" (p. 228).

Initial *brainstorming*, with or without the help of pictures to cue vocabulary and concepts, can be helpful in eliciting relevant information from the student's knowledge store. Generating *word lists* of topic-relevant vocabulary is also helpful with the transition from ideas to the language needed for writing. *Focus questions* prompting the types of information that should be included in a type of writing (e.g., who, what, where, when, and why for a factual piece; characters, setting, problem, action, and solution for a narrative story) are helpful in generating relevant information during the writing process. *Graphic organizers*, such as outlines, semantic maps, webs, and Venn diagrams, provide a way to organize information as well as generate it.

Story schemata, story grammars, and *text structures* are also helpful, because they provide frameworks that guide the storage and retrieval of information in memory that needs to be accessed when writing (Anderson, 1978; Englert & Thomas, 1987; Rentel & King, 1983; Scardamalia & Bereiter, 1986). *Story schemata* are the elements that, together, constitute a story. *Story grammars* are sets of rules that specify the elements of a story, along with the temporal and causal relationships between the elements. *Text structures* are frames for various types of expository textual forms (e.g., descriptive, enumeration, sequence, comparison/contrast). These three devices signal the types of information to be included in a particular piece of writing, as well as guidelines for the organization of the information. Story grammars and text structures also cue the writer to include the connections between the text/story elements — connections needed for text cohesion. Since each type of writing, especially expository writing, presents its own demands for content and organization (Englert et al., 1988), the writer must be able to remember the requirements for each one. For example, for an "explanation piece," there must be a clear introduction and inclusion of sufficient steps, sequenced correctly, with clear connections between steps made through the use of key or signal words (e.g., *then, after, not until, later*). The information must be relevant, not irrelevant or distracting — a task that requires a degree of inhibition foreign to many individuals with ADDs.

Typical learners increase their knowledge of story schemata with age. By 10 or 11 years of age, most children are thoroughly aware of narrative story structure and the elements that need to be included when writing (Stein & Glenn, 1979, 1982). The most basic narrative story includes temporally and causally related elements, including a beginning with a setting, a middle with some type of conflict, and an end that resolves the conflict. Many students with attention deficit disorders produce compositions that omit one or more of these fundamental components. Typical students first learn to include elements such as location, time, main characters and other characters, and relationships among the characters. Later, elements of plot are included, such as defining a complex problem, causal and temporal relationships between events, and plot resolutions such as achieving a goal or solving a problem. By third grade, most typical students are able to create narratives with all these elements (Laughton & Morris, 1989), but few students with attention deficit disorders are able to do so. Knowledge of various text structures develops over time, with comparison/contrast structures acquired later than enumeration and descriptive forms (Englert & Thomas, 1987). Students with ADDs may need procedural and memory support for story schemata and text structures. Graphic organizers and cue cards can be helpful devices for reminding students of key elements to include in their writing.

Of course, providing only story organizers and scaffolded instruction is likely to be insufficient for most severely disabled writers. Exposure to and experience with many types of texts, identifying the components and elements of stories and expository pieces that have been well written by others, and connecting reading comprehension strategies with writing instruction are all part of the instructional package. Additionally, many students will require instruction in some or all other specific skill areas.

PLANNING

Good writers spend time planning, and they continue to plan throughout the time they actually write (Gould, 1980; Humes, 1983). Goal setting is a critical step for expert writers (Hayes & Flower, 1980); during the planning periods, competent writers set goals including style choices, text structure choices, vocabulary choices, and actual text production (Beaugrande, 1984). When writing, good writers pause for a relatively long time between bursts of rapid writing, often between whole segments of texts, while poor writers pause for shorter periods, complete word- or sentence-level elements, and write more slowly (Van Bruggen, 1946). Students with writing disabilities spend significantly less time planning what they will write than nondisabled students (Hillocks, 1986; MacArthur, & Graham, 1987), and rarely continue the dynamic planning process once they begin writing (Flower & Hayes, 1980). Students with attention deficit disorders tend to record their thoughts as they occur to them, without planning. Or, even when there is a plan, the writer with ADD may be diverted by a more potent distraction and lose sight of his original design.

Planning is closely related to content knowledge. As mentioned earlier, expert writers are able to generate ideas with little effort, drawing on their background knowledge and using "metamemorial" searches, retrieving ideas and groups of related ideas, which can then be evaluated and edited to fit into the writer's plan (Bereiter & Scardamalia, 1984; Scardamalia & Bereiter, 1986). The writer must also hold in memory both the text structure requirements and the preceding sentences, in order to maintain coherence in the paragraph. When this process breaks down, coherence is disrupted by the omission of key connecting words, the inclusion of redundancies and irrelevancies, or early termination.

Immature writers typically use a "knowledge telling" strategy (Scardamalia & Bereiter, 1986): they pour out on paper whatever comes to mind, without much evidence of thought or planning. Bereiter and Scardamalia (1983) describe the knowledge-telling strategy as having five characteristics:

- lack of goal-related planning,
- lack of internal textual constraints on sentences,
- lack of interconnectedness,
- reliance on serial production, and
- lack of revision.

It is important for teachers to avoid encouraging knowledge-telling strategies by suggesting to their students that the purpose of writing is to tell all you know. *Knowledge telling can be a first step in generating material,* but that material then needs to be evaluated and organized during the drafting stage.

Evidence that writing-disabled students use this strategy is provided by Thomas, Englert, and Gregg (1987). Their writing-disabled subjects relied on a "knowledge telling" strategy, "dumping all their knowledge at once" (p. 26). Many writing-disabled subjects restated earlier sentences or extended them only slightly. This was especially apparent on the "description" text, where writing-disabled students focused on a single attribute and could not shift off it. Writing-disabled subjects viewed the writing process as a forward-directed, serial cognitive task, without the backward reflective process through which new information should be related to earlier statements and to the topic at hand.

Writing-disabled students were more likely than nondisabled students to include irrelevant information that was personally interesting to them. As Thomas et al. (1987) state, they "take tangential but familiar ideas and elaborate on them in an associative way" (p. 27). Writing-disabled subjects were also five times more likely than other subjects to terminate the writing too early. They had difficulty producing multiple statements, even within familiar topics. When prompted, however, they were often able to provide more detail.

Knowledge of the requirements for text structure, content, and organization can serve as procedural support, cueing the student as to what kinds of information are needed. However, writing-disabled students have deficient knowledge of text structure and story grammar, and have a great deal of difficulty meeting the requirements of writing stories and writing expository text (Montague, Maddux, & Dereshiwsky, 1990; Newcomer et al., 1988; Nodine, Barenbaum, & Newcomer, 1985; Vallecorsa & Garriss, 1990).

Montague, Graves, and Leavell (1991) used the Story Element Scale created by Graham and Harris (1989a) to quantify the degree of story development in their study of seventh- and eighth-grade students with and without writing disabilities. They found that the nondisabled subjects' stories were longer and included significantly more story elements than the writing-disabled subjects' compositions. However, when the students were provided with planning time and a cue card with the important elements of stories printed on it, the writing-disabled subjects were able to improve their story element scores to the level of the nondisabled subjects. The nondisabled subjects did not benefit from the planning and prompting condition, perhaps because they were already performing at their best. The results of this study suggest that writing-disabled students are not deficient in their knowledge store, but rather have inefficient retrieval strategies or do not know what types of information are needed in their compositions. However, it is yet to be established that equivalent story element scores reliably indicate comparable quality of the writing itself.

Graham (1989) also investigated the narrative compositions of students with writing disabilities. He found that writing-disabled students included some elements required by text structure, but often failed to include important features such as premise and conclusion. They also frequently included irrelevant information. Graham and his colleagues also found, like Montegue et al. (1991), that writing-disabled subjects who did not include basic story elements were able to generate content for specific parts of a story when prompted (Graham & Harris, 1988, 1989b; Graham et al., 1991).

Paralleling the research on students' narrative compositions is research on expository composition. Much of the work in this area has been done by Englert and her colleagues. Expository prose is more complicated than narration for most young writers. Each type of exposition presents its own demands for content and organization (Englert et al., 1988). For example, as noted earlier, the explanation format requires a clear introduction, the inclusion of sufficient steps in the correct sequence, and clear connections between steps through use of key or signal words. The comparison/contrast format has different requirements for content and organization. Sensitivity to textual organization is related to age (Englert & Hiebert, 1984) and reading comprehension (Hiebert, Englert, & Brennan, 1983). Students with learning problems often have difficulties perceiving textual structure (Wong & Wilson, 1984) and the relationships between major and minor ideas (Hanson, 1978).

In a series of elegant studies, Englert and her colleagues (Englert & Thomas, 1987; Thomas et al., 1987) demonstrated that students with writing disabilities had difficulty discriminating between information that was relevant and information that was irrelevant to the topic and text structure. Writing-disabled, low-achieving, and normally achieving students were given two-sentence paragraphs and asked to (1) read and judge the importance of sentences that were either very consistent, somewhat consistent, or inconsistent with the paragraphs; and (2) finish the paragraphs with two sentences. In the reading task, older subjects were more adept than younger subjects at detecting inconsistencies. Also, writing-disabled subjects were significantly poorer at the task than the low-achieving and normally achieving groups. Younger writing-disabled subjects had the most difficulty, and tended to rate all statements as "belonging in the paragraph." In the writing task, writing-disabled subjects were significantly poorer at generating relevant details that were also consistent with the text structure. This was so even when writing-disabled subjects were compared to their reading-level-matched peers.

In another study, when asked to read expository texts and summarize them in writing, writing-disabled students included fewer ideas and presented them in a less organized manner than both their low-achieving and their high-achieving peers (Englert et al., 1989). Even more important was the quality of the information in the summaries. Besides including more main ideas and details, high-achieving subjects' summaries showed conceptual organization. In contrast, the summaries of the writing-disabled group were less detailed, were very concrete, and showed no recognition of relationships among ideas. These writers seemed to process the ideas in the paragraphs as just a string of unrelated ideas. In the same study, a similar but even more dramatic pattern was noted in the original compositions of the subjects. Writing-disabled students included significantly fewer ideas than the low-achieving group, while the high-achieving group included significantly more ideas, details, and "signal" words than either the writing-disabled or the low-achieving group did. Signal words include adverbs, adjectives, pronouns, prepositions, and conjunctions that help to link ideas together and create more complex and interesting syntax.

Compared to other subjects, writing-disabled students have been shown to be less aware of textual requirements and less sensitive to conceptual organizations of ideas. Englert et al. (1988) interviewed 30 writing-disabled, high-achieving, and low-achieving students. They presented the students with three vignettes of students' "writing problems" and asked them questions about the writing and revising processes. They found that writing-disabled students didn't rely on text-structure criteria when evaluating writing. They focused on single sentences, evaluating them in egocentric terms such as whether they thought a sentence was "true" or not, or whether a detail was interesting to them personally. They used arbitrary standards such as length or conventions such as spelling to judge the merits of a composition. They were less able to make suggestions for organization of the whole text.

Englert et al. (1989) also conducted follow-up interviews with some of the subjects in this study, and noted a remarkable insensitivity to text structure among the writing-disabled subjects. When asked how to know when a composition was finished, the high-achieving students focused on text-structure elements such as needing more information to support a major point. The low-achieving subjects focused on the need to add more details, but were less conceptual than the high achievers. The writing-disabled subjects focused on arbitrary, external criteria (e.g., "show it to the teacher"), irrelevant criteria (e.g., "when you fill up the page"), or incorrect criteria (e.g., "when you put a period at the end"). In fact, when asked how to decide what order to put sentences into when summarizing, one writing-disabled subject suggested putting the sentences into alphabetical order.

The writing-disabled student's disposition to repeat information already stated in the text has been discussed by Bereiter (1985, cited in Thomas et al., 1987). He suggests that this may be a kind of coping strategy: when students do not fully understand a task, the best try may be to add a small amount of detail, staying close to what is available to them in the text. They avoid the high risk of error by staying away from higher-order responses. The evidence that writing-disabled students are not sensitive to the content and syntax requirements of different text structures (Raphael, Englert, & Kirschner, 1986; Taylor & Beach, 1984) is consistent with this fall-back strategy.

In a study by Raphael and her colleagues, writing-disabled subjects committed more spelling and syntax errors than nondisabled writers matched for reading level. However, they were even more likely to make text structure errors (50% text errors vs. 9% mechanical errors). Raphael et al. (1986) suggest that higher-order difficulties present a major barrier to performance, while lower-order elements such as spelling and syntax are easier to execute. That may be true, but it is also possible that the writing-disabled subjects exhausted their attention in the execution of difficult lower-order elements and had no reserves left to deal with the higher-order features. Others have noted that writing-disabled students' difficulty with the lower-level skills necessary to getting language onto paper interferes with planning and content processes (Graham et al., 1991).

SKILLED LANGUAGE GENERATION

Skilled writing depends on fluency in *language generation*, the ability to translate thoughts into a linguistic form that includes appropriate vocabulary and syntax (McCutchen, 1984). The language deficits of writing-disabled students, documented in the speech, language, and reading literature, create another barrier to writing performance. Problems with fluency can have a number of effects on the writing process. The writing-disabled writer may write fewer words (Deno et al., 1982) and may use fewer mature and interesting words and more commonplace, high-frequency words. He may write shorter, less complex sentences (MacArthur & Graham, 1987; Morris & Crump, 1982). Attending to lower-level language skills saps resources that might be used to plan the writing product or to generate content for it.

Once the writer has decided what he wants to say, he must translate his ideas into linguistic form. This is not an easy task; the ideas must be divided into smaller components so that the writer's working memory is neither overwhelmed with too much content nor bogged down in too much detail. There is evidence that the clause-length component is the basic unit of sentence planning (Kaufer, Hayes, & Flower, 1986). Expert writers pause longer at the boundaries of clauses, and errors are most likely to occur at clause boundaries (Daiute, 1984).

As mentioned in the preceding section, expert writers plan and execute larger portions of text than novices do. Drawing on their observations of expert writers, Kaufer et al. (1986) hypothesized that writers retrieve their thoughts from long-term memory and encode them in clause-like chunks (or, perhaps, retrieve in larger chunks but encode in units of clauses). The production capacity of even expert writers seems to be delimited by clause-length language.

The syntactical errors committed by writing-disabled writers (e.g., subject-verb disagreement, inconsistencies in tense, omissions and substitution, incoherence, etc.) may reflect a breakdown in the sentence generation process. Their attempts to compensate may be reflected in such strategies as using simple sentence structures (and thereby avoiding the attention demanded by on-line processing of complex sentence structure), decreased output, and low vocabulary level. Certainly one of the most frequently observed characteristics of the writing of students with attention deficits is limited output. Some bright students are able to develop sophisticated coping strategies, consciously choosing to use a pronoun in place of a more lengthy noun (e.g., *they* for "Robert and Nancy"); a contraction instead of two words (e.g., *won't* for "will not"); or a simpler word for a more lengthy one (e.g., *bad* for "terrible"). Bright, articulate writers with attention deficit disorders have explained to us that these strategies make writing "easier." Yet the attentional resources used to deploy these ink-conserving techniques consume energy that could be used to make the text more interesting or intelligible to the reader.

Michael, a bright 11-year-old with ADD, illustrates this difficulty. Michael's verbal language skills are excellent: his WISC-III Verbal Intelligence Quotient falls in the superior range. Yet, despite his oral language facility, he has extreme difficulty transcribing his ideas into print. Figure 10.5 shows his attempts to write single sentences (note the incomplete sentences and omission of words), and Figure 10.6 shows his failed attempt to write a story, after much encouragement.

COMMAND OF LOWER-ORDER ELEMENTS

The writer must have command of the conventions of writing and the motor demands of text production so that attention is available to devote to the higher-order components of the writing process (Berninger et al., 1992; Scardamalia & Bereiter, 1986). The search for a particular word, an approximate spelling, or even the formation of a letter symbol disrupts the associative processes involved in sentence generation: forgetting or confusion can result. The findings that novice writers and writers with writing disabilities concentrate on word-level or, at most, sentence-level processes — at the expense of text-level cohesion — may reflect just this problem. The lack of cohesion may be due to cognitive overload at a very basic level.

Some have argued that higher-level skills such as creating sentence variations, selecting form, communicating meaning, and presenting "voice" are not possible until lower-level skills such as handwriting, spelling, and conventions become automatic (Hayes & Flower, 1983; Humes, 1983). The secretary/author roles discussed by Isaacson (1989) are based on the theory that writing-disabled students must be able to manage both roles in order to become independent writers. Isaacson states that the "secretary" skills must be automatic in order to free up working memory to concentrate on higher-order, more purposeful and deliberate "author" tasks (Isaacson, 1992).

For nondisabled students, beyond the first few grades, mechanics do not seem to interfere with the quality of writing. But it may be different for writing-disabled students: their rate of writing (or typing) is so slow that remembering the thread of a main idea may be too difficult. It has been found that many writing-disabled students

Figure 10.5

TEST 27

Writing Samples (cont.)

6.

finbing in a cage on a perch

7.

The man on the right is The kin

8.

a chickling ishaching from an egg

9.

The unial on The left is a cow

10.

in the closet

The lost number so shaloo inan closet

Figure 10.6

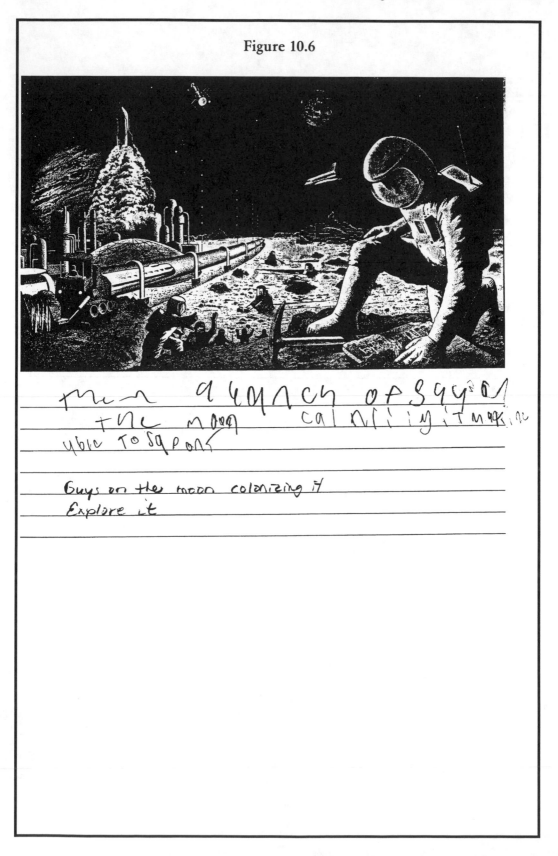

men   a lunch of sggon
   the moon   calnling; t mak;n
ubic To sgpons

Guys on the moon colonizing it
Explore it

continue to struggle with letter formation well after receiving years of instruction (Graham, Boyer-Schick, & Tippets, 1989).

McCutchen (1988), however, disagrees with the argument that basic writing skills must be automatic. She states that expertise in writing cannot be automatic, because the skilled writer must activate other subprocesses such as goal and audience awareness. "Goal-directed processes," she says, must be able to "intervene at any time and modify the language being generated" (p. 310). Automaticity, which by her definition is beyond conscious control, would prevent this metacognitive interaction. She cites the example of the immature writer, who can only use a knowledge-telling strategy (i.e., automaticity of language generation) because language generation under a more mature form (e.g., textual structure) would be too effortful. It is "through the over-simplification," she says, "that they [young writers] are able to manage the complexity of writing" (p. 312). An alternative explanation, however, is that information retrieval and language generation are *not automatic at all* for the knowledge-teller and that the disorganized and incohesive product reflects the cost of such consumption of cognitive attention. Rafal and Henik (1994) argue that the true measure of skill in print (reading and writing) is the ability to inhibit automatic processes when necessary.

TEXT COHESION AND WORKING MEMORY

Cohesion refers to the quality of "wholeness" or continuity in a story or text. Johnson-Laird (1983) asserts that cohesion is necessary for story grammar to be linked with content, and that cohesion depends on co-referencing (and therefore on working memory) so the reader can construct meaning. In other words, cohesion makes the connections between events clear for the reader.

Cohesion makes understanding the text easier for the listener or reader for two reasons. First, the reader is able to understand the writer's meaning when given only the information within the text; no extra-textual references are needed (Halliday & Hasan, 1976). Stories lack cohesion when the reader must make too many inferences or rely on information not present in the text in order to understand the actions of the characters or relationships between events. Second, the sentences are connected to one another through the use of lexical links. The sentences are built on the semantic commitments (i.e., word choices and content) of preceding sentences (McCutchen, 1988). At a simple level, this means using the right pronoun to coordinate with a previously-used noun, or a verb that agrees with the subject. At a more complex level, it means maintaining the syntactical and vocabulary style throughout a series of sentences.

King & Rentel (1981) describe four major types of lexical links:

1. **Conjunctions** (e.g., *but, and, since, furthermore, instead of, while, afterwards*) are especially helpful in creating cohesive ties between sentences (Fitzgerald & Spiegel, 1986). They signal temporal, causal, adversative, and additive relationships among information within the text.

2. **References** to information inside or outside the text include use of personal and possessive pronouns referring to a named character or object; demonstratives such as *the, those, that, this*; and use of comparatives such as *bigger* or *other*.

3. **Substitutions** for a removed word, phrase, or clause (e.g., *do, not, one, ones, same, so*) are used more rarely. Examples: "He remembered the first steps but couldn't remember the last *ones* [replaces *steps*]." "The father said, hurry up, hurry up. But the child *did not* [replaces *hurry up*]."

4. **Ellipsis** is the omission of sentence elements, and it requires the reader to refer back to earlier sentences in the text.

Consider the following passage:

Mary and I went to the store for some milk. I found *it, but she* wanted the *other* kind. *Then she* paid for *it and we* went home.

Within this passage, several elements of cohesion can be identified. The first *it* refers back to the *milk* (reference) mentioned in the first sentence. In the second sentence, *but* connects the first independent clause with the next independent clause (conjunction). *She* refers back to *Mary* (reference), again from the first sentence. *Other* refers back to some information outside the text. The reader has no idea what that might be, based on this text alone (unclear reference). It is implied that *other kind* is some type of milk, but this is not known for sure. In the last sentence, *Then* and *and* establish a sequential order between the first part of the passage and the last part (conjunction). The second *it*, in the last sentence, refers back to the unknown *other kind* (ellipsis). *We* refers back to the first sentence's *Mary and I* (reference).

In spoken narratives, the use of cohesion is fairly well established by age 6 or 7 (Liles, 1985). In written narratives, nondisabled children as young as 8 use cohesion when writing stories (Nodine et al., 1985). Older children are more skilled in recognizing coherent text than younger children (McCutchen, Perfetti, & Basick, 1983) and produce more coherent stories than younger children in both expository writing and narrative writing (McCutchen & Perfetti, 1982). In Newcomer et al.'s sample of third- and fifth-grade writing-disabled and nondisabled subjects, stories that included all the necessary elements of the narrative genre (beginning with setting, middle with conflict, end with problem resolution) were more cohesive than "Primitive Stories" (stories that omitted one element); both in turn were more cohesive than nonstories (pieces that omitted more than one element; Newcomer et al., 1988). For fifth-graders, narratives were more cohesive than opinion essays (Hidi & Hildyard, 1983).

Writing-disabled students' stories are less cohesive, less complete, and more disorganized than those by their nondisabled peers, and this pattern is pervasive across the grade levels (Montague et al., 1990). These students also make more errors in cohesion (e.g., unclear referents) than nondisabled students (Nodine et al., 1985). Reporting on case studies of writing-disabled and nondisabled fourth-graders, Tindal and Hasbrouck (1991) noted that the intersentence structure of writing-disabled students' writing was choppy and disconnected. The nondisabled students in this study used lexical strategies to create a cohesive text (e.g., use of key words such as *so*, use of synonyms, and repetition of words). In a study by Nodine et al. (1985), more than 18% of the writing-disabled 11-year-olds' compositions were judged holistically as incoherent; none of the nondisabled or reading-disabled students' compositions were judged to be incoherent.

Similar findings are reported by Vallecorsa and Garriss (1990) on sixth- and seventh-graders. The writing-disabled subjects in their study had difficulty with cohesion elements such as joining ideas and clarifying relationships. Their use of transitional and organizational ties was significantly less developed than that of the nondisabled subjects.

Cohesion is not limited to connecting information among different sentences. The elements of cohesion within a single sentence are commonly referred to as "good grammar." Within a single sentence, syntax and semantics are also vulnerable to such breakdowns as subject-verb disagreement (e.g., "The vase of flowers are pretty"; "The data looks good"), pronoun problems (e.g., "The chairman lost their place"), confusing references ("The student completed the worksheet and the teacher corrected *her* paper"), and split infinitives (e.g., "I tried to quickly move the papers"), etc.

Even when reading level is held constant, writing-disabled students commit more grammatical errors and errors of omission than their nondisabled peers (Johnson & Grant, 1989). Anderson (1982) investigated syntax use in an early study of writing-disabled fourth-grade students. With a small sample (N=10), she compared the written expression of writing-disabled subjects with that of normally achieving peers. She documented errors in four primary areas. The largest percentage of errors (46%) was due to substitutions and inconsistencies (e.g., beginning the story in the third person and switching to the first person) or using erroneous noun modifiers and prepositions). Another third (34%) of the errors involved additions, particularly the overuse of the connective *and*. A number of the compositions by the writing-disabled subjects connected all the elements in the story with *and,* as if the entire composition were a single thought unit. Another group of errors (29%) was due to omissions of words, especially subjects and verbs. Finally, a small proportion of errors involved word endings, including single-plural errors.

Sometimes, the ADD writer believes that she has transcribed her thoughts completely, while in reality she has omitted whole ideas or parts of words and sentences. Her mind was going faster than the transcription process. The writing makes sense to the writer, but the reader, who didn't think the thoughts, requires that everything be transcribed. We have found that having the writer read her sentences aloud will often provide the feedback necessary for her to add any missing words. This strategy is not as successful for text-level omissions, though. The writer must be able to remember what she originally thought in order to recognize missing pieces; of course, the greater the length or complexity of the text, the harder this is on working memory. Simultaneous monitoring of cohesion of form and of content may be too much for the student with attention deficit disorder. In this case, multiple passes through the composition during the revision process may be required: first checking for content and missing information, next checking for organization, then checking for grammar and syntax consistencies, etc.

Motor Planning, Spatial Organization, & Production Demands

Many individuals with attention deficit disorders suffer from poor fine motor and graphomotor skills. The hyperactivity associated with many ADDs produces a preference for gross motor activity at the expense of fine muscle movements (Zentall & Smith, 1993). As noted earlier, it has been found that many writing-disabled students continue to struggle with letter formation well after receiving years of instruction (Graham et al., 1989). Sometimes, as in the case of Michael (Figures 10.5 and 10.6), handwriting is virtually illegible. Often penmanship is characterized by poor letter formations, placement over, under, and through the lines, and inconsistent spacing between letters and words. Left hemifield neglect, which we discussed in Chapter 10 (Mesulam, 1990; Weintraub & Mesulam, 1983), results in "tornado writing," where the first line of writing begins in the left-hand margin, but each successive line is indented a bit more to the right, until only the right half of the page is used. The resultant product (Figure 10.7, p. 194) looks like a funnel cloud.

More importantly, difficulties in the manipulation of the equipment needed for writing can interfere with the planning and idea generation necessary for developing cohesive and elaborated compositions (Graham et al., 1991). A number of studies have shown that disabled writers produce longer compositions when they dictate, as compared to their handwritten products (Scardamalia, Bereiter, & Goelman, 1982). This has been demonstrated both in narratives and in opinion essays (Hidi & Hildyard, 1983). Although they were more fluent, however, there was no real improvement in the clarity or cohesion of their compositions (Hidi & Hildyard, 1983; Scardamalia et al., 1982).

Graham and his colleagues have investigated the written compositions of writing-disabled students in a variety of production modes. In one study (Graham, 1990) fourth- and sixth-grade writing-disabled students composed opinion essays under three conditions: writing, dictating, and "slow dictation." This last condition was designed to remove the effects of pencil-and-paper manipulation while keeping "time to compose" constant. The examiner recorded the dictation of subjects at the speed at which the subjects had done the actual writing. Graham found that the dictated essays were of significantly higher quality than the handwritten essays, although both modes produced very limited output (50 words or less). In the slow dictation condition, essays were longer, of higher quality, and, for sixth-graders, more cohesive. Thus, the handwriting condition, which made demands on the mechanical aspects as well as the organizational aspects of composing, was the most effortful for the subjects.

MacArthur and Graham (1987) compared the story compositions of fifth- and sixth-grade students with writing disabilities under three conditions: dictation, handwriting, and word processing on a computer. They found that the dictated stories were three to four times longer, were of higher quality, and contained fewer grammatical errors than those composed in the other two conditions. In addition, the dictated stories were composed nine times faster than handwritten stories, and twenty times faster than word-processed ones, despite subjects' familiarity with the computer. The two mechanical production modes were equally affected by spelling and other convention errors.

Computer technology offers some relief for ADD writers. Word processors provide a method of writing that produces neat, printed work; a method to make changes such as adding, deleting, and moving text without recopying; and a way to correct errors without messy erasures. Visibility of text on the screen (MacArthur, 1988) provides assistance to students with working memory weaknesses. Having a clear view of a large chunk of text relieves the burden of holding all the information on-line in memory during drafting or revising. Other advantages of having the text visible include a greater potential for peer collaboration (Daiute, 1986) and teacher interventions (Cochran-Smith, 1991; Morocco & Neuman, 1986). The task of spatial organization, too, is assumed by the computer. In addition, typing may be easier than handwriting, especially for students with fine motor or motor planning problems (MacArthur, 1996). Symbol formation merely requires finding the right letter on the keyboard and depressing the key. A *k* always looks like a *k*, never like an *b* or an *n* or an *l* as it can in cursive script. Naturally, facility with the keyboard is important for efficiency, so that attentional resources aren't consumed by the "hunt and peck" style of typing. (Many individuals with ADDs do have difficulty learning keyboarding skills.)

Software programs that provide word prediction and word bank assistance can reduce the need to type whole words, and spell checkers are helpful in identifying misspelled words and suggesting correct spellings. Like calculators for mathematics, though, these tools are best used to relieve the cognitive burden of having to execute lower-level skills in order to reserve attention resources for higher-level skills. They do not replace the need for the conceptual understanding of the print system that strong spelling abilities help to develop, nor do they fully match the efficiency that truly automatic spelling provides.

REVISION AND CONTROLLED ATTENTION TO DETAIL

Revision is an important aspect of the composing process that distinguishes expert writers from less skilled writers (Fitzgerald, 1987). During revision, the writer attempts to reconcile his composition draft with his goals. There is a great deal of evidence suggesting that the goals of the writing-disabled student are very different from those of nondisabled writers. When revising, expert writers stratify the process. They first concentrate on higher-level, meaning-based revisions, and later attend to lexical changes. Novices focus almost exclusively on the word level (Sommers, 1982), making mostly surface changes (Faigley & Witte, 1981).

Writing-disabled students at all levels revise more like novices than like experts. They equate revision with "tidying up," a process driven by mechanics rather than substance (Graham et al., 1991). Most of the revisions made by writing-disabled students are directed at mechanical areas such as spelling, capitalization, punctuation, and neatness, while their nondisabled peers attend to substantive revisions such as gathering more information to add to the text. Compared to their nondisabled peers, the writing-disabled subjects in a study by Englert et al. (1988) were less able to revise text, focusing on word order and mechanics more than text structure. Similar results were noted for stories (Barenbaum et al., 1987).

Other studies confirm that writing-disabled students focus on revising at a fairly low level. Isaacson and Mattoon (1990) asked 42 fifth- and sixth-grade writing-disabled students to write fables after an instructional lesson. Later, they asked the students about their thinking process when writing and revising. The writing-disabled subjects reported thinking the most about using good words and correct spelling, and writing sentences that made sense. They thought the least about the "moral" — the very element that set the goal and purpose for the writing and the element that had been emphasized in the lesson! They also reported being more concerned about how to start a story than about what to write next or how to end it, perhaps reflecting the difficulty they experienced in activating their knowledge store during the planning process.

Writing-disabled students have difficulty recognizing errors in their compositions; partly for this reason, their revisions tend to be ineffective or even counterproductive. Espin and Sindelar (1988) reported that writing-disabled sixth- and eighth-grade subjects and a younger, matched-for-reading-level group both identified fewer errors than nondisabled sixth- and eighth-grade students. Additionally, writing-disabled subjects had trouble distinguishing between correct and incorrect syntax and grammar. They also identified a number of errors falsely. Others have reported that writing-disabled students detect only about one third of the mechanical errors they make (Deshler, Ferrell, & Kass, 1978).

In another study on revision, writing-disabled students made some corrections in spelling, punctuation, and capitalization, but the proportion of errors did not change from the first draft to the second (MacArthur, Graham, & Skarvoed, 1986). MacArthur and Graham (1987) described the revisions made by fifth- and sixth-grade writing-disabled students as they worked on stories with pencil and paper and with a word processor. In both conditions, the writing-disabled students made approximately 20 revisions per 100 words. Nearly all of these focused at the word level only: minor word changes (20%) or spelling, punctuation, or capitalization conventions (57%). Furthermore, the revisions rarely changed the meaning of the text, and did not improve the quality of the final draft; there were just as many errors in mechanics as in the first draft. This same ineffective pattern was noted in a recent study by MacArthur, Graham, and Schwartz (1991). They noted that when students recopied their first draft, they introduced additional errors, thus defeating any improvements they may have made.

Others have replicated the finding that writing-disabled students' revisions on mechanics do not generally improve the content of a composition — sometimes even when interventions are provided to assist them. In a quasi-experimental study, Reynolds, Hill, Swassing, and Ward (1988) trained writing-disabled sixth-, seventh-, and eighth-grade students in revision strategies for mechanics and for sentence-level content. Their experimental groups improved their scores on the mechanics measures, but there was no improvement for general merit of the compositions: ideas, organization, and word use were intractable.

In a set of case studies, Graham and MacArthur (1988) analyzed the revision performance of three writing-disabled students in fifth and sixth grade before and after an instructional strategy intervention. They categorized each revision as to its purpose (make statement clearer, add more detail, make text more connected to main point, etc.) and awarded quality ratings to the effectiveness of the revisions as a whole (greatly improved, somewhat improved, no improvement, etc.). During the baseline condition, low to moderate levels of revision were observed. The vast majority (84%) of revisions were to add text (deletions or substitutions each constituting less than 10%), and fewer than 1% were rearrangements. Only one third of revisions affected meaning, and the revisions did not improve the quality of the compositions. Although improvements were noted after the strategy intervention training, the most remarkable finding was that *less than 1% of all revisions were directed at improving connections between sentences and main ideas.* Despite considerable training, the writing-disabled subjects still focused at the word or sentence level, not at the whole-text level.

Editing is particularly hard for students with attention deficits. Editing requires focused attention on individual elements of words and sentences. The impulsivity and poor focal attention associated with ADDs make it difficult to inspect every letter, every punctuation mark, every subject-verb agreement, and so on. In addition, their disinhibited, associative processing style leaves them ill prepared to detect poor cohesion in writing.

SPELLING

Writing-disabled students make more errors in spelling at all grade levels than their nondisabled peers (Deno et al., 1982; Moran, 1981; Poplin et al., 1980; Wong et al., 1989), even in studies that control for intelligence (Houck & Billingsley, 1989). To illustrate the seriousness of the spelling performance, Tindal & Hasbrouck (1991) presented case studies of two fifth-grade students with writing disabilities. They found that the two students, taken together, spelled only 14 of 96 words correctly.

The spelling performance of students with attention deficits often seems confusing to educators. These students often are able to study a list of vocabulary words, spell them correctly on a variety of daily activities during the week, and take the weekly test with good results. However, these same students misspell high-frequency words that they have seen in print and used a million times (e.g., *was, what, were*), and they do not seem to retain, for the long term, the vocabulary words that they are able to spell on weekly tests. They do not seem to be able to apply their spelling knowledge to their everyday writing. While the nondisabled student may be able to deduce the system independently within traditional instruction (e.g., via the weekly list-based unit) or without any instruction at all (via inventive spelling and reading experience), attention-disordered students do not seem to be able to do so. They do not independently attend to the systematic features of the print system, and thus do not acquire and retain spelling knowledge. Examination of the typical development of spelling ability, and of ADD students' divergence from it, helps explain why such problems occur.

Most children progress naturally from a primitive understanding of the spelling system toward increasingly standardized spelling over their elementary school years. At the first, *precommunicative* stage, children understand that letters printed on a page can stand for words. A child at this level might write "TRRNL" for *monster* and may not even write the letters in a row from left to right. At the next stage, the *semiphonetic*, the child understands that letters stand for sounds, although her understanding is limited and often reflects the sound of the letter name, e.g., writing *w* for /d/. She also omits many sounds that she doesn't hear clearly; a child at this level might spell "MTR" for *monster* (Gentry, 1984).

At the *phonetic* stage, the child's spelling includes a complete phonetic representation. This child has not learned to represent vowel sounds separately, as seen in her attempt at the word "MONSTR." The next stage is one of *transition*. Now the speller moves away from total dependence on phonological features and begins incorporating some of the orthographic conventions that she has encountered in print. The structure of the word is manifested in the spelling, even though all the letters may not yet be correct, as in "MONSTUR" (Gentry, 1984). The final stage is termed *correct* or *standard* (or *conventional* or *dictionary*) spelling. Here the child knows the spelling system and its basic rules: she understands rules about affixes, silent letters, root morphemes, and variations based on different languages of origin (sometimes thought of as irregularities). She has constructed generalizations and has a large number of orthographic principles to draw upon. She correctly spells most of the words she uses when writing. She is also attentive to her spellings, and uses a "spelling conscience" to monitor her writing. There is a sense of when a word "looks right" in print.[2]

The description above explains how children are supposed to progress. However, many children with attention disorders have difficulties spelling, especially moving from the transition stage to the correct spelling stage. Their spelling difficulties fall on a continuum. Some individuals have severe phonological processing disorders (see chapter 9) that interfere with perceiving and understanding the system of print used for reading and spelling. Some individuals devote limited attentional resources to

---

[2] It should be noted that these stages are only roughly defined, that often children operate in two or more stages simultaneously, and that there are no fixed age levels associated with individual stages.

monitoring their spelling, and thus do not catch errors that they make on known words (e.g., letter omissions, *b-d* reversals). They do not develop a strong "spelling conscience" because they cannot spare attentional resources for this purpose. Some ADD writers have a limited memory for words, and may be reluctant or unable to use references to check spellings. Others have combinations of problems, or fall elsewhere on the continuum. Of course, the appropriate interventions vary for these different types of problems.

Students with attention deficit disorders often do not carefully inspect printed words as they are reading, and thus fail to notice the important features of words. In spelling, even more than in reading, every single element is essential to remember. No letters can be skipped if the spelling is to meet dictionary standards. Because English orthography is complex, especially in polysyllabic words, students must *study* words to notice hidden roots. For example, the silent *g* in sign is important, because of the related words *signal* and *signature* in which the *g* is still pronounced. In a study of children who were asked to invent alternative spellings for words and justify their spellings, it was found that third- and fourth-grade children had almost no implicit awareness of morpho-phonemic spelling principles (Downing, Coughlin, & Rich, 1986). Instead, children at this age relied exclusively on phonological features. We have found that many individuals with attention deficit disorders remain at this level of spelling, well into secondary school and beyond.

The process of learning to spell involves much more than remembering the order of letters in a word, or representing as many sounds as one can. Rather, it is a process of determining the invariants in a complex but orderly system — a cognitive act that involves analysis and synthesis of orthographic units, and the construction of a "map" of the system. Spelling instruction and intervention for ADD students must be explicit and must capitalize on the regularities of the print system.

Instruction should capitalize on all three ordering principles of spelling. First, the *alphabetic principle:* letters tend to match sounds in a left-to-right sequence. Children who struggle with this principle need explicit instruction in phonological awareness (see Chapter 8). Mastery of this principle alone, though, is not enough. There are, in fact, many ways to spell a short *e,* and some words include silent letters. The other two principles, *within-word patterns* and *meaning-linked patterns,* clarify much of the seeming chaos in the orthography. Within-word patterns are those letter markers or combinations that indicate pronunciation, often dependent upon position within the word. For example, silent *e* in the final position indicates the preceding vowel has a long sound. *Gh* in the initial position (e.g., *ghost*) indicates the hard /g/ sound. *Ck* never comes at the beginning of a word, and usually is at the end of a word for the /k/ sound. English doesn't use *kw;* that sound is represented by *qu.* Meaning-linked patterns are based on the fact that words having similar root meanings will probably be spelled in similar ways (e.g., *meet* and *meeting*, not "meating"; *crux* and *crucial*, not "croocial"), even if the pronunciations change because of the affixes. The key to English orthography is that it tends to maintain orthographic patterns, not phonetic changes, once one moves beyond basic phonograms.

Most of the words in the English language are highly regular (Venezky & Massaro, 1979). Even within "irregular" words, most of the letter combinations are consistent with regular principles (Ehri, 1989). Teachers must point out these patterns explicitly: children will learn them when they know that the patterns exist, and that they need to watch out for them and attend to them. Children are ready to attend to simple orthographic patterns (e.g., silent *e*) and phonograms (e.g., -*at*) at the phonetic stage. The teacher can group words together so that the patterns are salient, and use color cues to highlight the critical features and direct students' attention to them.

Instruction should also use meaning as a scaffold. When morphemes (e.g., -*ed*, -*s*) and affixes (e.g., -*tion*, *pre*-) are taught, the meanings they bring to words can help students store the knowledge of these patterns in long-term memory in an organized way, thus increasing the chances that it can be accessed in the future. For example, the use of -*s* as a plural marker in *dogs* and *cats* illustrates a commonality, even though the letter sounds different in the two words: /dogz/; /cats/. An understanding of meaning helps prepare students to understand differences in stress and pronunciation of various related words when syllables are taught (e.g., *house, houses; photo, photography*). And when they encounter words with derivational roots, they can appreciate the effects on consonant and vowel sounds because they understand the meanings of the derivations (*muscle, muscular; sign, signature; explain, explanation*).

Once students acquire some skill in spelling, they need to use it. Progress in spelling is not measured by weekly tests of lists of words. Rather, it is measured by use of the salient features covered in spelling lessons on real pieces of writing, and by the ability to correct errors. We have found it helpful for students with attention deficit disorders to keep a personal list of "no excuse words" handy in their writing folder. These lists include the words that the student uses often in writing, usually high-frequency words that he has learned to spell, and that he is accountable for spelling correctly all the time. The lists are individualized, according to the needs and skills of the student. Such a reference can also be supplemented with extra words that might be needed for particular assignments (e.g., a social studies report), in an effort to relieve the burden of having to invent spellings, ask for assistance, or avoid spelling anticipated vocabulary words. For producing final copies, or "published" pieces (i.e., works that are shared with other readers), students with attention deficit disorders will need extra time to proofread and correct errors. Students with particular difficulties in focusing and sustaining attention may also need the assistance of a teacher, peer, or technological spell-checker to help catch all the errors, and the use of a dictionary or other references to correct them.

HIGHER-ORDER PROCESSES

We have spent much of this chapter talking about lower-order processes in writing: spelling, graphomotor skill, basic language generation, etc. This is, of course, not the entirety of written language. Truly proficient writers have command of higher-order processes: they demonstrate a sensitivity to the various needs of their audiences, varying the vocabulary level and complexity of syntax and articulation of ideas as necessary. They are able to create writing pieces that are *complete*, that stand on their own. Their texts or stories have cohesion throughout, so the reader does not have to work hard to track and understand the messages that are being conveyed. They are able to develop a style or "voice" of their own, so that it seems clear that they, the writers, are communicating with the reader. They are able to manage written language so that an emotional response can be evoked from the reader. This level of proficiency is rarely demonstrated by writers with attention deficit disorders, especially at the elementary and middle school level. They do not have the attentional resources needed for these higher-order processes because they have consumed them on lower-order processes.

We contend that these higher-order processes cannot be addressed head-on by instructional techniques or metacognitive strategies. These processes are not separate from the lower-order processes; they don't exist independently from them, and they cannot be isolated from them. They *emerge* out of facility and fluency with lower-level processes. Thus, intervention must focus on teaching and strengthening lower-order processes, ultimately to an automatic level. Then the writer may have enough surplus attentional resources available to consider tone, voice, audience, point-of-view, and other more expressive features of written language.

SUMMARY

Attention deficit disorders become written language disabilities whenever there is a need for controlled attention for the purpose of managing complex processes and complex information fields. In the process of writing, this occurs almost all of the time. Setting and keeping track of the goal for writing, making and modifying a plan, managing complex constructions, and automatizing orthographic principles all tax an already limited attention system. There are further issues of graphomotor, keyboarding, and word processing skill deficiencies.

Intervention may need to address any or all of these elements. Many students with attention deficit disorders will require specific instruction in spelling. Others will need direct instruction of other lower-order elements, as well as support for managing textual-level issues. Still others will need bypass strategies for managing graphomotor deficits. Most will need support to put it all together — the attention-demanding process that encompasses planning, drafting, and revising, moving between word-level and text-level considerations, and fine-tuning a piece of writing.

Each student, with his own unique combination of skills and weaknesses, will need a different combination of supports. The teacher's role will be to identify the place in the writing process to begin intervention, and to guide and support the student's growth as a writer.

11
Mathematics and Attention

The incremental nature of math and its demand for error-free procedure are particularly challenging for children and adults with ADDs. The cognitive difficulties associated with ADDs — inattention, difficulty with sustained attention, difficulty maintaining attention through repetitive tasks, difficulty with extended and complex information processing, working memory problems, difficulty with tracking and self-monitoring, cognitive impulsivity, and cognitive inflexibility, to name a few — interfere in various ways along the continuum of mathematics learning from preschool at least through high school. In fact, math performance tends to decline over the school years for children with ADDs (Ackerman et al., 1986).

Concepts Free for the Taking

The first math concepts to evolve with a child's experience are those involving cardinal property. Although Piaget placed a heavy emphasis on the "prerequisites" to the understanding of cardinal property, such as object permanence and one-to-one correspondence, in the post-Piagetian era we know that number concepts emerge in infants as early as 5 months of age. Strauss and Curtis (1984) have performed a series of studies establishing that infants can discriminate between amounts of two and three, even when spatial arrangement is manipulated to confound their awareness. Infants who habituate on a display showing two elements lined up horizontally will recognize at test that two elements on the diagonal are similar and that three aligned horizontally are novel (Strauss & Curtis, 1984). Using similarly clever paradigms, they have gone on to establish awareness of addition and subtraction properties in children under one year of age. One interesting finding from this line of research is that fairly advanced and abstract awareness can emerge as long as the quantity is three or fewer. It seems that the amount of information to be managed is critical.

Since infants are the prototypes of children with uncontrolled attention, it is informative to consider what is possible for them and why. Like infants, children with ADDs are capable of appreciating the critical features in their environments, including relational information such as cardinality and the reversibility of number operations (Piaget & Inhelder, 1969). They can recognize these relationships without instruction and without controlling their attention for the purpose of imposing order, since the order is inherent in their world (Gibson, 1979). They need simply to perceive the patterns that are there.

Interestingly, *degree of abstraction* does not seem to be an issue for early number awareness; rather, it is the *amount of relevant information* that makes a difference (Caron & Caron, 1981; Chi, 1985). The breakdown at the quantity three is informative. Studies of working memory have shown that three bits of information can be managed without controlled working memory strategies or controlled attention. Very young children can manage three bits of information, as can adults with severe mental retardation (Belmont & Butterfield, 1971; Spitz, 1966).

In situations where information can be learned through natural context, children with uncontrolled attention seem to be excellent math learners. Most children come to school with a strong sense of number, the ability to make more–less comparisons, and the awareness of the reversibility of addition and subtraction (if you take one away and then put it back, you have the original amount again). They have come to this awareness with little or no instruction. As the infant studies demonstrate, they need not even manipulate materials to understand these concepts, although action certainly helps enhance attention and perception (Adolph et al., 1993).

During the early grades, the ability to appreciate concepts and the meaning of relationships continues to be an asset for ADD children in some aspects of the math curriculum, at least for those children who don't have more specific mathematics disabilities. They seem to be able to comprehend the meanings of addition and subtraction with little difficulty. Whenever meaning is there for them to apprehend, they can do so. The presence of immediately perceived (that is, perceived without mediation) meaning alleviates the need for controlled information processing. Simple multiplication and division do not seem to create much of a challenge for them either, as long as they have time to use procedures such as repeated addition that are not dependent on automatized skills.

Attention and Arbitrary Associations

In kindergarten and the early elementary grades, children are also asked to learn math skills that cannot be discovered by observing natural relationships. They must learn the names of numerals, numeral–amount correspondences, and number facts at an automatic level. The learning of numeral names is sheer arbitrary association. To learn these associations, to commit them to a level of automatic association, it is necessary to practice them repeatedly and with full vigilance. Similarly, number facts, although not arbitrary, must in the long run be learned as if they were. Children who use their concept of number to add and subtract have not, in fact, learned their number facts. Although we do not argue that number facts are more important than the meaning that underlies them, we do suggest that automaticity with number facts is critical in freeing up attention for higher-level processing when children confront more complex tasks later on.

Poor achievement in mathematics is correlated with a lack of automaticity with math facts. Children with math difficulties tend to compute answers by counting rather than directly retrieve answers from memory. Reporting on a study by Fleishner, Connor (1983) reports that the computation approach manifests itself in a slow rate of answering and proneness to error. Reliance on a counting strategy rather than an easily accessed store of number facts usurps much of one's limited-capacity working memory and/or attentional space, and interferes with more complex cognitive activities. Diagnosticians have often observed youngsters who struggle through the substeps of a long division or word problem, exhaust themselves with the effort of multiple computations, and settle on an answer prematurely, before completing the last step. Even if they manage to perform all the steps of the algorithm correctly, a counting error somewhere along the way may ultimately result in an incorrect final answer. The importance of the efficient execution of simple mathematics operations for the solution of more complex problems has been well documented in the literature (Pelligrino & Goldman, 1987; Torgeson & Young, 1983).

Movement from a counting strategy to the automatic retrieval of math facts follows a developmental trend. Reaction time studies by Ashcraft and Fierman (1982) suggest that the third grade is a transitional period, when children begin to move away from a counting algorithm toward automatic retrieval from memory. Given enough time, third-graders can add as accurately as sixth-graders, but they respond significantly more slowly. Fourth-graders can add more quickly than third-graders, but they make more errors, perhaps because they are trusting their retrieval abilities more than third-graders, who are validating their answers with counting.

The process of driving an arbitrary association to the level of automaticity places large demands on the attention system. Since the relationship is not "there" to be perceived, it must be actively imposed. The typical way of imprinting the relationship is to have children rehearse the association repeatedly. In school this means independent work, paper-and-pencil tasks, and worksheets (often many of the same format), day in and day out — a prospect that elicits groans of dismay from the child with ADD. All of this makes demands on highly focused, sustained, distraction-free attention. The job requires a good deal of control. If the child is distracted, her consciousness is not directed toward forming the associations. Not only must the focus of attention be controlled and sustained; attention must also be active. The child has to be vigilant. She is, after all, *creating* an association, not receiving an impression as she would if she were understanding a naturally occurring relationship. She must keep the information active and alive in her mind, in working memory. Arousal and activation levels must be high. This is very hard for the child with ADD.

To make it worse, this degree of arousal, activation, and focus must be maintained over time and over repetitious tasks such as worksheet drills. Even if the task required less vigilance, the sheer repetitiveness of the worksheet format and the content itself would challenge the ADD child's need for novelty, i.e., for shifts in activity or thoughts. And usually, the child is asked to practice the material independently.

Most practice drills also require a child to use a pencil and paper. A high percentage of children with ADDs also have graphomotor problems and/or slowed motor responding (Zentall & Smith, 1993), and must allocate some of their precious and limited attentional resources to the writing that the drill process requires. If they attend to their writing enough to make it legible and neat (qualities so highly valued in the early grades), they will most likely fail to attend fully to the number facts themselves.

Working Memory and Automaticity with Facts and Operations

There is good reason to believe that adequate working memory functions are critical to the learning of number facts. In order for the full association to be made (e.g., $3 + 5 = 8$ or $7 \times 8 = 56$), all the terms of the equation must be held in working memory simultaneously. If working memory capacity is too limited to allow this, the loss of information in working memory is fatal to the association (Geary, 1993). Of course, focal, sustained, and vigilant attention is essential to the maintenance of information on-line in working memory (Cherkes-Julkowski & Stolzenberg, 1992). It is not surprising, then, that children with ADDs who begin to take stimulant medication are able to improve their learning of math facts (Badian, 1983).

We know few children with ADDs who actually *know* their number facts. Most understand what the process is all about and can count up, or down, or by 5's, etc., to get the right answer. And children with ADDs are predictably fast. It may seem to their teachers that their number facts are automatic. Accuracy is a problem, however. The counting procedure is also an attention-intensive task. We have watched children with ADDs try to set up their materials so they can add up two amounts or take away a given amount. They are likely to disrupt their work with excess motor activity which disorganizes the arrangement of their materials. Or they simply do not sustain the one-to-one correspondence necessary for counting. They lose track of the items and cannot remember which ones they have accounted for already.

Children who have difficulty with math facts often use immature counting procedures. They tend to count more slowly, in part because of their disorganized efforts at tracking themselves. There may be generally slowed processing and word retrieval difficulties associated with many mild neurologic impairments (Mesulam, 1990), ADDs among them. Slowed access to numeral names and/or to the process of operating with one-to-one correspondence creates a bottleneck for working memory. First of all, precious capacity must be allocated for the purpose of accessing labels and tracking the counting process, thereby siphoning off resources from the math concepts at hand. And second, the inefficiency created by slow access has serious consequences. Efficiency is a necessity if working memory is to be exploited to its fullest potential. Only with rapid movement of information in and out of the limited-capacity working memory store is it possible to juggle information of any complexity at all.

Immature counting often involves "counting all" (Geary, 1990) rather than "counting-on" (Carpenter & Moser, 1984). To add two numbers, rather than starting with the larger number and simply counting the remaining amount of the smaller, immature counters will count all the way through both numbers. The demands for increased attention and the cost to working memory are obvious. Processes that bog down in this way, preventing simultaneous awareness of all relevant information in working memory, hinder the automatization of facts and procedures. It is not surprising, then, that faster counting is associated with greater working memory capacity (Kail, 1992).

It is important to assess efficiency even at the lowest levels of skill to ensure that higher-level functions such as adding with renaming are not being undermined by inefficiency with basic procedures such as counting. In this example, more drill or explanation in renaming principles would not help performance. Instruction would have to create a way to increase automaticity with number facts, and promoting more efficient counting procedures would be an important first step.

Given the multiple sources of disruption which are both causes and effects of breakdowns in the attention/working memory system, it is important to separate out individual functions and to strengthen them individually. The concept of number and the meaning of operations would make up one level for instruction. Increased efficiency with counting would be another. Still other levels would include automatization of math facts and automatization of each of the algorithms necessary for the range of operations. Automaticity with math facts might best be achieved through paired-associative learning activities, i.e., practicing pairing the terms of the problem with the answers — simply memorizing that *3 + 4* goes with the answer *7*, and so on. This would eliminate the crowding of working memory with counting procedures.

To support the practice of number facts, it is important to ensure that attention is fully activated and available to drive working memory processes. One suggestion is to have children with ADDs practice their number facts using computer games. The right game would be interactive and sufficiently arousing in terms of timing and graphic presentation. It has been found, for example, that the use of color in instructional materials improves performance among children with ADD (Zentall, Falkenberg, & Smith, 1985). It is important, however, that the game not be too competitive or too intense in terms of time demands, since overarousal is as disruptive to attention regulation as underarousal.

Any form of interactive instruction is likely to increase attention. Interactive computer games provide one form of interaction. Teacher-coordinated drills can also be helpful, especially if they are done orally so that the child need not write and attend to the number combinations at the same time. The advantage of teacher-coordinated drills is that the ADD child can be helped to use verbal rehearsal to maintain activation of the material during practice.

Creative teachers can think of a number of ways to vary practice drills. Board games can be adapted so that flash cards rather than dice are used to determine the number of moves, thereby enforcing automatic association in the absence of counting. The teacher can play student, so that it becomes the role of the child with ADD to find and correct her errors.

If a child is to perform counting procedures in order to calculate or to explore the meaning of operations, it might be beneficial to give her a prepared worksheet. The worksheet would contain a series of marks (X's or hash marks) that can be checked off to represent the amount of units in each number. Such a format would eliminate the need to draw or set up elements, would diminish the chances that materials would get disorganized, and would avoid excessive graphomotor demands, all of which would spare attention/working memory resources. For example, if the child is to add 3 + 4, she would put a box around 4 X's, then 3 (choosing the larger set first) and then count the total. Figure 11.1 on the next page illustrates this procedure. Subtraction can be done on the same worksheet. In fact, the worksheet can be duplicated and used for practice of a number of different operations and number combinations. An artistic teacher or student might draw favorite objects in place of the X's. If tracking is a problem, each marker can be drawn differently to facilitate place keeping. The worksheet can even suggest place value by organizing the marks in groups of 10 (see Figure 11.2 below). Eventually, as the child adds sums greater than 10, she will need to use more than one group of markings for each problem. At the appropriate point in the curriculum, the notion of place value can be attached to the idea of grouping.

Just as automaticity with number facts can be a problem, so can automaticity with the procedural aspects of basic algorithms. The problems of limited capacity and information management are thus compounded. Added to the load associated with number facts is the load of tracking one's progress through the necessary steps of an algorithm. This reaches its peak as a source of confusion when a child with ADD is asked to work her way through a long division problem. She must know subtraction and multiplication facts automatically, she must know the seemingly arbitrary steps of the algorithm, and she must know where she is in the process — what is and is not

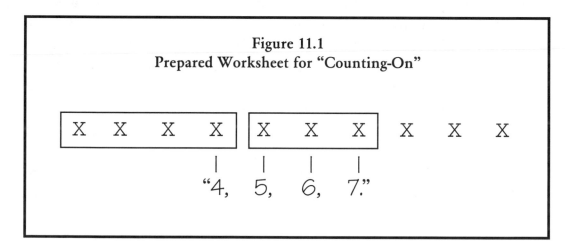

Figure 11.1
Prepared Worksheet for "Counting-On"

X   X   X   X │ X   X   X │ X   X   X

"4, 5, 6, 7."

Figure 11.2
Prepared Worksheet to Facilitate Tracking and Place Value

XS*h@	XS*h@	XS*h@	XS*h@	XS*h@	XS*h@	XS*h@
t#R$B	t#R$B	t#R$B	t#R$B	t#R$B	t#R$B	t#R$B
XS*h@	XS*h@	XS*h@	XS*h@	XS*h@	XS*h@	XS*h@
t#R$B	t#R$B	t#R$B	t#R$B	t#R$B	t#R$B	t#R$B

as yet accounted for in the operation. Maintaining an organized record of the work done thus far is crucial. Attention difficulties jeopardize all of these contributing factors, as well as the executive function of tracking and orchestrating among the steps of the process.

Careless vs. Accidental Errors

Teachers and parents often refer to errors in number combination (7 + 9 = 15) or procedural errors, such as failing to add the carried number, as *careless*. However unintended, the message is that the child did not care and that more care would solve the problem. Anyone who has watched a child count up to solve a problem knows that *lack of care* is not the issue. A typical child with ADD will set up his materials for counting, begin, abort that effort when he loses track or disrupts his materials, and begin again. This cycle can repeat itself any number of times. In the end, the answer is likely to be off — and then the child is told that he has been careless.

Furthermore, *care* itself can cause problems; the conscious attention required to work one's way through iterative procedures, and to be explicit about each step in an algorithm, consumes precious attention/working memory commodities. If care comes with worry, there can be further use of capacity for non-math-related issues.

Lack of automaticity at any level creates additional processing demands (Schiffrin & Dumais, 1984). Each additional demand competes for attention/working memory resources. The losers in this competition become sources of errors. But these errors are the accidental fallout *of insufficient resources, not lack of care.* The fallout can be at any place within the computational process; accidental errors are likely to appear in different places or functions at different times. One time, the child will manage a given step correctly. Next time, that step is the one to give way. This inconsistency adds to the impression that the child *can* succeed, and *would* if she just tried harder. Of course, she can, but if she does, the high probability is that another error will result as the cost of "caring" about this operation. We make an issue of this fact — that perceptions of carelessness are so often misguided — because children with ADDs do not need any more negative feedback about their character.

Executive Functions: Tracking, Mental Flexibility, Self-Monitoring

The increased number of steps necessitated by lack of automaticity require *tracking*. It is ironic that the children who have particularly limited attentional capacity create an even greater load for themselves through failure to automatize lower-level skills. As part of the executive function component of the attention system (Benson, 1991;

Denckla, 1996b; Mirsky et al., 1991), the process of tracking is a problem for those with poorly regulated attention. Tracking one's mental manipulations is an especially challenging task since it consumes the working memory capacity that is much needed for the conceptual aspects of the task.

The greater the information load, the more there is to track and, therefore, the more likely it is that breakdowns due to poor tracking will occur. Despite a child's knowledge of a complex algorithm, he may fail to take certain steps. For example, during addition of mixed numbers with unlike denominators, allocating attention to finding a common denominator can make it difficult to simultaneously monitor the goal, the steps required for solution, and one's progress along the continuum. The result in one case looked like this:

$$4 \tfrac{4}{5} \times \tfrac{7}{7} = \tfrac{28}{35}$$
$$+ 3 \tfrac{6}{7} \times \tfrac{5}{5} = \tfrac{30}{35}$$
$$\tfrac{58}{35} = 1 \tfrac{23}{35}$$

This error was corrected when the child was prompted to take a second pass through the problem. Layering task demands in this way seems to relieve the tracking/attentional demands. At the same time, comparing prompted and unprompted performance provides insight into the roles of tracking and self-monitoring as possible sources of breakdown. If the child can be successful with external prompting of this sort, it is most likely that her original difficulty was based in poor self-monitoring.

Tracking is required for analyzing the problem itself as well as for monitoring one's mental and physical execution of the steps to solve it. For example, the child who committed the self-monitoring/tracking error described above also failed to attend to operation signs in very simple problems. In addition to mental tracking, systematic scan of extrapersonal space can be disrupted when the attention network is impaired (Mesulam, 1990). The attention network includes frontal eye fields which contribute to the execution of controlled and systematic tracking of "things out there." Failure to examine all of the information in the stimulus field can threaten learning and performance in profound as well as relatively trivial ways.

Deep effects are realized when a child's scan of the environment is so disrupted that critical information is simply not noticed. One child, age 8 years 10 months, had failed to acquire spatial concepts related to *more* and *less* and had not yet managed to count effectively. Her rote recitation of the counting sequence was fine, but she could not coordinate the correspondence between each count word and the items to be counted. Since she failed to attend to all of the elements involved, she had no foundation for developing the relationship between counting and cardinal property. This same child gave a random and incomplete performance on a cancellation task, in which she was asked to cross out each instance of a given letter embedded in a series of randomly arranged letters. Again, prompting that provided the tracking for her was highly effective, making it possible for her to gather the information critical to concept formation. On her own, however, she would be unlikely to develop sound concepts based on physical properties, i.e., "things out there."

More trivial manifestations of neglecting areas of the stimulus field include failures to notice operation signs, such as adding instead of subtracting, and making intermittent counting errors. Minor counting errors of this kind can lead teachers to erroneously attribute breakdowns in performance to carelessness. Given this interpretation, the only remediation offered is "Try harder." This approach not only precludes giving remediation that *might* work, such as devising a set-up for the child's work that will promote tracking, or prompting the child through the counting process; it could also create the kind of attentional "burnout" described by Kahneman (see chapter 3, p. 42).

Tracking often requires the combined processes of monitoring "things out there" and "things in here." Complicated calculations, such as those required in the problem $\{2x + y = 16; 3x - y = 3; x = \_\_, y = \_\_\}$ (Woodcock & Johnson, 1989), necessitate keeping track of the terms of the problem, perceiving the goal, envisioning the steps to solution, and then executing them — while maintaining awareness of what has been accounted for already, where one has set out to go in the first place, and what remains to be done. In the above problem, failure to monitor the big picture while working through the problem can result in following a valid yet nonproductive path:

$$3x - y = 3$$
$$-y = 3 - 3x$$
$$y = -3 + 3x$$
$$3x - (-3 + 3x) = 3$$
$$3 = 3$$

Another frequent monitoring error in problems such as the one above is failure to track all manipulations of positive and negative signs. As is typically the case with tracking errors, the deeper conceptual aspects of the task are not at issue. When a scheme for tracking performance is provided, performance improves markedly.

Maintaining the ultimate goal in mind while working through computational steps is a function served by the executive branch. At times, the steps can dominate at the expense of the goal. For example, a child with ADD who is quite competent with math concepts was asked to solve a problem requiring the addition of two fractions with like denominators. He immediately began to convert the fractions to *another* like denominator, worked through the process, and duly reduced the answer he found. Only when the original problem was pointed out to him did he recognize that he had taken more steps than were necessary.

A history of tracking and monitoring difficulties can cause a child to feel overwhelmed once she intuits the complexity of a problem and/or its solution. One delightful, intellectually gifted, and highly motivated seventh-grade algebra student with ADD declined to solve a lengthy but arithmetically simple problem because "that takes too much mind."

Teacher intervention in the form of orchestrating the tracking process (prompting) for the student is almost always effective. This may be a necessary first-level intervention. However, it is always more helpful in the long term to find supports that encourage more independent functioning. Approaches that provide an organizational structure and thus condense and systematize the problem field would be most effective. For example, for addition of mixed numbers, a work space like the one in Figure 11.3 (below) might be provided. The organizational structure for each skill would vary depending upon the process being taught or practiced.

Intuition vs Meta-awareness

A challenge for many children with ADDs comes when they are required to shift from their intuitive sense of number to a more scientific, more formal, and more

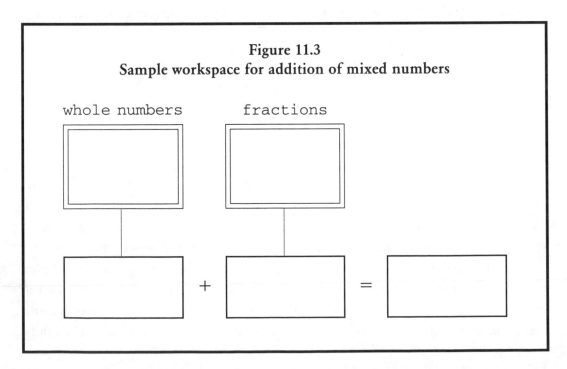

Figure 11.3
Sample workspace for addition of mixed numbers

whole numbers   fractions

algorithmic, procedural awareness. The first shift of this kind happens when the child must deal with multidigit, difficult-to-envision numbers. It is hard to intuit how much *3,685 × 248* might be, although ADD children who have a strong intuitive grasp of number can come very close, very quickly. Still, regardless of their aptitude for math, their motivation, and their common sense, intuition rarely, if ever, leads to a correct answer in such a case. An algorithm for computation is necessary.

The algorithm for multidigit multiplication appears obscure enough that it can seem to be another case of arbitrary association. Of course, this need not be so. But to make the traditional algorithm meaningful, the child would have to understand place value and the distributive property of multiplication over addition. For a child with ADD, added instruction in these concepts would place the algorithm back into the intuitively meaningful range and thus reduce the need for controlled attention. If there is deep understanding of the algorithm, it can be derived, if not automatized.

An awareness of the meaning of the multidigit multiplication algorithm might even provide the child with some defense against the inevitable obstacle of the long division algorithm. Children with ADDs nearly always fall apart in math at the point of long division, if not before. They can get correct answers by using repeated multiplications, and they endure the cumbersomeness of this approach especially well if their math intuitions make them good estimators. However, again, the process is error-prone because of its lengthiness and increased demands on sustained attention and tracking. It also fails if the answer is not a whole number.

From long division onward, the style of mathematics instruction often changes — to the grave disadvantage of children with ADDs. There are fewer demonstrations and less hands-on activity. Instruction primarily takes the form of verbal explanation, accompanied by teacher-provided examples and followed by independent practice on the part of the child. This is, of course, the *worst possible format of instruction* for a child with ADD. The meaning of the algorithm is not readily apparent. Listening requires unflagging attention. Automatization of the algorithm depends on sustained, active, and repeated practice of steps that are apparently arbitrary and therefore lack the organizing and condensing effects of meaning.

The Perils of Purely Didactic Instruction

The curriculum usually proceeds from long division to fractions (4th or 5th grade), decimals, and percentages. Simple fraction notation and concepts (e.g., addition and subtraction with like denominators) can often be intuited by children with ADDs if instructors provide even a few pictures or demonstrations. Beyond this, however, their inability to benefit from orally delivered instruction and the need to shift from meaning to formal procedure make the challenge just too great. As instruction is given concerning a particular algorithm — e.g., long division, division by a fraction, multiplication of mixed numbers, or placement of the decimal in a multiplication problem — the ADD child's attention may be erratic. Even if she manages to avoid distraction and to stay oriented toward the lesson, she is not likely to listen actively and to actively recode the information into an explicit formulation.

ADD children often perceive their difficulties as problems with memory retrieval. In reality, it seems, they have never adequately stored the information in the first place. Any procedure that would elicit more active processing would be helpful. Pairing the lesson with some kind of motor involvement, if possible, would help the child to maintain arousal. Other approaches would be to ask the student to paraphrase what has been said, or ask her to teach the concept to another child (real or imagined). A child who can write easily might write out the justification for each step as he goes through the algorithm. These approaches serve two functions: invoking a more active, explicit awareness; and allowing the teacher to observe whether the child has missed critical information.

Instruction in fractions is often not thorough enough for children with ADDs. They are told and often shown that a fraction is "less than one." Yet on their own, they don't seem able to perform the processing required to infer that there can be a fraction *of a set* or that fraction notation can indicate an amount *greater* than one (e.g., $15/6$). A common problem among children with ADDs is their inability to draw a picture of an improper fraction. When asked to draw a picture of $15/6$, for example, many start out by drawing a circle or rectangle and dividing it into six parts. They can see that there are not 15 parts to be shaded in. Many resolve their problem by drawing in 9 more parts. Some shade in six, and others shade in all 15 segments. When asked to write the fraction numeral for what they have drawn, they can often do so correctly, but are still at a loss for how to draw an accurate picture of the designated fraction. However, when presented with the situation of ordering pizzas for a party with 15 people, when each pizza has 6 slices and each person will eat one piece, they see immediately what the issue is. They understand the concepts involved, but have never explicitly linked them with the notation or computation system.[1]

Since decimals and percentages involve some of the same concepts as fractions, a problem in one is likely to accompany a problem in the others. Despite this reality, many children *appear* to have mastered decimals quite well. They can add and subtract them and arrive at a correct answer. Many of those same children, however, can neither read their answer (e.g., *11.206* may be read as *11,206*) nor answer correctly

---

[1] Of course we are only describing a general trend among children with ADDs. There are those who have more severe math disabilities as well, and a small number who escape the problems we are describing.

when asked if their solution is, for example, greater than 100.

Children with ADDs are often given calculators to perform operations from long division on. This certainly serves many useful purposes. It eliminates errors due to problems with number facts or with keeping track of counting procedures or lengthy algorithms. If the child is doing calculations in the process of solving a problem, the calculator will free limited attention resources for the higher-level activity of problem solving itself. Nevertheless, exclusive use of the calculator for these procedures makes it difficult — if not impossible — for the child to see what the algorithm is really all about. We often find that youngsters who find themselves in advanced algebra or physics, when they have in the past relied extensively upon calculators, don't have the background to understand the arithmetic logic of the procedures they must use.

Gaps in Skill Acquisition

Often the extent of gaps in math learning are not discovered until the children are well beyond the grades in which the material was part of the curriculum. Even when the gaps are recognized, they may be overlooked in the interest of keeping the children progressing to more advanced topics. Once it is time to study algebra, for example, children with deficient fraction computation skills are nevertheless moved along, under the illusion that they don't truly need those skills to do algebra. The reality is that fractions operations are frequently required in solving algebraic equations, such as $\{3x - 5 = 9\}$ or $\{2x + 4 = x + 8\}$.

A further obstacle at the point of transition to algebra is the frequent tendency of ADD children to work from their intuition about numbers. At the beginning stages of algebra, it is quite easy for youngsters to use number estimation procedures to solve for an unknown quantity. Many children with ADDs can look at the equation $\{3x + 1 = 10\}$ and see that x must be quite small. Having established that boundary, estimation procedures are easy, effective, and efficient. These youngsters can perform a good number of straightforward examples and achieve a high degree of accuracy without ever being aware of or practicing formal algebraic procedures. But since they have never actually used algebraic procedure to achieve their successes, it is quite confusing for them when they have to solve equations involving two unknowns; the estimation procedure is far more cumbersome, and the increased need for attention-intensive tracking procedures makes accurate solution elusive. Without a more formal awareness of what is lawful in algebra, the ability to construct proofs in geometry is also jeopardized, as is all further math performance.

The shift to algebra is not qualitatively different from the shift a young child has to make when learning algorithms. Both require the child to give up his more intuitive orientation and work at a meta-awareness level. Working at such a level requires controlled information processing that is dependent on controlled and well-modulated attention.

Invented Algorithms

Because instruction can be so hard for a child with ADD to follow and the traditional algorithms can seem so obscure, children and adolescents with ADD often develop their own, more or less valid procedures for computation. Most often these procedures are conducted mentally, not written down. In fact, when these children are asked to write out their work, it becomes apparent that they don't know what their procedures would look like in writing. When they are asked to talk through what they are thinking and doing, it can often be seen that at least one aspect of their work is essentially valid. It becomes the challenge of special instruction to work with the child's own procedures to show her how these would look in writing, and ultimately how they translate into the traditional algorithm.

Without this intervention, the child must maintain all of her work on-line in working memory. As the operations exceed more than one or two steps, the load is simply too great for the child with ADD. If she can record her work in writing, the stress on the on-line holding function of working memory is greatly reduced, errors become less likely, and the extreme frustration that comes from losing track of one's thinking is alleviated. If graphomotor responding is so difficult for a particular child that writing is not an advantage, we recommend the use of an adding machine, i.e., a calculator that produces a tape with a record of each step.

Many of the algorithms invented by the children, however, are invalid. They are built out of partial awareness of what the teacher has explained and demonstrated. The rest is patched together with whatever sense the child can make of it all, based on her background knowledge and intuitions. Sometimes, what is learned in a later context can reorganize an earlier algorithm to disadvantage. One intellectually competent high school student, for example, believed that to divide mixed numbers, you could divide first the two whole numbers, and then the fractions. This idea seems to be influenced by her awareness of the distributive property. But she fails to extend the rule fully.

There are cases in which the invented algorithm can be applied correctly as long as the examples are similar enough to those that the child has been shown how to do. A child who has added decimals in the standard format, with an equal number of decimal places in all addends, might be very confused about what to do in a problem such as:

$$235.16$$
$$+ \; 122.3$$

Some invalid algorithms can yield the correct solution under some circumstances; for example, adding or subtracting from left to right yields correct solutions as long as no renaming is involved. When this is true, the child has an opportunity to practice an invalid algorithm until it becomes automatic. The problem for the teacher becomes one of dissuading the child from using his or her own creation — one that is now a habitual response — in favor of a more valid approach.

It is not necessarily effective to treat the invalid algorithm as an unfortunate annoyance. It is, after all, the child's own creation, one she has invented in the process of actively trying to figure out what should be done. If it has already been used repeatedly, it has the force of an automatic, unconscious response, which may not easily come under the control of what the teacher now has to say about the "right" way to do things.

One approach is to set up an example that will demonstrate dramatically how the algorithm is not working. A child might be asked to estimate a solution. Once the estimate is a close one, the teacher could write it down and make it clear that it is a close approximation. The child would then perform her calculation and be asked to compare it with the estimation to see whether the calculated answer could be correct. At that point the child is ready to examine her approach at a more conscious level. Another approach is to show a child how to use her algorithm as a basis for a more valid one. If a child adds from left to right, she could be shown how to do so while respecting place value.

In our opinion, it is a mistake simply to begin instruction in the "right" way to do things. The child comes to the situation with his or her own expectations, formulations, and beliefs; *these cannot be ignored*, because they will color what is understood about subsequent instruction. Individual instruction is necessary at this point, since simply including such a child in a group of other children learning the same algorithm would not take into consideration the need to approach instruction from the child's unique point of view.

Verbal Problem Solving

Word problems compound the issues of extended information processing: solving them requires the processing of complex language as well as the use of higher-level math procedures. The more that is loaded into a task, of course, the greater demand there is on attention resources. Complex word problems aggravate all the vulnerabilities associated with executive functions. Conversely, the more directly stated the problem, the fewer terms, and the fewer steps to solution, the more likely it is that a child with ADD will have adequate attention resources to solve it.

The aggregated demands of problem solving are particularly difficult to meet when lower-level skills have not been automatized. The same child who can add correctly, albeit laboriously, when performing a straight calculation may begin to make errors when she must perform the same non-automatic procedures in service of problem solution. She simply cannot keep track of all the task demands. Similarly, if algorithms are not automatized, calculation errors may occur despite use of a correct procedure.

When algorithms haven't been automatized or even learned, children will often invent their own, usually attention-draining, procedures. For example, one student could not manage the procedure for finding a percentage. The problem called for finding the price after a cost reduction of 10%. He reasoned that *percent* meant 1 per 100, so there would be a reduction of one penny for every dollar if the discount were 1%, and 10 cents per dollar at 10%. Having gone this distance down a rather long, detoured path, he could not remember the problem. He tried to find his place in the problem but then lost track of his subsolution. All of this work took considerable time and mental effort. In the end he was frustrated and overwhelmed. He quit and had only discouragement and failure to show for his insight and diligence. This youngster is identified as oppositional in his school and runs the risk of not finishing high school. This situation seems particularly ironic given the amount of effortful compliance and intelligence revealed in his performance.

Of course, the deep solution to this predicament is to ensure both understanding and automatization of lower-level skills. When this hasn't been or can't be done, it is important to ensure that the student keeps a record of her work. Since children with ADDs often have difficulty with graphomotor functions, writing can be an effortful process that creates a further drain on attention resources. When they do write, the work is often disorganized and nearly illegible, and thus cannot be used as a way to facilitate tracking. This is another case in which using a calculator with a tape can be a helpful alternative.

A number of ADD students with whom we have worked fail to adhere to the exact nature of the question asked. Impulsively, they assume that they know what the problem is asking of them before they have read or heard it all. Even when they have read it all, they simply cannot keep track of the question while simultaneously beginning a solution. For example, a problem on the Woodcock-Johnson—R applied problems test (1989) gives the amounts spent in a week by a family for vegetables, fruit, dairy, and meat. The question is stated at the end and asks for the average cost to feed each member in the family of four for a week. Children with ADDs often produce the total cost, neglecting the specific requirements of the question. Or they insist that they don't know how many people are in the family. When the question is re-read for them, most are quick to realize how to find the solution.

Problems that state the information in the order in which it is used for calculation decrease information-processing demands. The child can listen, operate, download, listen, operate, download, and so on. Some problems, however, offer information in an order that is different from the order of operations. One example is a problem which states that you have given the clerk $2.00 to buy three notebooks that cost 55 cents each, and asks for the amount of change received (Woodcock-Johnson, 1989). Some students with ADDs will set up the following computation:

$$
\begin{array}{r}
\$2.00 \\
.55 \\
.55 \\
-\ \ .55 \\
\hline
\end{array}
$$

If the goal were to help the student understand the mathematical relationships in this problem, it could be restated to bring the order of information presentation in alignment with the order of operations. However, if the goal were information management and problem solving *per se*, then it would be important to work with the student to set up a strategy for listing problem information, restating the question, and then beginning solution.

There are some problems that are simply overwhelming from the beginning. Another example from the Woodcock-Johnson–R applied problems test demonstrates how the sheer amount of information can discourage a student with ADD, despite the relatively simple arithmetic demands of the task:

When Dave walks to school, he averages ninety steps per minute. Each of his steps is eighty centimeters long. It takes him ten minutes to get to school. His brother Jack, going to the same school by the same route, averages one hundred steps per minute. Jack's steps are sixty centimeters long. How long does it take Jack to get to school?

(Woodcock & Johnson, 1989, p. 169)

When students with ADDs in middle school through high school are presented with this problem, most of them are obviously overwhelmed. Most can give a reasonable estimate but have judged that they will never be able to find their way through the morass of information. It simply "takes too much mind." Some will realize that there is a piece of information missing but fail to recognize that they could derive it. Some will begin well, but then get lost in the subroutines, never to find their way out again, as depicted in Figure 11.4 below.

The traditional technique of listing the information given in the problem and then rewriting the question is particularly useful for students with ADDs. By layering the information, it wards off the need to consider it all in a single mental sweep. Furthermore, it gives the child something she can do even when she feels overwhelmed in the face of a problem that "takes too much mind." Of course, once she has considered each piece of information individually, it is likely that some sense of the problem space will begin to emerge.

The goal of nearly all interventions for children with ADDs who are having difficulty with complex processing is to divide the task into more manageable units of information. Some verbal math problems lend themselves to pictorial representation. Drawing the picture brings attention to individual pieces of information, as

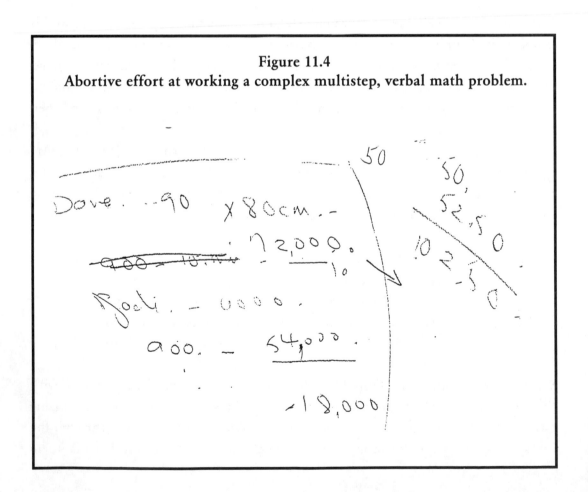

Figure 11.4
Abortive effort at working a complex multistep, verbal math problem.

does listing problem data. The picture has the potential to condense information into a single, simultaneous presentation, thus reducing information load.

Of course, the picture only facilitates solution to the extent that it represents problem information correctly. When it does not, it provides valuable diagnostic information about the erroneous way in which the child has organized the elements of the problem. For example, another problem from the Woodcock-Johnson—R (1989) asks:

> Sue walks thirteen blocks to school, Mary walks six blocks, and Robert walks eight
> blocks. How many more blocks does Sue walk than Robert? (p. 157)

The child who understands the demands of the comparison is likely to draw a picture with the houses of the children placed correctly along a single path, as in Figure 11.5a below. A more poorly integrated grasp of the problem space has produced pictures like Figure 11.5b. In addition, overfocused children can spend a very long time detailing the windows, flag, and playground of the school — emerging from their drawing only to wonder what it was they had set out to do in the first place.

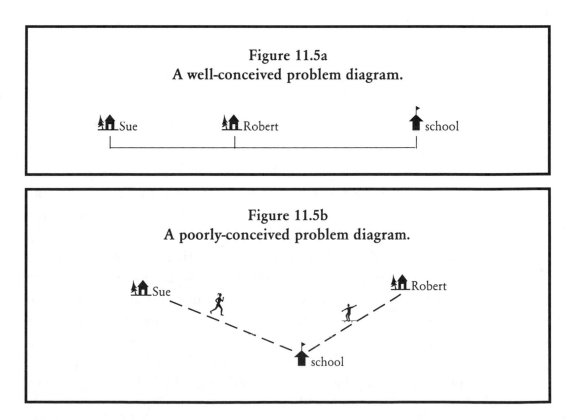

Figure 11.5a
A well-conceived problem diagram.

Sue   Robert   school

Figure 11.5b
A poorly-conceived problem diagram.

Sue   Robert

school

Language Processing Demands

Particular forms of linguistic expression increase demands on the working memory/ executive function component of the attention system (Shankweiler & Crain, 1986; see also chapter 9 of this volume). Any sentence beginning with a relative rather than a main clause creates the need to hold subordinate information on-line until the actual subject of thought can be found. Embedded phrases create a similar disruption in the intake of the main thought and thus require more information to be held on-line before completing the thought. Negations and indirect references are likewise challenging in terms of their effective increase in processing load. Problems stated using these kinds of constructions are likely to be difficult for the child whose attentional capacity cannot support adequate working memory/executive functioning. This is not to say that students with ADDs should not confront these demands, only that they are likely to need support in order to do so.

One approach might be to have the student rewrite complex sentences into a series of simple, direct statements. Consider the following example:

> Sue, who is 6 years younger than Jane, is 5 years older than Bob, who is 11. How old are the two girls?

The rewrite might look like this:

> Bob is 11.
> Sue is 5 years older than Bob.
> Jane is 6 years older than Sue.
> Sue's age = _____
> Jane's age = _____

Of course, revisions of this kind will need to be demonstrated by the teacher and supported in a teacher–student joint effort for a period of time before the child can begin to weed his way through the language more independently.

Function words also challenge the information processing of a child with limited attention capacity. Function words are those that are low in semantic but high in syntactic value (such as *and, or, if, each, the,* conjunctions, demonstratives, articles, and auxiliary verbs). Because they are so rich in syntactic information, they carry a good deal of the information concerning the critical relationships in the problem. At the same time, they tend to elude the ADD child, as attention deficits both promote impulsive emphasis on more directly meaningful, semantically loaded vocabulary and limit the ability to maintain not-yet-meaningful function words in working memory until enough context is gleaned that full meaning can be appreciated (Shankweiler & Crain, 1986). When these words are missed, the child is likely to form an erroneous conceptualization of the problem.

A problem from the Woodcock-Johnson—R applied problems test (1989) makes the point:

> Tom and Sue each earn five dollars a day and Dave earns four dollars a day. How much money will Tom, Sue, and Dave earn together in three days? (p. 161)

The word *each* often escapes children with ADDs. They therefore have reason to assume that together the earnings of Tom and Sue equal five dollars daily. The answer they give is 27. Simply pointing to the word *each* often is enough to prompt an accurate solution.

The benefits of presenting this kind of syntactic challenge to the student with ADD, and supporting the careful linguistic analysis that is necessary, certainly exceed those associated with just math functions.

Mental Flexibility and Inflexibility

Flexible thinking is extremely important for many aspects of problem solving. Many problems can be approached and solved in a number of different ways. The deeper and more fluid the child's understanding of essential concepts and relationships, the more likely it is that novel alternative solution paths will emerge. A child who does not know division but understands the nature of the question "If there are 12 cookies and 3 children, what would be an equal share for each child?" could derive a strategy of successive subtractions. On the surface, the following problem requires knowledge of division by a mixed number:

> Bakeries use a lot of flour and sugar each day. If seventy-five pounds of flour lasted
> a bakery two and one-half days, how much flour was used per day?
> (Woodcock-Johnson—R, 1989, p. 165)

A child who has insufficient knowledge of fractions, but a good understanding of number concepts and some mental flexibility, might reason that the bakery would use 150 pounds of flour in 5 days, and hence 30 pounds in one day.

Flexibility of this kind is promoted by the availability of adequate working memory resources. On-line capacity allows alternative approaches to be generated and compared with each other. The nonlinear quality of this kind of thinking lacks the attentional efficiency of sequential processing, which conserves working memory resources by serially moving information in and out (Johnson-Laird, 1983). It is encouraging to see that math curricula are beginning to emphasize fluid, self-generated, bottom-up solutions to a variety of complex problems.

Were it not for his limitations in working memory, the typical disinhibited child with ADD might be expected to demonstrate mental flexibility — perhaps to a fault. Uninhibited associations yield a potential source of fluidity out of which novel frameworks for problem solving might emerge. They are, however, only an asset insofar as associations remain *within* the problem space, however broadly that is defined.

In contrast, the overfocused subtype of ADD is characterized by mental rigidity and anxiety, both of which may be reflections of the same underlying biochemistry. Children in this category may prefer to work within clearly defined guidelines for problem solving. They are likely to respond well to a prototypical example with a carefully delineated algorithm for solution. Progressive examples might provide increasingly distant variations on the theme.

The question remains, though, whether such an orchestrated and restricted approach can be considered to be authentic problem solving. The overfocused child might be moved more productively toward flexibility by being given the solution and asked for at least two different ways the solution might be derived. If the child is socially competent, working in groups can also help him experience different ways of viewing the same problem.

It is possible, although far from clearly established, that stimulant medications decrease mental flexibility (see Chapter 6, pp. 104-105). When a child with ADD who is taking stimulants presents inflexibility as a particular problem, it is important to pursue the possibility of changing medication or altering the dosage of the current medication.

The Special Case of ADD with Nonverbal Learning Disability

Difficulty with math is one of the defining features of Nonverbal Learning Disability (NLD), otherwise referred to as right-hemisphere syndrome. It is strongly suspected that right parietal dysfunction contributes to this syndrome (Semrud-Clikeman & Hynd, 1990; Weintraub & Mesulam, 1983). Since this area is considered to be an integral part of the attention system as well, it would be logical to assume some comorbidity between NLD and ADDs. In fact, attentional disturbances are often found in NLDs (Weintraub & Mesulam, 1983). A recent study (Gross-Tsur, Shalev, Manor, & Amir, 1995) found ADHD in 100% of its NLD subjects (N=20).

The typical profile of math problems in this group of children includes procedural errors, failure to shift set, and difficulty with spatial organization and visual detail. Some of the error types in this list appear to be closely associated with the attention network and have been discussed already (i.e., procedural errors, failure to shift set, and to some degree difficulty attending to visual detail). The issue of spatial organization, however, may introduce an additional element into the math dysfunction of children with ADDs who also have NLD.

Spatial organization may play a role in the evolution of math concepts and math skills at several points along the course of development. Early number concept is often learned in the context of spatial arrangement. And certainly more–less comparisons can be facilitated through perception of space (Piaget & Inhelder, 1969). It is suspected that spatial organization is made possible by parallel processing, in which the right hemisphere is thought to have particular aptitude (Semrud-Clikeman & Hynd, 1990). Parallel processing contributes to the ability to manage complex, simultaneously perceived information as an integrated unit. As such, it promises to support appreciation of cardinal property.

Although visuospatial disturbances are unlikely to account fully for problems with calculations, there are a number of obstacles that they can impose. Problems with orientation in space can certainly interfere with the orderly progression of counting or with the left-right or right-left procedures used in computational algorithms. Losing one's place in the visual field can interfere with the conceptual aspects of learning place value. Visuospatial disorders may make it difficult for young children to arrange and manipulate materials as a way to represent early math concepts and operations.

Hartje (1987, p. 126) lists a variety of errors that might occur in written calculations due to spatial difficulties:

- distortion of digits in shape or spatial orientation
- inversion of single digits
- misplacement of digits in multidigit numbers
- dissociation of single digits in complex numbers
- irregular horizontal alignment of digits in complex numbers
- irregular vertical alignment of digits or numbers in columns
- omission of digits on left or right side of a number
- omission or displacement of auxiliary lines (e.g., to differentiate the operator from the product)
- starting the calculation from the wrong place
- local errors in the process of "carrying" or "borrowing"

- skipping rows or columns during the process of calculation ("losing one's place")
- disregard of the local values of the decimal system in the placement of intermediate results

In extreme cases of right hemisphere syndrome, there may be left hemifield neglect — the neglect of any material in the left visual field. Any information which falls within the neglected field is simply not noticed. There is complete inattention to, and therefore lack of awareness of, any information appearing in this area. Inattention persists in whatever field is to the left of the individual's orientation. (A shift in position would occlude a different set of information.) Typically, copy drawings by individuals affected by this disorder fail to represent the part of the picture depicted in the left visual field. Their writing tends to begin at the left margin, but each successive line ignores more of the left field until only half of the page is used for writing (Mesulam, 1990; Weintraub & Mesulam, 1983); this phenomenon was termed "tornado writing" by one middle-school teacher.

To illustrate, we present some examples of the work of an 11-year-old child with both NLD and ADD. The copy of the Rey-Osterrieth complex figure (Figure 11.6) demonstrates the absence of the left side of the figure and some distortion of spatial relationships. The writing sample (Figure 11.7) confirms the left hemifield neglect and reveals some graphomotor difficulty. A child with this kind of visuo-spatial processing disorder must tackle math procedures within the context of this distorted perception. In this case, the child's numeral formation is awkward (Figure 11.8). It is not clear whether the child has (a) missed the spatial ordering of digits around the decimal or (b) failed to notice the presence or meaning of the decimal point, representing his answer as a 4-digit whole number with a comma properly placed.

Although the spatial features of computational procedures are rather superficial, they play a role in developing notions of place value and in managing traditional algorithms. Instructionally, one defense against visuospatial confusion would be to build a strong conceptual base. Estimation based on the conceptual properties of the task, rather than on right-left arrangement, would at least allow a child to recognize when her answer had gone too far afield. At the moment we are trying to use a computer application with one child who has both ADD and NLD. The goal is to position him facing a computer screen and to move all of the material he must work with to the right of the screen. Of course, this will require him to maintain a constant focal point and not shift so that the midpoint of his vision is the midpoint of the material.

Figure 11.6
The Rey-Osterrieth complex figure, with a copy drawing by one 10-year-old
ADD/NLD child, illustrating the phenomenon of left hemifield neglect.

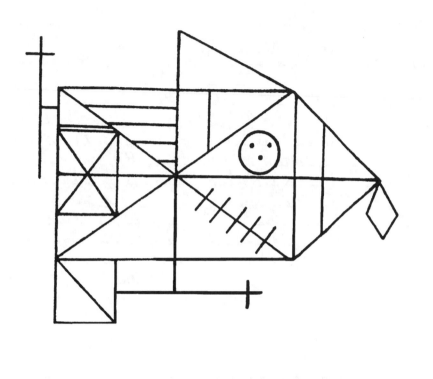

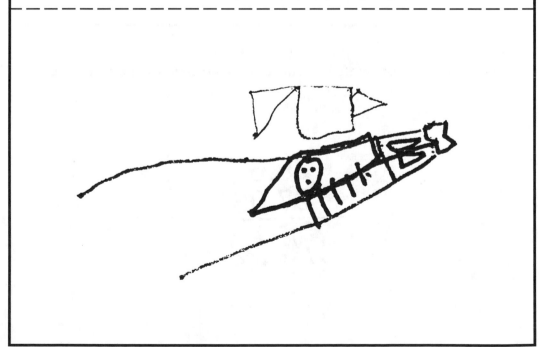

Figure 11.7
The "tornado" effect of left hemifield neglect on a child's writing performance.

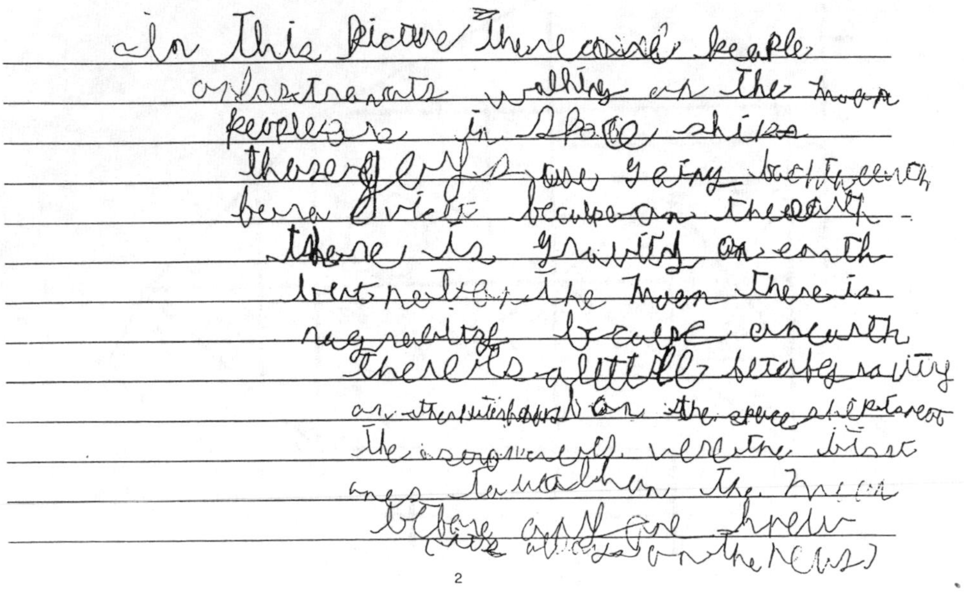

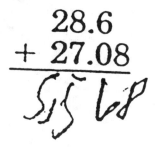

Figure 11.8
The effects of visuospatial dysfunction on arithmetical performance.

$$28.6$$
$$+\ 27.08$$

Conclusion

Attention disorders can interfere significantly with math understanding and performance. The impairment goes beyond the child's capacity for on-task behavior and commitment to repetitive practice. At a deeper level, attention disorders disrupt a number of cognitive processes that make possible the learning of math facts and concepts, including the management of complex operations. Instruction will need to support the impaired cognitive functions at a deep level, rather than providing more superficial strategies or simply more opportunity to practice.

12

Summary and Directions for Intervention

ATTENTION AS A SELF-ORGANIZING SYSTEM

Attention is a complex concept. So too is the dysfunction of attention. Attention deficit disorder cannot be distilled into a handful of behaviors listed on a checklist without losing the richness of meaning inherent in the concept, and therefore its myriad ramifications on human behavior, thought, and emotion. Nevertheless, the history of defining and treating ADDs consists of a series of attempts to reduce them to simplistic formulations with overly simplistic "solutions."

We have shown that attention is an intricate, self-organizing system. It is nonlinear and recursive, a set of feedback and feedforward loops that allow multiple aspects of the cognitive and emotional systems to communicate with one another, drawing upon prior knowledge and capitalizing on the human drive to notice novelty. Learning is, after all, the process of noticing something new, associating it with something familiar, perceiving relationships and consolidating the knowledge, and getting ready for more. This is not a serial, linear, unidirectional process, even though the constraints of language require us to describe it in that way. Rather, it is a dynamic, interactive process. The attention system attempts to maintain a balance between activation and arousal, perceiving novel stimuli without becoming overwhelmed — which might lead to avoidance or overfocusing — or bored, which might lead to distractibility.

Attention is a limited-capacity system that must function in a world with infinite demands. The more complex a notion, the more information it contains and the more intricately it is intertwined with other concepts. Thinking involves managing all the elements in a controlled and modulated manner, so that the system has just enough information to appreciate the relationships, but not so much that it becomes overwhelmed. A sense of the right "cut," so that the amount of information is optimal, comes with experience and prior knowledge, but its emergence absolutely depends on a well-regulated attentional system. When the system is disordered, it is vulnerable either to overloading with detail, thus missing the big picture, or to underfocusing, resulting in a vague sense of the information and jeopardizing retention.

Because attention is a limited-capacity system, it is essential that the cognitive system store information efficiently in order to preserve capacity — or reserve resources — so that the system can continue to process information. After all, learning never ends! The cognitive system, of which attention is so critical a part, perceives, stores, and knows information in an integrated way. Information is organized into concepts, thereby reducing the consumption of attentional capacity and freeing attentional resources for further work.

We have described the neurological and biological connections that manage this remarkable system. Research from the medical and psychological fields has contributed enormously to our understanding of the brain. The neurotransmitters dopamine, norepinephrine, and serotonin in particular have been found to have critical roles in the regulation of attention, but other neurotransmitters and the endocrine and sympathetic nervous systems are also involved. The frontal areas of the brain play a primary role, but many other parts of the brain are involved in regulating attention. The most important feature of the attentional system, though, is its dynamic nature. Everything interacts. Each component — whether a neurotransmitter, a hormone, a cell assembly, or a brain structure — affects other components and is affected by other components. Nothing comes first. Nothing is "in charge." Nothing is unimportant. And because everything is mutually interdependent, the entire system is vulnerable to disturbance.

The biological system is not a closed one; it does not exist in a vacuum. Neurological and biological connections interact with the individual's experiences in complex ways, creating human behavior: learning, feeling, and moving. To observe behaviors and fail to appreciate the dynamic biological system that helped create them is to miss their most fundamental and meaningful aspects. To then *judge* the behaviors and place a value on them, without regard to the biological underpinnings that support them, is the height of arrogance. Attempts to change the behaviors based only on such judgments, with no respect for the biological foundations and personal experiences of the individual, are doomed to fail. What we have sought to do in this work is to restore the entire person, in all her complexity, to the consideration of ADD, moving the focus of diagnosis and treatment away from control of the surface behaviors.

Appreciation of the biological foundations of behavior helps one to comprehend the concept of motivation. Motivation is a complex phenomenon, much of which is embedded in the biochemistry of attention, below the level of consciousness. It is not under the conscious control of "will," but rather is driven by the forces of novelty, emotion, the nature of a situation, expectations built by experience, and above all, the need to preserve homeostasis. It is foolishness to expect that such a complex phenomenon would be susceptible to change that is forced by external constraints imposed by someone else. Behavior modification techniques are at best blunt instruments, and are not terribly effective in dealing with the intricacies of behavior. We believe that any type of change can be facilitated only if it takes place in the context of an individual's organizational state at that point in time. In other words, it must respect the individual's tendencies toward preservation of homeostasis or toward homeorhesis, reorganization at a more advanced level. If an intervention does not acknowledge this principle, the system will perceive it as disruptive or irrelevant, and it will not be effective.

The first step toward change, then, is understanding the function of the behavior. As a result of the neuropsychological and cognitive dynamics of attention dysfunction, behavior, cognition and affect interact and create distinct, idiosyncratic methods of coping. Avoidance behaviors serve to protect the individual from overstimulation, understimulation, or frustration. They become evident in various ways: refusals to start, stop, or continue with a task; socializing; clowning; fidgeting; talking out; and acting out. The behaviors listed on the checklists used for diagnosis of attention dysfunction are, in some individuals, evidence of their attempts at coping. The key to diagnosis, though, is determining *with what difficulties* the individual is trying to cope.

THE ADD CHILD AS LEARNER

The second major focus of our argument relates to how ADDs impact on a child's learning and how instruction might be structured to support the child's efforts to learn. As we have repeatedly stressed, the usual approaches to children with ADDs focus almost exclusively on managing the student's behaviors more effectively. The usual expectation regarding drug treatment — that drugs enable more behavioral control, and with that control the child's learning will take care of itself — is not a supportable assumption. Many (if not most) children with ADDs continue to experience difficulties in learning even after medication has curbed most behavioral disturbances, and they must expend considerable effort to manage their learning, above and beyond the effort it takes to manage their behavior. In short, while drugs do seem to help a student manage his behavior, the unpredictable impact of the chemicals affecting his attentional system continues to influence his attempts to learn effectively. There has been too little attention paid to these effects. Cognitive functioning and performance on school tasks must be addressed even after behavioral control is attained. Teachers who have become sensitive to an ADD child's difficulties can structure his learning by establishing various supports, and can learn to understand and tolerate behaviors that she sees as part of the student's attempts to learn.

The second half of the book has reviewed the attention demands of specific areas of school performance — providing analyses of what may pose difficulties for ADD students and suggestions for handling these difficulties within classrooms. In the following discussion, we present more general descriptions of instruction, guidelines for assessing a child's cognitive strengths and weaknesses, and suggestions for appropriate instructional interventions.

The Dynamics of Instruction

Intentions may bridge the gap between attention and learning (Denckla, 1996b; Shaw et al., 1992). Intentions serve as focal points to which attention is drawn and around which thought and action are mobilized. When a learner accepts a goal as her own intention, she has entered the instructional situation. At the moment when intention is shifted to a specific instructional goal, that goal becomes the organizer that activates attention and attunes and stabilizes its direction.

However, children enter instructional situations with their own intentions. After all, instruction involves the teaching of something new; how could the learner hold an intention about something he does not yet know? His attention will be attuned to those goals that he is able to perceive. The art of instruction is to move the child from his original intention to ones that more closely approximate the instruction goal, in a cycle of smooth transitions.

Children with ADDs are in need of even greater support than their peers in order to stabilize attention for adopting the intentions of the instructor. For these children, it is absolutely critical that the instructor begin by sharing the child's intentions. It is at that moment that effective instruction can begin and the child can be induced to progress gracefully in the direction of the instructor's goal.

It is the instructor who must make the adaptation to the intentions of the child with ADD. Once she has come to share the child's intention, she is inside the learning system and can affect change from within. When she remains outside the system, by setting goals that cannot be incorporated by the child, she sets up a dynamic of force ("learn this") and counterforce ("No, I won't"). Once this dynamic is set in motion, the situation can only get worse. Adaptive instructors — who give up the original goal in its pure form, who begin by assessing the current status of the learner's intents and then joining the learner at that level — have more success in reaching the ultimate goal than those who insist on that goal relentlessly (Cherkes-Julkowski & Mitlina, submitted for publication).

The Need For Assessment

It is essential to understand the ADD child's behaviors as fully as possible in order to optimize interventions for improvement in any attention-regulated area (that is to say, any area whatsoever). Ongoing, diagnostic assessment is a fundamental component of any interaction between a child with an attention deficit disorder and his or her teacher, parent, physician, or other planner of intervention.

Where to begin? Pragmatically, beginning anywhere, on any "task," is probably fine. The key is in observing and gathering data in a systematic or organized way so that patterns of strengths and weaknesses begin to emerge, and so that hypotheses about the child's coping style(s) can be formulated and examined.

The diagnostician (i.e., the parent, teacher, psychologist, or other evaluator) should be attentive to how the child responds to stimuli. For example, what types of stimulation catch the child's attention, and for how long does he remain engaged? And then what happens? Is the child able to select appropriate types and amounts of stimulation? Is he easily distracted by noises or movements or objects in the environment, or by his own impulsive thoughts? How disruptive to the task at hand is the interruption? Can the child reorient back to the task, or does he require external supports to do so? Can the child shift her attention appropriately throughout the task, or does she become "stuck" or overwhelmed when she is on her own?

It is important to assess the child's performance on various tasks. How much of a particular task can the child manage on her own: all of it, some of it, or none at all? Where does the process seem to break down for her: getting started, knowing where to go in the middle of it, or knowing when she is done? Since the answers to these questions will certainly vary according to the specific type of task, it's important to determine what kinds of tasks are handled, and with what degree of competence. This analysis must take the following dimensions into account:

- the various types of information involved in the task: e.g, verbal or printed, linguistic or non-linguistic, symbolic or concrete, visuo-spatial, temporarily presented or present throughout, random or arbitrary information versus organized, abstract or concrete concepts
- the complex processing demands of the task: e.g, single-step, multiple-step, multiple steps that require a specific sequence, seemingly arbitrary algorithms or procedures
- the response demands of the task: e.g, writing, speaking, drawing, building, manipulation of materials
- the length of the task
- the content of the task: e.g, mathematics, reading, writing, spelling, science, social interactions

All attention-deficient children would benefit from a battery of individually administered diagnostic instruments. The nature and scope of the assessment will vary according to the specific needs of the child, but should certainly consider all appropriate academic areas, language processing, motor skills, and social skills. Many children will require thorough sensory processing evaluations (such as occupational therapy, central auditory processing, physical therapy, or assistive technology evaluations) or more comprehensive speech and language evaluations.

Assessment of academic achievement must be multidimensional. Certainly, basic skills — such as letter and sound knowledge, word recognition, word attack skills, number concepts, math facts, symbol recognition, and so forth — will need to be evaluated. Furthermore, the application of skills on more integrated tasks, particularly those requiring extended information processing, is essential. A student may be able to solve isolated computation problems, yet not have math facts automatized; this deficiency might show up in a slow rate of speed as the student relies on a counting procedure rather than retrieval of facts from memory. The same student may make errors when attempting to solve story problems, because the counting procedure she uses places too large a burden on her working memory, and she does not have enough resources remaining to solve the problem effectively. She also may not attend to the key words in the problem, missing important cues for what numbers and procedures are relevant to a solution. Similarly, a student might be able to write a single, simple sentence quite appropriately, but be unable to sustain the attention and manage the organizational demands required for writing a cohesive paragraph. Spelling, mechanics, or grammar might break down during such sustained written language tasks.

Nowhere is the effect of increased information processing load more detrimental, and possibly nowhere is it less appreciated, than in the area of reading comprehension (Brock & Knapp, 1996; Cherkes-Julkowski & Stolzenberg, 1991). Children with ADDs may be able to read and understand short passages using simple, direct linguistic constructions. As the length increases, so do the demands on attention. Comprehension begins to fall. This effect has been demonstrated (Cherkes-Julkowski & Stolzenberg, 1991) and confirmed (Brock & Knapp, 1996). Unfortunately, reading comprehension is ordinarily assessed using very short passages of two or three sentences. A child assessed by such methods as having no reading comprehension problems may still not comprehend typical middle-school-length reading assignments. Given the findings of no reading difficulties, teachers often turn to the motivation explanation, ultimately blaming the child for his disability.

The attention system can be evaluated through observation of the student's performance on academic and cognitive tasks. The diagnostician considers all the demands placed on the attentional system by each task handled successfully and by each task handled unsuccessfully. She considers the role of attention span, working memory, automaticity, executive functions, and complex information processing. For instance, how does the student allocate his attentional resources? How does he deploy his attention? Can he initiate, select, sustain, inhibit, and shift attention when needed? Is disinhibited thought so rich that it leads to a multitude of associations, vast enough to further disorganize his thought? Does the student use language as a mediator or mechanism for keeping information active as she processes it? Or does she rely on other strategies, such as visualization or recording? (One fourth-grade child we evaluated used the vent openings on a radiator in the examination room to construct a makeshift "number line," which she used for a variety of placekeeping purposes.)

The diagnostician makes judgments about the student's knowledge networks. Are they well integrated, or do they consist of scattered bits and pieces of information? Impoverished knowledge stores impede learning because they make retrieval inefficient, and they fail to provide adequate frames for chunking, compressing, organizing, associating, and elaborating upon information, so span and capacity are not optimized. Lack of automaticity is another factor that impedes learning. The diagnostician determines if any skills are automatic, so that the student has some capability for non-effortful attention processing. If some processes that should be automatic (for age, experience, intelligence, and so on), are not, the diagnostician considers *why*. Perhaps the student lacks the ability to sustain attention, be vigilant, and control the need for arousal in order to engage in repeated associations; these associations are necessary for him to learn the arbitrary associations for a skill to be developed to an automatic level.

It is also important to determine the child's mechanisms for coping with his difficulties. Consider what the child does when he cannot cope with the demands of

a task. Does he guess randomly, or respond impulsively? Does he try and then aban-
don the task just before its conclusion? Does he refuse to try? Or does he display some
"inappropriate" behavior to avoid it completely? Data on these coping mechanisms
help to describe the child's attempts at self-organization and regulation, and provide
essential information about where to begin to provide support. These behaviors will
likely be the most meaningful to the child, since they have emerged out of his own
attempts at self-regulation. They should *never* be ignored or disrespected. Instruction
that treats coping behaviors as unfortunate sources of interference on the path toward the goal is doomed to failure. Coping strategies are active and constructive
attempts at self-organization that can and must be recruited into the learning process.

Planning Interventions

When the diagnostician begins to understand the child's cognitive strengths and
weaknesses, and identifies where in the curriculum to begin, she is ready to plan
intervention. This is not a simple process. She must devise strategies and methods of
instruction that begin at a point where the child is comfortable, and that stretch his
resources just a bit at a time. She will need to constantly be a vigilant observer of the
instructional interaction, particularly of the child's reactions, and will need to make
the subtle adjustments (and sometimes dramatic changes) needed to provide more
support here, less support there.

At various points in this book, we have talked about "top-down" and "bottom-
up" approaches to instruction. The top-down teacher's message to the student is "Do
it my way, because it's the best, it will avoid error, and I know what's best for you."
Unfortunately, top-down methods don't respect — and cannot capitalize upon —
what the child has already constructed as a concept or as a strategy. The "bottom up"
approach sends a different message: "Let's look at what you're doing now, what part
of it works and can be built upon, and where we should go from here." This is the way
learning develops.

The teacher brings to the learning situation her knowledge of the end result and
her vision of multiple ways to achieve it. She knows the elements essential to a concept or a procedure, and she can select examples and activities that highlight those
features. She can choose the road that best matches the one that the student has
already embarked upon — while shaping it toward the desired destination — and
provide gentle guidance as he travels along it. Thus, the two travel together, and the
journey is meaningful to the student. This method has a far better chance of success
than simply lifting the student up and plopping him down on the "right path,"
outside of any context.

Instruction becomes effective when the teacher and the learner share a joint intention. It is that intention that serves as the focal point around which behavior organizes. Since the child with attention deficits cannot readily assume the intentions of
another (or even hold his own for very long), it is critical that the instructor work
within those intentions held by the child at the outset of instruction.

We endorse the apprenticeship model of instruction discussed in earlier chapters.
For any complex new skill, the student or "apprentice" will not be able to handle all
the attentional and cognitive components independently, but he will be able to handle
some part or parts. The student learns and practices the parts that he can manage,
within the context of the entire operation. The teacher manages the executive function of organizing, regulating, and monitoring the process as an entirety — the relationship, the action, and the repetitions. This is not to say that particular component
skill should never be practiced in isolation. Basketball players routinely practice shoot-
ing lay-ups and foul shots outside of the context of the game; cake decorators practice
forming rose petals out of frosting over and over again; and children need to practice
addition facts. Basic component skills need to be learned to automaticity, so that the
student will not have to allocate effortful attention to them when she eventually
masters the entire task.

It is important for the teacher to remember, though, that learning component
skills to automaticity, by practicing them outside the context of the whole process or
task, requires a tremendous amount of controlled attention to override the natural
decline in arousal that occurs when doing repetitive tasks. Such massed practice will
need to be made as interesting as possible, in order to maintain arousal as much
aspossible. This can be done in several ways:

- Incorporating movement and/or color into the task materials or presentation can help keep the child focused on them.
- Response requirements that involve a gross motor movement (verbal responding, pointing, reaching, retrieving, etc.) keep the child active.
- Math facts presented in different colored inks or varied fonts may maintain interest far longer than the standard commercial flashcards.
- Computer games can be excellent, but the teacher will need to preview
  the software and monitor the child carefully. They won't be effective if
  the student can respond to them randomly or inattentively.
- Social interaction can also help; for some children working with a peer or
  an adult is helpful in maintaining arousal levels and not disrupting
  attentional control.
- Switching tasks frequently can also facilitate arousal. Break up practice

into smaller chunks of time, and provide opportunities for movement in between sitting-and-concentrating times.

Importantly, practice should not begin until the child has appreciated the role of the skill in meaningful context. Complex tasks requiring sustained attention or execution of multiple steps (writing and editing a paragraph, long division, reading a science chapter for information, etc.) can be especially problematic for students with attention deficits. When possible, the tasks should be made meaningful. Writing a paragraph on a topic completely foreign to the student will be far more difficult than writing on a familiar or self-selected one. Keeping tasks meaningful may require preteaching about underlying concepts — i.e., building the knowledge network. It may require making concepts concrete in some way, such as teaching long division with expanded notation, teaching the multiplication of fractions with manipulatives or pictures, or teaching students to use a writing web to organize ideas. The teacher can provide verbal cues to support the student's intake of information and pacing. The teacher might suggest when to switch from collecting pieces of information to condensing them into a whole (e.g., consolidating facts into a main idea).

The teacher needs to remember the arousal/activation loop, as well as the neurological biases for attending to novelty and habituating rapidly that are so dramatic in students with attention deficit disorders. However, she must also guard against the threat of overstimulation (when too much is attempted too fast), which further disorganizes the student. The teacher can use environmental resources to bring about dynamic processes that impact on alert states. For example, some students will need periodic breaks to down-regulate. Medication schedules affect attentional resources as the medication works through its half-life. Teachers must be aware of what times of the day the student's attention is best, and what times it is worst (e.g., right before a second dose). Teachers can then capitalize on optimal times of attention, scheduling instruction on new and complex tasks at those times, or expecting more independent work to be accomplished at those times. Conversely, when medication has worn off, or at other times when attention is just not optimal, teachers should avoid presenting new information, complex tasks, independent work, andrepetitive, rote tasks. These times might be ideal for movement activities, enjoyable activities, self-selected activities, and so on, that do not demand highly controlled attention. Remember the lesson of the Blue Bear experiments we mentioned in chapter 4: respond to the child's attempts at self-regulation, and do not impose some arbitrary rhythm.

References

Abikoff, H. (1991). Cognitive training in ADHD children: Less to it than meets the eye. *Journal of Learning Disabilities, 24(4),* 205-209.

Abikoff, H., Ganeles, D., Reiter, G., Blum, C., Foley, C., & Klein, G.R. (1988). Cognitive training in academically deficient ADDH boys receiving stimulant medication. *Journal of Abnormal Child Psychology, 16,* 411-432.

Abikoff, H., Gittelman, R., & Klein, D.F. (1980). Classroom observation code for hyperactive children: A replication of validity. *Journal of Consulting and Clinical Psychology, 48,* 555-565.

Ackerly, S.S. (1950). Prefrontal lobes and social development. *Yale Journal of Biological Medicine, 22,* 471-482.

Ackerman, P.T., Anhalt, J.M., & Dykman, R.A. (1986). Arithmetic automatization failure in children with attention and reading disorders: Associations and sequela. *Journal of Learning Disabilities, 19(4),* 222-232.

Adams, M.J. (1990). *Beginning to read.* Cambridge, MA: MIT Press.

Adler-Grinberg, D., & Stark, L. (1978). Eye movements, scanpaths, and dyslexia. *American Journal of Optometry and Physiological Optics, 55,* 567-570.

Adolph, K., Eppler, M., & Gibson, E. (1993). Development of perception of affordances. In C. Rovee-Collier & L. Lipsitt (Eds.), *Advances in Infancy Research* (Vol. 8, pp. 51-98). Norwood, NJ: Ablex.

Alkon, D.L. (1989, July). Memory storage and neural systems. *Scientific American,* 42-51.

American Psychological Association (1968). *Diagnostic and statistical manual of mental disorders* (2nd ed.). Washington, DC: American Psychiatric Association.

American Psychological Association (1980). *Diagnostic and statistical manual of mental disorders* (3rd ed.). Washington, DC: American Psychiatric Association.

American Psychological Association (1987). *Diagnostic and statistical manual of mental disorders* (3rd ed., rev.). Washington, DC: American Psychiatric Association.

American Psychiatric Association (1994). *Diagnostic and statistical manual of mental disorders* (4th ed., rev.). Washington, DC: American Psychiatric Association.

Anderson, P.L. (1982). A preliminary study of syntax in the written expression of learning disabled children. *Journal of Learning Disabilities, 15(6),* 359-362.

Anderson, R.C. (1978). Schema-directed processes in language comprehension. In A. Lesgold, J. Peligrino, S. Fokhema, & R. Glaser (Eds.), *Cognitive psychology and instruction* (pp. 67-82). New York: Plenum.

Applebee, A.N. (1984). *Contexts for learning to write: Studies of secondary school instruction.* Norwood, NJ: Ablex.

Arend, R., Gove, F., & Sroufe, L.A. (1979). Continuity of individual adaptation from infancy to kindergarten: A predictive study of ego-resiliency and curiosity in preschoolers. *Child Development, 50,* 950-999.

Ashcraft, M.H., & Fierman, B.A. (1982). Mental addition in third, fourth, and sixth graders. *Journal of Experimental Child Psychology, 33,* 216-234.

ATTENTION! (1995). Interview with Dr. John Werry. *2*(1), pp. 7-8, 30-31.

Ausubel, D.P., & Fitzgerald, D. (1962). Organizer, general background, and antecedent learning variables in sequential verbal learning. *Journal of Educational Psychology, 53,* 243-249.

Bachevalier, J. (1994). Medial temporal lobe structures and autism: A review of clinical and experimental findings. *Neuropsychologia, 32,* 627-648.

Badian, N.A. (1983). Dyscalculia and nonverbal disorders of learning. In H.R. Myklebust (Ed.), *Progress in learning disabilities* (Vol. 5, pp. 235-264). New York: Stratton.

Barenbaum, E., Newcomer, P., & Nodine, B. (1987). Children's ability to write stories as a function of variation in task, age, and developmental level. *Learning Disabilities Quarterly, 10*, 175-188.

Barkley, R. (1981). *Hyperactive children: A handbook for diagnosis and treatment.* New York: Guilford.

Barkley, R. (1984). *Do as we say, not as we do: The prblem of stimulus control and rule-governed behavior in children with Attention Deficit Disorder with Hyperactivity.* Paper presented at the Highpoint Conference, Toronto.

Barkley, R. (1990a). *Attention deficit hyperactivity disorder: A handbook for diagnosis and treatment.* New York: Guilford.

Barkley, R. (1990b). A critique of current diagnostic criteria for attention deficit hyperactivity disorder: Clinical and research implications. *Developmental and Behavioral Pediatrics, 11*(6), 343-352.

Barkley, R. (1991). The ecological validity of laboratory and analogue assessment methods of ADHD symptoms. *Journal of Abnormal Child Psychology, 19*, 149-178.

Baron-Cohen, S., Tager-Flusberg, H., & Cohen, D. (1993). *Understanding other minds: Perspectives from autism.* Oxford: Oxford University Press.

Barrickman, L., Noyes, R., Kuperman, S., Schumacher, E., & Verda, M. (1991). Treatment of ADHD with fluoxetine: A preliminary trial. *Journal of the American Association of Child and Adolescent Psychiatry, 30*, 762-767.

Barrickman, L., Perry, P., Allen, A.J., Kuperman, S., Arndt, S.V., Herrmann, K.J., & Schumacher, E. (1995). Buproprion versus methylphenidate in the treatment of attention deficit hyperactivity disorder. *Journal of the American Academy of Child and Adolescent Psychiatry, 34*(5), 649-657.

Barton, S. (1994). Chaos, self-organization and psychology. *American Psychologist, 49*, 5-14.

Baumgaertel, A., Wolraich, M.L., & Dietrich, M. (1995), Comparison of diagnostic criteria for Attention Deficit Disorders in a German elementary school sample. *Journal of the American Academy of Child and Adolescent Psychiatry, 34*(5), 629-638.

Beaugrande, R. de. (1984). *Text production: Toward a science of composition.* Norwood, NJ: Ablex.

Belmont, J.M., & Butterfield, E.C. (1971). Learning strategies as determinants of memory deficiencies. *Cognitive Psychology, 2*, 411-420.

Bender, L. (1942). Postencephalitic behavior disorders in children. In J.B. Neal (Ed.), *Encephalitis: A clinical study.* New York: Grune and Stratton.

Beninger, R.J. (1989). Dopamine and learning: Implications for attention deficit disorder and hyperkinetic syndrome. In T. Sagvolden & T. Archer (Eds.), *Attention deficit disorder: Clinical and basic research* (pp. 323-338). Hillsdale, NJ: Erlbaum.

Benson, D.F. (1991). The role of frontal dysfunction in Attention Deficit Hyperactivity Disorder. *Journal of Child Neurology, 6* (Supplement): s9-s12.

Bereiter, C. (1985). Children need more complete reading strategies. In J. Osborne, P.T. Wilson, & R.C. Anderson (Eds.), *Reading education: Foundations for a literate America* (pp. 311-318). Lexington, MA: D.C. Heath.

Bereiter, C., & Scardamalia, M. (1983). Does learning to write have to be so difficult? In A. Freedman, I. Pringle, & J. Yolden (Eds.), *Learning to write: First language, second language* (pp. 20-33). London: Longman's Internations.

Bereiter, C., & Scardamalia, M. (1984). Information-processing demands of text composition. In H. Mandl, N.L. Stein, & T. Trabasso (Eds.), *Learning and comprehension of text* (pp. 407-428). Hillsdale, NJ: Erlbaum.

Berninger, V., Abbott, R.D., Whitaker, D., Sylvester, L., & Nolen, S.B. (1995). Integrating low- and high-level skills in instructional protocols for writing disabilities. *Learning Disability Quarterly, 18*, 293-309.

Berninger, V., & Alsdorf, B. (1989). Are there errors in error analysis? *Journal of Psychoeducational Assessment, 7*, 209-222.

Berninger, V., Mizolawa, D.T., & Bragg, R. (1991). Theory-based diagnosis and remediation of writing disabilities. *Journal of School Psychology, 29*, 57-79.

Berninger, V., Yates, C., Cartwright, A., Rutberg, J., Remy, E., & Abbott, R. (1992). Lower-level developmental skills in beginning writing. *Reading and Writing: An Interdisciplinary Journal, 4*, 257-280.

Biederman, J., Baldessarini, R.J., Wright, V., Knee, D., Harmatz, J.S. (1989). A double-blind placebo controlled study of desipramine in the treatment of ADD: Efficacy. *Journal of the American Academy of Child and Adolescent Psychiatry, 28*, 777-784.

Biederman, J., Faraone, S.V., & Chen, W.J. (1993). Social adjustment inventory for children and adolescents: Concurrent validity in ADHD children. *Journal of the American Academy of Child and Adolescent Psychiatry, 32*(5), 1059-1064.

Biederman, J., & Jellinek, M.S. (1984). Psychopharmacology in children. *New England Journal of Medicine, 310,* 968-972.

Blackwell, S.L., McIntyre, C.W., & Murray, M.E. (1983). Information processed from brief visual displays by learning disabled boys. *Child Development, 54,* 927-940.

Borden, K.A., Brown, R.T., Jenkins, P., & Clingerman, S.R. (1987). Achievement attributions and depressive symptoms in attention deficit-disordered and normal children. *Journal of School Psychology, 25,* 399-404.

Breslin, N.A., & Weinberger, D.R. (1991). Schizophrenia and the normal functional development of the prefrontal cortex. *Development and Psychopathology,* 409-424.

Brock, S., & Knapp, P.K. (1996). Reading comprehension abilities of children with Attention Deficit/Hyperactivity Disorder. *Journal of Attention Disorders, 1*(3), 173-183.

Brown, A.L., Bransford, J.D., Ferrara, R.A., & Campione, J.C. (1983). Learning, remembering and understanding. In P.H. Mussen (Ed.), *Handbook of child psychology: Cognitive development* (pp. 77-166). New York: John Wiley.

Brown, A.L., Campione, J.C., & Murphy, M.D. (1977). Maintenance and generalization of trained metamnemonic awareness by educable retarded children. *Journal of Experimental Psychology, 24,* 191-211.

Bruner, J. (1985). Vygotsky: An historical and conceptual perspective. In J. Wertsch (Ed.), *Culture, communication and cognition: Vygotskian perspectives.* Cambridge, England: Cambridge University Press.

Buitelaar, J., Gaag, R., Swaab-Barneveld, H., & Kuiper, M. (1995). Prediction of clinical response to methylphenidate in children with attention-deficit hyperactivity disorder. *Journal of the American Academy of Child and Adolescent Psychiatry, 34,* 1025-1033.

Byers, R.K., & Lord, E.E. (1943). Late effects of lead poisoning on mental development. *American Journal of Diseases of Children, 66,* 471-494.

Campbell, S.B., & Cluss, P. (1982). Peer relationships of young children with behavior problems. In K.H. Rubin & H.S. Ross (Eds.), *Peer relationships and social skills in childhood* (pp. 323-351). New York: Springer-Verlag.

Cantwell, D. (1977). Hyperkinetic syndrome. In M. Rutter & L. Hersove (Eds.), *Child psychiatry: Modern approaches.* Oxford, England: Blackwell Scientific Publications.

Cantwell, D.P., & Baker, L. (1988). Issues in the classification of child and adolescent psychopathology. *Journal of the American Academy of Child and Adolescent Psychiatry, 27,* 521-533.

Cantwell, D., & Baker, L. (1991). Association between Attention Deficit – Hyperactivity Disorder & learning disorders. *Journal of Learning Disabilities, 24*(2), 88-95.

Caplan, R., Foy, J.G., Asarnow, R.F., & Sherman, T. (1990). Information processing deficits of schizophrenic children with formal thought disorder. *Psychiatry Research, 31,* 169-177.

Carlisle, J.F. (1989). Diagnosing comprehension deficits through listening and reading. *Annals of Dyslexia, 39,* 159-178.

Carlson, C.L., Lahey, B.B., Frame, C.L., Walker, J., & Hynd, G.W. (1987). Sociometric status of clinic-referred children with Attention Deficit Disorders with and without Hyperactivity. *Journal of Abnormal Child Psychology, 15,* 537-547.

Caron, A., & Caron, R. (1981). Processing of relational information as an index of infant risk. In S. Friedman & M. Sigman (Eds.), *Preterm birth and psychological development.* New York: Academic Press.

Carpenter, P.A., & Just, M.A. (1989). The role of working memory and language comprehension. In D. Klahr & K. Kotovsky (Eds.), *Complex information processing* (pp. 31-68). Hillsdale, NJ: Erlbaum.

Carpenter, P., Just, M.A., & Shell, P. (1990). What one intelligence test measures: A theoretical account of the processing in the Raven Progressive Matrices test. *Psychological Review, 97*(3), 404-431.

Carpenter, T.P., & Moser, J.M. (1984). The acquisition of addition and subtraction concepts in grades one through three. *Journal of Research in Mathematics Education, 15,* 179-202.

Cherkes-Julkowski, M. (in press). Learning disability, attention deficit disorder and language impairment as outcomes of prematurity: A longitudinal study. *Journal of Learning Disabilities.*

Cherkes-Julkowski, M., Davis, L., Fimian, M., Gertner, N., McGuire, J., Norlander, K., Okolo, C., & Zoback, M. (1986). Encouraging flexible strategy usage in handicapped learners. In J.M. Berg (Ed.), *Science and service in mental retardation* (pp. 189-196). London: Methuen.

Cherkes-Julkowski, M., & Gertner, N. (1989). *Spontaneous cognitive processes in handicapped children.* New York: Springer-Verlag.

Cherkes-Julkowski, M., & Mitlina, N. (submitted for publication). Self-organization of mother-child instructional dyads and later attention disorder.

Cherkes-Julkowski, M., & Stolzenberg, J. (1991, October). *Reading comprehension, extended processing and attention dysfunction.* Paper presented at the National Council on Learning Disabilities. Minneapolis, MN. (ERIC Abstracts, 1991, microfiche collection, ED 3440194).

Cherkes-Julkowski, M., & Stolzenberg, J. (1991). *Information processing demands, reading comprehension, and attention dysfunction.* Paper presented at the Council of Learning Disabilities Conference, Minneapolis, Minnesota.

Cherkes-Julkowski, M., & Stolzenberg, J. (1991). The learning disability of attention deficit disorder. *Learning Disabilities: A Multidisciplinary Journal,* 2(1), 9-16.

Cherkes-Julkowski, M., & Stolzenberg, J. (1992). Working memory: The problem is not the problem. *Learning Disabilities: A Multidisciplinary Journal,* 3(1), 19-28.

Cherkes-Julkowski, M., Stolzenberg, J., Hatzes, N., & Madaus, J. (1995). Methodological issues in assessing the relationships among ADD, medication effects and reading performance. *Learning Disabilities: A Multidisciplinary Journal,* 6(2), 21-30.

Cherkes-Julkowski, M., Stolzenberg, J., & Segal, L. (1991). Prompted Cognitive Testing as a diagnostic comprehension for attentional deficits: The Raven Standard Progressive Matrices and attention deficit disorders. *Learning Disabilities: A Multidisciplinary Journal,* 2(1), 1-8.

Chess, S. (1960). Diagnosis and treatment of the hyperactive child. *New York State Journal of Medicine,* 60, 2339-2385.

Chi, M. (1985). Interactive roles of knowledge and strategies in the development of organized sorting and recall. In S. Chipman, J. Segal, & R. Glaser (Eds.), *Thinking and Learning Skills* (Vol. 2). Hillsdale, NJ: Erlbaum.

Chi, M., & Koeske, R.D. (1978). Knowledge structure and memory development. In R. Siegler (Ed.), *Children's thinking: What develops.* Hillsdale, NJ: Erlbaum.

Clark, M.L., Cheyne, J.A., Cunningham, C.E., & Siegel, L.S. (1988). Dyadic peer interaction and task orientation in attention-deficit-disordered children. *Journal of Abnormal Child Psychology,* 16, 1-15.

Clements, S.D. (1966). *Task Force One: Minimal brain dysfunction in children* (National Institute of Neurological Diseases and Blindness, Monograph No. 3). Rockville, MD: U.S. Department of Health, Education and Welfare.

Cochran-Smith, M. (1991). Word processing and writing in elementary classrooms: A critical review of related literature. *Review of Educational Research,* 61, 107-155.

Cohen, B.D. (1978). Referential communication disturbances in schizophrenia. In S. Schwartz (Ed.), *Language and cognition in schizophrenia.* Hillsdale, NJ: Erlbaum.

Colby, C.L. (1991). The neuroanatomy and neurophysiology of attention. *Journal of Child Neurology,* 6 (Supplement): s88-s116.

Comings, D.E., & Comings, B.G. (1990). A controlled family history study of Tourette Syndrome: I. Attention deficit disorder, learning disorders and school problems. *Journal of Clinical Psychiatry,* 51, 275-280.

Connor, F.P. (1983). Improving school instruction for learning disabled children: The Teachers College Institutes. *Exceptional Education Quarterly,* 4(1), 23-24.

Conrad, P. (1975). The discovery of hyperkinesis: Notes on the medicalization of deviant behavior. *Social Problems,* 23, 12-21.

Courchesne, E. (1989). Neuroanatomical systems involved in infantile autism: The implications of cerebellar abnormalities. In G. Dawson (Ed.), *Autism: Nature, diagnosis and treatment* (pp. 119-143). New York: Guilford Press.

Courchesne, E., Chisum, H., & Townsend, J. (1994). Neural activity-dependent brain changes in development: Implications for psychopathology. *Development and Psychopathology,* 6(4), 697-722.

Craik, F.I.M., & Lockhart, R.S. (1972). Levels of processing: A framework for memory research. *Journal of Verbal Learning and Verbal Behavior,* 11, 671-684.

Csikszentmihalyi, M., & Larson, R. (1984). *Being adolescent*. New York: Basic Books.

Cunningham, C.E., & Barkley, R.A. (1979). The interactions of hyperactive and normal children with their mothers during free play and structured task. *Child Development, 50,* 217-224.

Cunningham, C.E., Siegel, L.S., & Offord, D.R. (1985). A developmental dose response analysis of the effects of methylphenidate on the peer interactions of attention deficit disordered boys. *Journal of Child Psychology and Psychiatry, 26,* 955-971.

Daiute, C. (1984). Performance limits on writers. In R. Beach & L. Bridwell (Eds.), *New directions in composition research* (pp. 205-224). New York: Guilford Press.

Daiute, C. (1986). Do 1 and 1 make 2? Patterns of influence by collaborative authors. *Written Communication, 3,* 382-408.

Damasio, A. (1994). *Descartes' error*. New York: Grosset/Putnam.

Damasio, A., & Damasio, H. (1992). Brain and language. *Scientific American, 267*(3), 89-95.

Davy, T., & Rogers, C.L. (1989). Stimulant medication and short attention span: a clinical approach. *Journal of Developmental and Behavioral Pediatrics, 10,* 313-318.

Dawson, G., Klinger, G., Panagiotides, H., Hill, D., & Spieker, S. (1992). Frontal lobe activity and affective behavior of infants and mothers. *Journal of Abnormal Child Psychology, 18,* 335-345.

Denckla, M.B. (1991, December). Academic and extracurricular aspects of nonverbal learning disabilities. *Psychiatric Annals,* 717-724.

Denckla, M.B. (1991). Attention Deficit Disorder – Residual Type. *Journal of Child Neurology, 6* (Supplement): s42-s48.

Denckla, M.B. (1996a). Biological correlates of learning and attention: What is relevant to learning disability and attention-deficit hyperactivity disorder? *Developmental and Behavioral Pediatrics, 17*(2), 114-119.

Denckla, M.B. (1996b). Neuropsychological perspective on executive function. In G. R. Lyon & N.A. Krasnegor (Eds.), *Attention, memory and executive functions* (pp. 263-278). Baltimore: Brookes.

Denckla, M.B., & Rudel, R.G. (1976). Rapid automatized naming (R.A.N.): Dyslexia differentiated from other learning disabilities. *Neuropsychologia, 14,* 471-479.

Dennett, D.C. (1991). *Consciousness explained*. Boston: Little, Brown.

Deno, S.L., Marston, D., & Mirkin, P. (1982). Valid measurement procedures for continuous evaluation of written expression. *Exceptional Children, 48*(4), 368-371.

Derryberry, D., & Reed, M.A. (1996). Regulatory processes and the development of cognitive representations. *Development and Psychopathology, 8*(1), 215-234.

Deshler, D.D., Alley, G.R., Warner, M.M., & Schumaker, J.B. (1981). Instructional practices for promoting skill acquisition and generalization in severely learning disabled adolescents. *Learning Disabilities Quarterly, 4*(4), 415-421.

Deshler, D.D., Ferrell, W.R., & Kass, C.E. (1978). Monitoring of schoolwork errors by LD adolescents. *Journal of Learning Disabilities, 11*(7), 10-23.

Diamond, A. (1985). Development of the ability to use recall to guide action, as indicated by infants' performance on AB. *Child Development, 56,* 868-883.

Diamond, A., Zola-Morgan, S., & Squire, L.R. (1989). Successful performance by monkeys with lesions of the hippocampal formation on AB and object retrieval, two tasks that mark developmental changes in human infants. *Behavioral Neuroscience, 103*(3), 526-537.

Doehring, D.G. (1976). Acquisition of rapid reading responses. *Monograph of the Society for Research in Child Development, 41.*

Donnelly, M., Zametkin, A.J., Rapoport, J.L. (1986). Treatment of hyperactivity with desipramine: Plasma drug concentrations, cardiovascular effects, plasma and urinary catecholamine levels and clinical response. *Clinical Pharmacological Therapy, 39,* 72-81.

Douglas, V.I. (1972). Stop, look, and listen: The problem of sustained attention and impulse control in hyperactive and normal children. *Canadian Journal of Behavioural Science, 4,* 259-282.

Douglas, V.I. (1980). Treatment and training approaches to hyperactivity: Establishing internal or external control. In C.K. Whalen & B. Henker (Eds.), *Hyperactive children: The social ecology of identification and treatment* (pp. 283-317). New York: Academic Press.

Douglas, V.I., Barr, R.G., Desilets, J., & Sherman, E. (1995). Do high doses of stimulants impair flexible thinking in attention-deficit disorders? *Journal of the American Academy of Child and Adolescent Psychiatry, 34*(7), 877-885.

Douglas, V.I., Barr, R.G., O'Neill, M.E., & Britton, B.G. (1988). Dosage effects and individual responsivity to methylphenidate in attention deficit disorder. *Journal of Child Psychology and Psychiatry, 29*, 453-475.

Douglas, V.I., & Peters, K.G. (1979). Toward a clearer definition of the attentional deficit of hyperactive children. In G.A. Hale & M. Lewis (Eds.), *Attention and the development of cognitive skills* (pp. 173-248). New York: Plenum.

Downing, J., Coughlin, R.M., & Rich, G. (1986). Children's inventive spellings in the classroom. *The Elementary School Journal, 86*, 295-303.

Downings, J. (1979). *Reading and reasoning*. New York: Springer-Verlag.

Dweck, C. (1987). *Children's theories of intelligence: Implications for motivation and learning*. Invited address, AERA Annual Meeting, Washington, D.C.

Dykman, R.A., Ackerman, P.T., Clements, S.D., & Peters, J.E. (1971). Specific learning disabilities: An attention deficit syndrome. In H.R. Myklebust (Ed.), *Progress in learning disorders* (pp. 56-98). New York: Grune & Stratton.

Dyme, I.Z., Sahakian, B.J., Golinko, B.E., & Rabe, E.F. (1982). Perseveration induced by methylphenidate in children: preliminary findings. *Progress in Neurological Psychopharmacology & Biological Psychiatry, 6*, 269-273.

Edelman, G.M. (1992). *Bright air, brilliant fire: On the matter of the mind*. New York: Basic Books.

Ehri, L. (1989). The development of spelling knowledge and its role in reading acquisition and reading disability. *Journal of Learning Disabilities, 22*, 356-365.

Ehri, L., & Wilce, L.S. (1983). Development of word development and word identification speed in skilled and less skilled beginning readers. *Journal of Educational Psychology, 75*, 3-18.

Englert, C.S. (1992). Writing instruction from a sociocultural perspective: The holistic, dialogic, and social enterprise of writing. *Journal of Learning Disabilities, 25*, 153-172.

Englert, C.S., & Hiebert, E.H. (1984). Children's developing awareness of text structures in expository materials. *Journal of Educational Psychology, 76*, 65-75.

Englert, C.S., & Palincsar, A.S. (1991). Reconsidering instructional research in literacy from a sociocultural perspective. *Learning Disabilities Research & Practice, 6*, 225-229.

Englert, C.S., & Raphael, T.E. (1988). Constructing well-formed prose: Process, structure, and metacognitive knowledge. *Exceptional Children, 54*(6), 513-520.

Englert, C.S., Raphael, T.E., Anderson, L.M., Gregg, S.L., & Anthony, H.M. (1989). Exposition: Reading, writing, and the metacognitive knowledge of learning disabled students. *Learning Disabilities Research, 5*(1), 5-24.

Englert, C.S., Raphael, T.E., Fear, K.L., & Anderson, L.M. (1988). Students' metacognitive knowledge about how to write informational texts. *Learning Disabilities Quarterly, 11*, 18-46.

Englert, C.S., & Thomas, C.C. (1987). Sensitivity to text structures in reading and writing: A comparison of learning disabled and non-learning disabled students. *Learning Disabled Quarterly, 10*, 93-105.

Epstein, M.A., Shaywitz, S.E., Shaywitz, B.E., & Woolston, J.L. (1991). Boundaries of attention deficit disorder. *Journal of Learning Disabilities, 31*, 262-270.

Espin, C.A., & Sindelar, P.T. (1988). Auditory feedback and writing: Learning disabled and nondisabled students. *Exceptional Children, 55*(1), 45-51.

Eysenck, M.W. (1982). *Attention and arousal: Cognition and performance*. Heidelberg: Springer-Verlag.

Fagan, J. (1982). Infant memory. In T. Field, A. Huston, H. Quay, L. Troll, & G. Finley (Eds.), *Review of Human Development*, (pp. 79-92). New York: Wiley and Sons.

Faigley, L., & Witte, S. (1981). Analyzing revision. *College Composition and Communication, 32*, 400-414.

Feingold, B. (1975). *Why your child is hyperactive*. New York: Random House.

Fitzgerald, J. (1987). Research on revision in writing. *Review of Educational Research, 57*, 481-506.

Fitzgerald, J., & Spiegel, D.L. (1986). Textual cohesion and coherence in children's writing. *Research in the Teaching of English, 20*, 263-280.

Flavell, J.H. (1985). *Cognitive development*. Englewood Cliffs, NJ: Prentice Hall.

Flower, L.S., & Hayes, J.R. (1980). The dynamics of composing: Making plans and juggling constraints. In L.W. Gregg & E.R. Steinberg (Eds.), *Cognitive processes in writing* (pp.31-50). Hillsdale, NJ: Erlbaum.

Flower, L., & Hayes, J.R. (1981). A cognitive process theory of writing. *College Composition and Communication, 35*, 365-387.

Fodor, J. (1983). *The modularity of mind*. Cambridge, MA: MIT Press.

Foley, G., & Hobin, M. (1981). *Attachment-Separation-Individuation Scale*. Reading, PA: Albright College.

Foley, M.A., Passalacqua, C., & Ratner, H. (1993). Appropriating the actions of another: Implications for children's memory and learning. *Cognitive Development, 8*, 373-401.

Forness, S.R., Cantwell, D.P., Swanson, J., Hanna, G., & Yonpa, D. (1991). Differential effects of stimulant medication on reading performance of boys with hyperactivity with and without conduct disorder. *Journal of Learning Disabilities, 24*(5), 304-310.

Freud, S. (1965). *The interpretation of dreams*. New York: Avon Books.

Fuster, J. (1989). *The prefrontal cortex*. New York: Raven.

Gammon, G.D., & Brown, T.E. (1993). Fluoxetine and methylphenidate in combination for treatment of ADD and Comorbid Depressive Disorder. *Journal of Child and Adolescent Psychopharmacology, 3*(1), 1-10.

Garfinkel, B.D., & Wender, P.H. (1989). In H.I. Kaplan & B.J. Saddock (Eds.), *Textbook of comprehensive psychiatry* (Vol. V, p. 1828). Baltimore: Williams & Wilkins.

Geary, D. (1990). A componential analysis of an early learning deficit in mathematics. *Journal of Experimental Child Psychology, 49*, 363-383.

Geary, D. (1993). Mathematical disabilities: Cognitive, neuropsychological, and genetic components. *Psychological Bulletin, 114*(2), 345-362.

Gell-Mann, M. (1994). *The quark and the jaguar*. New York: Freeman.

Gentry, J.R. (1984). Developmental aspects of learning to spell. *Academic Therapy, 20*, 11-19.

Gibson, J.J. (1979). *The ecological approach to visual perception*. Boston: Houghton Mifflin.

Goldman-Rakic, P.S. (1992). Working memory and the mind. *Scientific American, 267*(3), 110-117.

Goldstein, K. (1936). Modification of behavior consequent to cerebral lesion. *Psychiatric Quarterly, 10*, 539-610.

Goldstein, S., & Goldstein, M. (1990). *Managing attention disorders in children: A guide for practitioners*. New York: Wiley.

Goodman, R., & Stevenson, J. (1989). A twin study of hyperactivity: II. The aetiological role of genes, family relationships, and perinatal adversity. *Journal of Child Psychology and Psychiatry, 30*, 691-709.

Gough, P., Ehri, L.C., & Treiman, R. (1992). *Reading acquisition*. Hillsdale, NJ: Erlbaum.

Gough, P.B., & Walsh, M.A. (1991). Chinese, Phoenicians and the orthographic cipher of English. In S. Brady & D. Shankweiler (Eds.), *Phonological Processing in Literacy, A Tribute to Isabelle Y. Liberman* (pp. 199-210). Hillsdale, NJ: Erlbaum.

Gould, J. (1980). Experiments on composing letters: Some facts, some myths, and some observations. In L.W. Gregg & E.R. Steinberg (Eds.), *Cognitive processes in writing* (pp. 97-127). Hillsdale, NJ: Erlbaum.

Graham, S. (1989, April). *The role of production factors in learning disabled students' compositions*. Paper presented at the Annual Meeting of the American Educational Research Association, San Francisco.

Graham, S. (1990). The role of production factors in learning disabled students' compositions. *Journal of Educational Psychology, 82*, 781-791.

Graham, S., Boyer-Schick, K., & Tippets, E. (1989). The validity of the handwriting scale from the Test of Written Language. *Journal of Educational Research, 82*, 166-171.

Graham, S., & Harris, K.R. (1988). Instructional recommendations for teaching writing to exceptional students. *Exceptional Children, 54*, 506-512.

Graham, S., & Harris, K.R. (1989a). Components analysis of cognitive strategy instruction: Effects on learning disabled students' compositions and self efficacy. *Journal of Educational Psychology, 81*(3), 353-361.

Graham, S., & Harris, K.R. (1989b). Improving learning disabled students' skills at composing essays: Self-instructional strategy training. *Exceptional Children, 56*(3), 201-214.

Graham, S., Harris, K.R., MacArthur, C.A., & Schwartz, S. (1991). Writing and writing instruction for students with learning disabilities: Review of a research program. *Learning Disabilities Quarterly, 14,* 89-114.

Graham, S., & MacArthur, C. (1988). Improving learning disabled students' skills at revision essays produced on a word processor: Self-instructional strategy training. *The Journal of Special Education, 22*(2), 133-152.

Grattan, L.M., & Eslinger, P.J. (1991). Frontal lobe damage in children and adults: A comparative review. *Developmental Neuropsychology, 7*(3), 283-326.

Grattan, L.M., Eslinger, P.J., Damasio, A., & Damasio, H. (1989). Cognitive developmental study of childhood frontal lobe lesion. *The Clinical Neuropsychologist, 3,* 287.

Graves, D.H. (1983). *Writing: Teachers and children at work.* Exeter, NH: Heinemann Educational Books.

Gray, J.A. (1987). *The psychology of fear and stress.* Cambridge, England: Cambridge University Press.

Greenberg, K. (1987). Defining, teaching, and testing basic writing competence. *Topics in Language Disorders, 7,* 31-41.

Greenhill, L.L. (1992). Pharmacotherapy: Stimulants. In G. Weiss (Ed.), *Child and adolescent psychiatry clinics of North America,* Vol. 1 (pp. 411-447). Philadelphia: Saunders.

Greenhill, L.L., Abikoff, H.A., Arnold, L.E., Cantwell, D.P., Conners, C.K., Elliott, G., Hechtman, L., Hinshaw, S.P., Hoza, B., Jensen, P., March, J.S., Newcorn, J., Pelham, W., Severe, J.B., Swanson, J., Vitiello, B., & Wells, K. (1996). Medication treatment strategies in the MTA study: Relevance to clinicians and researchers. *Journal of the American Academy of Child and Adolescent Psychiatry, 35*(10), 1304-1313.

Gregg, S., Raphael, T.E., & Englert, C.S. (1987, April). *The expository writing and reading performance of regular and special education students.* Paper presented at the Annual Meeting of the American Educational Research Association, Washington, D.C.

Gross-Tsur, V., Shalev, R.S., Manor, O., & Amir, N. (1995). Developmental right-hemisphere syndrome: Clinical spectrum of the nonverbal learning disability. *Journal of Learning Disabilities, 28*(2), 80-86.

Haenlein, M., & Caul, W.F. (1987). Attention Deficit Disorder with Hyperactivity: A specific hypothesis of reward dysfunction. *Journal of the American Academy of Child and Adolescent Psychiatry,* 356-362.

Halliday, M.A.K., & Hasan, R. (1976). *Cohesion in English.* London: Longman.

Hallowell, E.M., & Ratey, J.J. (1994). *Driven to distraction.* New York: Pantheon Books.

Hanson, C.L. (1978). Story retelling with average and learning disabled readers as a measure of reading comprehension. *Learning Disabilities Quarterly, 1,* 62-69.

Hardy, B.W., McIntyre, C.W., Brown, A.S., & North, A.J. (1989). Visual and auditory confusability in students with and without learning disabilities. *Journal of Learning Disabilities, 22,* 646-651.

Harris, K.R. (1986). Self-monitoring of attentional behavior versus self-monitoring of productivity: Effects on on-task behavior and academic response rate among learning disabled children. *Journal of Applied Behavior Analysis, 19,* 417-423.

Hartje, W. (1987). The effect of spatial disorders on arithmetic skills. In G. Deloche & X. Seron (Eds.), *Mathematical disabilities: A cognitive neuropsychological perspective* (pp. 121-136). Hillsdale, NJ: Erlbaum.

Hayes, J.R., & Flower, L.S. (1980). Identifying the organization of writing processes. In L.W. Gregg & E.R. Steinberg (Eds.), *Cognitive processes in writing* (pp. 3-30). Hillsdale, NJ: Erlbaum.

Hayes, J.R., & Flower, L.S. (1983). *A cognitive model of the writing process in adults: Final report.* (ERIC Document Reproduction Service No. ED 240 608). Pittsburgh, PA: Carnegie Mellon University.

Hayes, J.R., & Flower, L.S. (1986). Writing research and the writer. *American Psychologist, 41*(10), 1106-1113.

Hayes-Roth, B. (1977, March). *Structurally integrated versus structurally memory representations: Implications for the design of instructional materials* (Rand Paper P-5841). Santa Monica, CA.

Hebb, D. (1949). *The organization of behavior: A neuropsychological theory.* New York: Wiley.

Heilman, K.M., Voeller, K.K.S., & Nadeau, S.E. (1991). A possible pathophysiologic substrate of attention deficit disorder. *Journal of Child Neurology, 6* (Supplement), s74-s79.

Hess, R.D., & Shipman, V. (1965). Early experience and the socialization of cognitive modes in children. *Child Development, 36,* 869-886.

Hidi, S., & Hildyard, A. (1983). The comparison of oral and written productions of two discourse types. *Discourse Processes, 6,* 91-105.

Hiebert, E.H., Englert, C.S., & Brennan, S. (1983). Awareness of text structure in recognizing and producing expository discourse. *Journal of Reading Behavior, 15*(4), 63-80.

Hillocks, G. (1986). *Research on written composition: New directions for teaching.* Urbana, IL: National Conference for Research in English.

Hinshaw, S.P. (1987). On the distinction between attentional deficits/hyperactivity and conduct problems/aggression in child psychopathology. *Psychological Bulletin, 101,* 443-463.

Hinshaw, S.P., Henker, B, & Whalen, C.K. (1984). Cognitive-behavioral and pharmacological interventions for hyperactive boys: comparative and combined effects. *Journal of Consulting and Clinical Psychology, 12,* 55-77.

Hobson, J.A. (1994). *The chemistry of conscious states.* Boston: Little, Brown.

Hockey, R. (1984). Varieties of attentional states: The effects of environment. In R. Parasuraman & D.R. Davies (Eds.), *Varieties of attention.* New York: Academic Press.

Høeg, P. (1994). *Borderliners.* New York: Bantam Doubleday Dell.

Hofstadter, D. (1979). *Gödel, Escher, Bach: An eternal golden braid.* New York: Basic Books.

Hofstadter, D. (1985). *Metamagical themas.* New York: Basic Books.

Hofstadter, D. (1995). *Fluid concepts and creative analogies.* New York: Basic Books.

Hohman, L.B. (1922). Post-encephalitic behavior disorder in children. *John Hopkins Hospital Bulletin, 33,* 372-375.

Houck, C.K., & Billingsly, B.S. (1989). Written expression of students with and without learning disabilities: Differences across the grades. *Journal of Learning Disabilities, 22*(9), 561-567, 572.

Huessy, H.R. (1974). The adult hyperkinetic (letter). *American Journal of Psychiatry, 131,* 724-725.

Huessy, H., & Wright, A.I. (1970). The use of imipramine in children's behavioral disorders. *Acta Paedopsychiatry, 37,* 194-199.

Humes, A. (1983). Research on the composing process. *Review of Educational Research, 53,* 201-216.

Individuals with Disabilities Education Act (1990). *20 United States Code* (Sections 1400-1485). Washington, DC: U.S. Government Press.

Isaacson, S. (1989). Role of secretary vs. author: Resolving the conflict in writing instruction. *Learning Disabilities Quarterly, 12,* 209-217.

Isaacson, S. (1992). Volleyball and other analogies: A response to Englert. *Journal of Learning Disabilities, 25*(3), 173-177.

Isaacson, S., & Mattoon, C.B. (1990). The effect of goal constraints on the writing performance of urban learning disabled students. *Learning Disabilities Research, 5*(2), 94-99.

Iverson, S., & Tunmer, W. (1993). Phonological processing skills and the Reading Recovery Program. *Journal of Educational Psychology, 83,* 112-126.

James, W. (1902). *The principles of psychology.* New York: Henry Holt & Co.

Johnson, D.J., & Grant, J.O. (1989). Written narratives of normal and learning disabled children. *Annals of Dyslexia, 39,* 140-158.

Johnson-Laird, P.N. (1983). The coherence of discourse. *Mental models: Towards a cognitive science of language, inference, and consciousness.* Cambridge, MA: Harvard University Press.

Johnson-Laird, P.N. (1985). Logical thinking: Does it occur in daily life? Can it be taught? In S. Chipman, J. Segal, & R. Glaser (Eds.). *Thinking and Learning Skills* (Vol. 2, pp. 293-318). Hillsdale, NJ: Erlbaum.

Kahneman, P. (1973). *Attention and effort.* Englewood Cliffs, NJ: Prentice-Hall.

Kail, R. (1992). Processing speed, speech rate, and memory. *Developmental Psychology, 28,* 899-904.

Karmel, B.Z., Gardner, J.M., & Magnano, C.L. (1991). Attention and arousal in infancy. In M.J.S. Weiss & P.R. Zelazo (Eds.), *Newborn attention, biological constraints and the influence of experience* (pp. 339-376). Norwood, NJ: Ablex.

Kaufer, D., Hayes, J., & Flower, L. (1986). Composing written sentences. *Research in the Teaching of English, 20,* 121-140.

Kaufman, A., & Kaufman, N.L. (1985). *Assessment Battery for Children.* Circle Pines, MN: American Guidance Service.

Kaye, K. (1982). Organism, apprentice and person. In E.Z. Tronick (Ed.), *Social interchange in infancy.* Baltimore: University Park Press.

Kendall, P.C., & Braswell, L. (1982). Cognitive-behavioral self-control therapy for children: A components analysis. *Journal of Consulting and Clinical Psychology, 50,* 672-689.

Kendall, P.C., & Wilcox, L.E. (1980). Cognitive-behavioral treatment for impulsivity: concrete versus conceptual training in non-self-controlled problem children. *Journal of Consulting and Clinical Psychology, 48*(1), 80-91.

King, M.L., & Rentel, V.M. (1981). Research update: Conveying meaning in written texts. *Language Arts, 58,* 721-728.

Kinsbourne, M. (1990). Overfocusing: An apparent subtype of Attention Deficit-Hyperactivity Disorder. *Pediatric Adolescent Medicine, 12*(44), 1-18.

Kleiman, G.M. (1975). Speech recoding in reading. *Journal of Verbal Learning and Verbal Behavior, 14,* 323-339.

Klorman, R., Brumaghim, J.T., Salzman, L.F., Strauss, J., Borgstedt, A.D., McBride, M.C., & Loeb, S. (1990). Effects of methylphenidate on processing negativities in patients with Attention-Deficit Hyperactivity Disorder. *Psychophysiology, 27,* 328-337.

LaBerge, D., & Samuels, S.J. (1974). Toward a theory of automatic information processing in writing. *Cognitive Psychology, 6,* 293-323.

Lahey, B.B., Pelham, W.E., Schaughency, E.A., Atkins, M.S., Murphy, H.A., Hynd, G.W., Russo, M., Hartdagen, S., & Lorys-Vernon, A. (1988). Dimensions and types of attention deficit disorder with hyperactivity in children: A factor and cluster analytic approach. *Journal of the American Academy of Child and Adolescent Psychiatry, 27,* 330-335.

Lahey, B.B., Piacentini, J.C., McBurnett, K., Stone, P., Hartdagen, S., & Hynd, G. (1988). Psychopathology in the parents of children with conduct disorder and hyperactivity. *Journal of the American Academy of Child and Adolescent Psychiatry, 27,* 163-170.

Landau, S., & Milich, R. (1988). Social communication patterns of attention deficit disordered boys. *Journal of Abnormal Child Psychology, 16,* 69-81.

Laufer, M.W. (1967). Brain disorders. In A.M. Friedman & H.I. Kaplan (Eds.), *Textbook of modern psychiatry* (pp. 1442-1452). Baltimore: Williams & Wilkens.

Laufer, M., & Denhoff, E. (1957). Hyperkinetic behavior syndrome in children. *Journal of Pediatrics, 50,* 463-474.

Laughton, J., & Morris, N.T. (1989). Story grammar knowledge of learning disabled students. *Learning Disabilities Research, 4*(2), 87-95.

Lave, J. (1988, May). *The culture of acquisition and the practice of understanding* (Report No. IRL 88-0007). Palo Alto, CA: Institute for Research of Learning.

Lesgold, A.M., & Resnick, L.B. (1982). How reading difficulties develop: Perspectives from a longitudinal study. In J.P. Das, R.F. Mulcahy, & A.E. Wall (Eds.), *Theory and research in learning disabilities* (pp. 155-187). New York: Plenum.

Leventhal, D. (1990). *Developmental neurobiology.* Paper presented at the American Academy of Child and Adolescent Psychiatry Fifteenth Annual Conference, Chicago, Illinois.

Levin, P.M. (1938). Restlessness in children. *Archives of Neurology and Psychiatry, 39,* 764-770.

Levine, D.F. (1989). Neural network principles for theoretical psychology. *Behavior Research Methods Instruments and Computers, 21*(2), 213-224.

Lezak, M. (1983). *Neuropsychological assessment.* New York: Oxford University Press.

Liberman, A.M., Cooper, F.S., Shankweiler, D.P., & Studdert-Kennedy, M. (1967). Perception of the speech code. *Psychological Review, 74,* 431-461.

Liberman, I., & Shankweiler, D. (1987). Phonology and the problems in learning to read and write. In H.L. Swanson (Ed.), *Memory and learning disability* (pp. 203-224). Greenwich, CT: JAI Press.

Liles, B.Z. (1985). Cohesion in the narratives of normal and language disordered children. *Journal of Speech and Hearing Research, 28,* 123-133.

Lou, H.C., Henriksen, L., & Bruhn, P. (1984). Focal cerebral hypoperfusion in children with dysphasia and/or Attention Deficit Disorder. *Archives of Neurology, 41,* 825-829.

Lou, H.C., Henriksen, L., Bruhn, P., Borner, H., & Nielsen, J.B. (1989). Striatal dysfunction in attention deficit and hyperkinetic disorder. *Archives of Neurology, 46,* 48-52.

Luria, A.R. (1966). *The higher cortical functions in man.* New York: Basic Books.

MacArthur, C.A. (1988). The impact of computers on the writing process. *Exceptional Children, 54,* 536-542.

MacArthur, C.A. (1996). Using technology to enhance the writing processes of students with learning disabilities. *Journal of Learning Disabilities, 29*(4), 344-354.

MacArthur, C.A., & Graham, S. (1987). Learning disabled students' composing under three methods of text production: Handwriting, word processing, and dictation. *Journal of Special Education*, *21*(3), 22-42.

MacArthur, C.A., Graham, S., & Schwartz, S. (1991). Knowledge of revision and revising behavior among learning disabled students. *Learning Disabilities Quarterly*, *14*, 61-73.

MacArthur, C.A., Graham, S., & Skarvoed, J. (1986). *Learning disabled students' composing with three methods: Handwriting, dictation, and word processing*. (Tech. Rep. No. 109). College Park, MD: Institute for the Study of Exceptional Children and Youth.

Mahler, M.S. (1979). *The selected papers of Margaret S. Mahler*. New York: Jason Aronson.

Markham, L.R. (1976). Influences of handwriting quality on teacher evaluation of written work. *American Educational Research Journal*, *13*, 277-283.

Mash, E.J., & Johnston, C. (1983). Sibling interactions of hyperactive and normal children and their relationship to reports of maternal stress and self-esteem. *Journal of Clinical Child Psychology*, *12*, 91-99.

Mayron, L.M., Ott, J.N., Nations, R., & Mayron, E.L. (1974). Light, radiation, and academic behavior: Initial studies on the effects of full-spectrum lighting and radiation shielding on behavior and academic performance of school children. *Academic Therapy*, *10*, 33-47.

McCutchen, D. (1984). Writing as a linguistic problem. *Educational Psychologist*, *19*, 226-238.

McCutchen, D. (1988). "Functional automaticity" in children's writing. A problem of metacognitive control. *Written Communication*, *5*(3), 306-324.

McCutchen, D., & Perfetti, C.A. (1982). Coherence and connectedness in the development of discourse production. *Text*, *2*, 113-139.

McCutchen, D., Perfetti, C.A., & Basick, C. (1983, April). *Young writers' sensitivity to local coherence*. Paper presented at the meeting of the American Educational Research Association, Montreal.

McEvoy, R., Rogers, S., & Pennington, R. (1993). Executive function and social communication deficits in young, autistic children. *Journal of Child Psychology and Psychiatry*, *34*, 563-578.

McGuiness, D., & Pribram, K. (1980). The neuropsychology of attention: Emotional and motivational controls. In W.C. Wittrock (Ed.), *The brain and psychology* (pp 93-139). New York: Academic Press.

Meichenbaum, D., & Goodman, J. (1971). Training impulsive children to talk to themselves: A means of developing self-control. *Journal of Abnormal Psychology*, *77*, 115-126.

Meldman, M.J. (1970). *Diseases of attention and perception*. Oxford, England: Pergamon Press.

Meltzer, L., Fenton, T., Ogonowski, M., & Malkus, K. (1988, April). *Automaticity, cognitive strategies, and academic achievement in students with and without learning disabilities*. Paper presented at the annual meeting of The American Educational Research Association, New Orleans, LA.

Mesulam, M.M. (1981). A cortical network for directed attention and unilateral neglect. *Annals of Neurology*, *10*(4), 309-325.

Mesulam, M.M. (1990). Large-scale neurocognitive networks and distributed processing for attention, language, and memory. *Annals of Neurology*, *28*, 597-613.

Meyer, A. (1904). The anatomical facts and clinical varieties of traumatic insanity. *American Journal of Insanity*, *60*, 373-441.

Meyer, E., & Byers, R.K. (1952). Measles encephalitis: A follow-up study of sixteen patients. *American Journal of Diseases of Children*, *84*, 543-579.

Miller, G.A. (1956). The magical number seven, plus or minus two: Some limitations on our capacity for processing information. *Psychological Review*, *63*, 81-87.

Mirsky, A.F., Anthony, B.J., Duncan, C.C., Ahearn, M.B., & Kellam, S.G. (1991). Analysis of elements of attention: A neuropsychological approach. *Neuropsychology Review*, *2*(2), 109-145.

Montague, M., Graves, A., & Leavell, A. (1991). Planning, procedural facilitation, and narrative composition of junior high students with learning disabilities. *Learning Disabilities Research & Practice*, *6*, 219-224.

Montague, M., Maddux, C.D., & Dereshiwsky, M.I. (1990). Story grammar and comprehension and production of narrative prose by students with learning disabilities. *Journal of Learning Disabilities*, *23*(2), 190-197.

Moran, M.R. (1981). Performance of learning disabled and low achieving secondary students on formal features of a paragraph-writing task. *Learning Disabilities Quarterly, 4,* 271-280.

Morocco, C.C., & Newman, S.B. (1986). Word processors and the acquisition of writing strategies. *Journal of Learning Disabilities, 19,* 243-247.

Morris, N.T., & Crump, W.D. (1982). Syntactic and vocabulary development in the written language of learning disabled and non-learning disabled students at four age levels. *Learning Disabilities Quarterly, 5,* 163-172.

Mundy, P. (1995). Joint attention in autism. *Developmental Psychopathology, 7*(1), 63-82.

Murphy, L. (1962). *The widening world of childhood: Paths toward mastery.* New York: Basic Books.

Navon, D., & Gopher, D. (1979). On the economy of the human processing system. *Psychological Review, 86,* 214-255.

Nelson, N.W. (1995). Scaffolding in the secondary school: A tool for curriculum-based language intervention. In D.F. Tibbits (Ed.), *Language disabilities beyond the primary grades* (pp. 377-421). Austin, TX: PRO-ED.

Newcomer, P.L., Barenbaum, E.M., & Nodine, B.F. (1988). Comparison of the story production of LD, normal-achieving, and low-achieving children under two modes of production. *Learning Disabilities Quarterly, 11,* 82-96.

Nichols, P.L., & Chen, T.C. (1981). *Minimal brain dysfunction: A prospective study.* Hillsdale, NJ: Erlbaum.

Nicolis, G., & Prigogine, I. (1989). *Exploring complexity.* New York: Freeman and Co.

Nigg, J.T., Swanson, J., & Hinshaw, S.P. (1993). *Posner individual orienting task with ADHD children.* Paper presented at S.R.C.A.P.

Nodine, B.F., Barenbaum, E., & Newcomer, P. (1985). Story composition by learning disabled, reading disabled, and normal children. *Learning Disabilities Quarterly, 8,* 167-179.

O'Connor, M., Foch, T., Sherry, T., & Plomin, R. (1980). A twin study of specific behavioral problems of socialization as viewed by parents. *Journal of Abnormal Child Psychology, 8,* 189-199.

O'Leary, K.D., Rosenbaum, A., & Hughes, P.C. (1978). Fluorescent lighting: A purported source of hyperactive behavior. *Journal of Abnormal Child Psychology, 6,* 285-289.

Parmalee, A.H. (1989). The child's physical health and the development of relationships. In A.J. Sameroff & R.N. Emde (Eds.), *Relationship disturbances in early childhood: A developmental approach* (pp 76-91). New York: Basic Books.

Pauls, D.L., Leckman, J.F., & Cohen, D.J. (1993). Familial relationship between Gilles de la Tourette's Syndrome, attention deficit disorder, learning disabilities, speech disorders, and stuttering. *Journal of the American Academy of Child and Adolescent Psychiatry, 32*(5), 1044-1050.

Pelham, W.E., & Bender, M.E. (1982). Peer relationships in hyperactive children: Description and treatment. In K.D. Gadow & I. Bialer (Eds.)., *Advances in learning and behavioral disabilities* (Vol. 1, pp. 365-436). Greenwich, CT: JAI Press.

Pelham, W.E., McBurnett, K., Harper, G.W., Milich, R., Murphy, D.A., Clinton, J., & Thiele, C. (1990). Methylphenidate and baseball playing in ADHD children: Who's on first? *Journal of Consulting and Clinical Psychology, 58* (1), 130-133.

Pelligrino, J.W., & Goldman, S.R. (1987). Information processing and elementary mathematics. *Journal of Learning Disabilities, 20,* 23-32.

Penrose, R. (1990). *The emperor's new mind.* Oxford, England: Oxford University Press.

Perfetti, C.A., & Lesgold, A.M. (1977). Discourse comprehension and sources of individual differences. In M.A. Just & P.A. Carpenter (Eds.), *Cognitive processes in comprehension* (pp. 141-183). Hillsdale, NJ: Erlbaum.

Perfetti, C.A., & Lesgold, A.M. (1979). Coding and comprehension in skilled reading and implications for reading instruction. In L.B. Resnick & P.A. Weaver (Eds.), *Theory and practice in early reading* (Vol. 1, pp. 57-84). Hillsdale, NJ: Erlbaum.

Perfetti, C.A., & Roth, S.F. (1981). Some of the interactive processes in reading and their role in reading skill. In A.M. Lesgold & C.A. Perfetti (Eds.), *Interactive processes in reading* (pp. 269-297). Hillsdale, NJ: Erlbaum.

Piaget, J., & Inhelder, B. (1969). *The psychology of the child.* New York: Basic Books.

Pinker, S. (1994). *The language instinct.* New York: William Morrow.

Pliszka, S.R., McCracken, J.T., & Maas, J.W. (1996). Catecholamines in Attention-Deficit Hyperactivity Disorder: Current perspectives. *Journal of the American Academy of Child and Adolescent Psychiatry, 35*(3), 264-272.

Poplin, M.S., Gray, R., Larsen, S., Banikowski, A., & Mehring, T. (1980). A comparison of components of written expression abilities in learning disabled and non-learning disabled students at three grade levels. *Learning Disabilities Quarterly, 3*(4), 46-53.

Popper, C.W., & Elliot, G.R. (1990). Sudden death and tricyclic antidepressants: Clinical considerations for children. *Journal of Child and Adolescent Psychopharmacology, 1*, 125-132.

Porges, S.W. (1983). Heart rate patterns in neonates: A potential diagnostic window to the brain. In T. Field (Ed.), *Infants born at risk* (pp. 3-22). New York: Grune & Stratton.

Porrino, L.J., Esposito, R.U., Seeger, T.F., Crane, A.M., Pert, A., & Sokoloff, L. (1984). Metabolic mapping of the brain during rewarding self-stimulation. *Science, 224*, 306-309.

Posner, M. I. (1978). *Chronometric explorations of mind.* Hillsdale, NJ: Erlbaum.

Poteet, J.A. (1978). Characteristics of written expression of learning disabled and non-learning disabled elementary school students. *Diagnostique, 4*, 60-74.

Price, B.H., Daffner, K.R., Stowe, R.M., & Mesulam, M.M. (1990). The comportmental learning disabilities of early frontal lobe damage. *Brain, 113*, 1383-1393.

Rafal, R., & Henik, A. (1994). The neurology of inhibition: Integrating controlled and automatic processes. In D. Dagenbach & T.H. Carr (Eds.), *Inhibitory processes in attention, memory and language* (pp. 1-52). New York: Academic Press.

Raphael, T.E., Englert, C.S., & Kirschner, B.W. (1986). *The impact of text structure instruction and social context on students' comprehension and production of expository text.* (Research Series No. 177). East Lansing, MI: Michigan State University, Institute for Research on Teaching.

Rapport, M.D., Carlson, G.A., Kelly, K.L., & Pataki, C. (1993). Methylphenidate and desipramine in hospitalized children: I. Separate and combined effects on cognitive function. *Journal of the American Academy of Child and Adolescent Psychiatry, 32*(2), 333-342.

Rapport, M.D., Denney, C., DuPaul, G.J., & Gradner, M. (1994). Attention Deficit Disorder and methylphenidate: Normalization rates, clinical effectiveness, and response prediction in 76 children. *Journal of the American Academy of Child and Adolescent Psychiatry, 33*(6), 882-893.

Rapport, M.D., Stoner, G., DuPaul, G.J., Birmingham, B.K., & Tucker, S. (1985). Methylphenidate in hyperactive children: Differential effects of dose on academic, learning and social behavior. *Journal of Abnormal Psychology, 13*, 227-244.

Reader, M.J., Harris, E.L., Schuerholz, L.I., & Denckla, M.B. (1994). Attention Deficit Hyperactivity Disorder and executive dysfunction. *Developmental Neuropsychology, 10*(4), 493-512.

Rentel, V., & King, M. (1983). Present at the beginning. In P. Mosenthal, L. Tamor, & S.A. Walmsley (Eds.), *Research on writing: Principles and methods* (pp. 139-376). New York: Longman.

Reynolds, C.J., Hill, D.S., Swassing, R.H., & Ward, M.E. (1988). The effects of revision strategy instruction on the writing performance of students with learning disabilities. *Journal of Learning Disabilities, 21*(9), 540-545.

Richards, G.P., Samuels, S.J., Turnure, J.E., & Ysseldyke, J.E. (1990). Sustained and selective attention in children with learning disabilities. *Journal of Learning Disabilities, 23*, 129-136.

Richardson, E., Kupietz, S.S., Winsberg, B.G., Maitinsky, S., & Mendell, N. (1988). Effects of methylphenidate dosage in hyperactive reading-disabled children: Reading achievement. *Journal of the American Academy of Child and Adolescent Psychiatry, 27*(1), 78-87.

Risser, M.G., & Bowers, T.G. (1993). Cognitive and neuropsychological characteristics of attention deficit hyperactivity disorder children receiving stimulant medications. *Perceptual and Motor Skills, 77*, 1023-1031.

Robbins, J.W. (1984). Cortical noradrenaline, attention and arousal. *Psychological Medicine, 14*, 13-21.

Rogeness, G.A., Javors, M.A., & Pliszka, S.R. (1992). Neurochemistry, child and adolescent psychiatry. *Journal of the American Academy of Child and Adolescent Psychiatry, 31*(5), 765-781.

Rogoff, B. (1990). *Apprenticeship in thinking.* New York: Oxford.

Rosch, E. (1977). Classification of Real-World objects: Origins and representations in cognition. In P.N. Johnson-Laird and P.C. Wason (Eds.), *Thinking* (pp. 264-273). New York: Cambridge University Press.

Rosner, J., & Simon, D.P. (1971). The auditory analysis test: An initial report. *Journal of Learning Disabilities, 4*, 384-392.

Rourke, B.P. (1987). Syndrome of nonverbal learning disabilities: The final common pathway of white matter disease/dysfunction? *The Clinical Neuropsychologist, 1,* 209-234.

Ruhl, K.L., & Suritsky, S. (1995). The pause procedure and/or an outline: Effect on immediate free recall and lecture notes taken by college students with learning disabilities. *Learning Disability Quarterly, 18*(1), 2-12.

Ruthen, R. (1993). Adapting to complexity. *Scientific American, 268*(1), 130-140.

Sameroff, A. (1982). Development and the dialectic: The need for a systems approach. In W.A. Collins (Ed.), *The concept of development* (pp. 83-104). Hillsdale, NJ: Erlbaum.

Sameroff, A., & Chandler, M.J. (1975). Reproductive risk and the continuum of caretaking casualty. In F.D. Horowitz (Ed.), *Review of child development research* (pp. 207-220). Chicago: University of Chicago Press.

Samuels, S.J. (1987). Why it is difficult to characterize the underlying cognitive deficits in special education populations. *Exceptional Children, 54*(1), 60-62.

Samuels, S.J., LaBerge, D., & Bremer, C.D. (1978). Units of word recognition: Evidence for developmental changes. *Journal of Verbal Learning and Verbal Behavior, 17,* 715-720.

Samuels, S.J., Miller, N., & Eisenberg, P. (1979). Practice effects on the unit of word recognition. *Journal of Educational Psychology, 71,* 514-520.

Samuels, S.J., & Peterson, E. (1986). *Toward a theory of word recognition: Integrative data from subjects, materials, task, and context.* Washington, DC: National Institutes of Education.

Sandler, A., Hooper, S., Watson, T., Coleman, W., Footo, M., & Levine, M. (1993). Talkative children: Verbal fluency as a marker for problematic peer relationships in clinic referred children with attention deficits. *Perceptual and Motor Skills, 76,* 943-951.

Satir, V. (1988). *The new peoplemaking.* Mountainview, CA: Science and Behavior Books.

Scardamalia, M., & Bereiter, C. (1986). Research on written composition. In M.C. Wittrock (Ed.), *Handbook of research on teaching* (pp. 778-803). New York: Macmillan.

Scardamalia, M., Bereiter, C., & Goelman, H. (1982). The role of production factors in writing ability. In M. Nystrand (Ed.), *What writers know: The language, process, and structure of written discourse* (pp. 173-210). New York: Academic Press.

Schachar, R., & Tannock, R. (1995). Test of four hypotheses for the comorbidity of Attention-Deficit Hyperactivity Disorder and conduct disorder. *Journal of the American Academy of Child and Adolescent Psychiatry, 34*(5), 639-648.

Schiffrin, R.M., & Dumais, S. (1984). The development of automatism. In J.K. Anderson (Ed.), *Cognitive skills and their acquisition* (pp. 111-140). Hillsdale, NJ: Erlbaum.

Schleifer, M., Weiss, G., Cohen, N.J., Elman, M., Cvejic, H., & Kruger, E. (1975). Hyperactivity in preschoolers and the effect of methylphenidate. *American Journal of Orthopsychiatry, 45,* 38-50.

Schneider, W., & Schiffrin, R.M. (1977). Controlled and automatic human information processing: II. Perceptual learning, automatic attending, and a general theory. *Psychological Review, 84,* 127-190.

Schrag, P., & Divoky, D. (1975). *The myth of the hyperactive child.* New York: Pantheon.

Schwartz, C.E., Snidman, N., & Kagan, J. (1996). Early childhood temperament as a determinant of externalizing behavior in adolescence. *Development and Psychopathology, 8,* 527-537.

Semrud-Clikeman, M., & Hynd, G.W. (1990). Right hemisphere dysfunction in nonverbal learning disabilities: Social, academic, and adaptive functioning in adults and children. *Psychological Bulletin, 107,* 196-209.

Sergeant, J. (1988). From DSM-III attentional deficit disorder to functional defects. In L. Bloomingdale & J. Sergeant (Eds.), *Attention deficit disorder: Criteria, cognition, and intervention* (pp. 183-198). New York: Pergamon Press.

Shaffer, D., Campbell, M., Cantwell, D., Bradley, S., Carlson, G., Cohen, D., Denckla, M., Frances, A., Garfinkel, B., Klein, R., et al. (1989). Child and adolescent psychiatric disorders in DSM-IV: Issues facing the work group. *Journal of the American Academy of Child and Adolescent Psychiatry, 28*(6), 830-835.

Shankweiler, D., & Crain, S. (1986). Language mechanisms and reading disorder: A modular approach. *Cognition, 24,* 139-168.

Shapiro, E.G., Hughes, S.J., August, G.J., & Bloomquist, M.L. (1993). Processing of emotional information in children with attention deficit hyperactivity disorder. *Developmental Psychology, 9*(3-4), 207-224.

Shapiro, K.L., Ogden, N., & Lind-Blad, F. (1990). Temporal processing in dyslexia. *Journal of Learning Disabilities, 23,* 99-107.

Shaw, R., Kadar, E., Sim, M., & Repperger, D.W. (1992). The intentional spring: A strategy for modeling systems that learn to perform intentional acts. *Journal of Motor Behavior, 24*(1), 3-28.

Shaywitz, S.E., Cohen, D.J., & Shaywitz, B.E. (1980). Behavior and learning difficulties in children of normal intelligence born to alcoholic mothers. *Journal of Pediatrics, 96,* 978-982.

Shaywitz, S.E., & Shaywitz, B.E. (1988). Attention deficit disorder: Current perspectives. In J.F. Cavanagh & T.J. Truss, Jr. (Eds.), *Learning Disabilities: Proceedings of the National Conference* (pp. 369-523). Parkton, MD: York Press.

Shenker, A. (1992). The mechanism of action of drugs used to treat attention-deficit hyperactivity disorder: focus on catecholamine receptor pharmacology. *Advances in Pediatrics, 39,* 337-82.

Shirley, M. (1939). A behavior syndrome characterizing prematurely born children. *Child Development, 10,* 115-128.

Silva, R., Munoz, D.M., & Alpert, M. (1996). Carbamazepine use in children and adolescents with features of attention-deficit hyperactivity disorder: A meta-analysis. *Journal of the American Academy of Child and Adolescent Psychiatry, 35*(3), 352-358.

Silver, L. (1990). Attention Deficit – Hyperactivity Disorder: Is it a learning disability or a related disorder? *Journal of Learning Disabilities, 23*(7), 394-397.

Smith, L. (1975). *Your child's behavior chemistry.* New York: Random House.

Solanto, M.V., & Wender, E.H. (1989). Does methylphenidate constrict cognitive functioning? *Journal of the Academy of Child and Adolescent Psychiatry, 26,* 897-902.

Sommers, N. (1982). *Revision strategies of student writers and experienced adult writers* (ERIC Document Reproduction Service No ED 220 839). (Contract No. NIE-P-0029). Washington, DC: National Institution of Education.

Spencer, T.J., Biederman, J., Harding, M., O'Donnell, D., Faraone, S.V., & Wilens, T.E. (1996). Growth deficits in ADHD children revisited: Evidence for disorder-associated growth delays? *Journal of the American Academy of Child and Adolescent Psychiatry, 35*(11), 1460-1469.

Spitz, H.H. (1966). The role of input organization in the learning and memory of mental retardates. In N. R. Ellis (Ed.), *International review of research in mental retardation,* (Vol.2, pp. 29-56). New York: Academic Press.

Spitzer, R.L., Davies, M., & Barkley, R.A. (1990). The DSM-III-R field trial for the Disruptive Behavior Disorders. *Journal of the American Academy of Child and Adolescent Psychiatry.*

Spitzer, R.L., & Williams, J.B.W. (1980). Classification of mental disorders and DSM-III. In A.M. Freedman & B.J. Sadock (Eds.), *Comprehensive textbook of psychiatry.* Baltimore: Williams & Wilkins.

Spoont, M.R. (1992). Modulatory role of serotonin in neural information processing: Implications for human psychopathology. *Psychological Bulletin, 112*(2), 330-350.

Sprague, R.L., & Sleator, E.K. (1977). Methylphenidate in hyperkinetic children: Differences in dose effects on learning and social behavior. *Science, 198,* 1274-1276.

Sroufe, L.A. (1990). Considering normal and abnormal together: The essence of developmental psychopathology. *Developmental Psychopathology, 2,* 335-347.

Stein, M.A., Szumowski, E., & Blondis, T.A. (1995). Adaptive skills dysfunction in ADD and ADHD children. *Journal of Child Psychology and Psychiatry and Allied Disciplines, 36,* 663-670.

Stein, N., & Glenn, G. (1979). An analysis of story comprehension in elementary school children. In R. Freedle (Ed.), *New directions in discourse processing* (Vol. 2, pp. 53-120). Norwood, NJ: Ablex.

Stein, N.L., & Glenn, C.G. (1982). Children's concept of time: The development of a story schema. In W. Freedman (Ed.), *The developmental psychology of time* (pp. 255-282). New York: Academic Press.

Stevenson, J., Pennington, B.F., Gilger, J.W., DeFries, J.C., & Gillis, J.J. (1993). Hyperactivity and spelling disability: Testing for shared genetic aetiology. *Journal of Child Psychology and Psychiatry, 34*(7), 1137-1152.

Still, G.F. (1902). Some abnormal psychical conditions in children. *Lancet, I*, 1008-1012, 1077-1082, 1163-1168.

Stolzenberg, J., & Cherkes-Julkowski, M. (1991). The LD–ADHD connection. *Journal of Learning Disabilities, 24*(4), 194-195.

Stone, B.H., Merritt, D.D., & Cherkes-Julkowski, M. (in press). Language and reading: Phonological connections. In D.D. Merritt & B. Culatta (Eds.), *Collaborative language intervention in the classroom*. San Diego, CA: Singular Publishing Group.

Strauss, A.A., & Lehtinen, L.E. (1947). *Psychopathology and education of the brain-injured child*. New York: Grune & Stratton.

Strauss, M.S., & Curtis, L.E. (1984). Development of numerical concepts in infancy. In C. Sophian (Ed.), *Origins of cognitive skills* (pp. 131-156). Hillsdale, NJ: Lawrence Erlbaum Associates.

Stuss, D.T., & Benson, D.F. (1986). *The frontal lobes*. New York: Raven Press.

Sullivan, H.S. (1953). *The interpersonal theory of psychiatry*. New York: Norton.

Swanson, H.L. (1981). Vigilance deficit in learning disabled children: A signal detection analysis. *Journal of Child Psychology and Psychiatry, 22*, 393-399.

Swanson, H.L. (1983). A developmental study of vigilance in learning disabled and nondisabled children. *Journal of Abnormal Child Psychology, 11*, 415-429.

Swanson, H.L. (1985). Effects of cognitive-behavioral training on emotionally disturbed children's academic performance. *Cognitive Therapy and Research, 9*(2), 201-216.

Swanson, H.L. (1994). The role of working memory and dynamic assessment in the classification of children with learning disabilities. *Learning Disabilities Research and Practice, 9*(4), 190-202.

Swanson, J., Cantwell, D., Lerner, M., McBurnett, K., & Hanna, G. (1991). Effects of stimulant medication on learning in children with ADHD. *Journal of Learning Disabilities, 24*(4), 219-230.

Swanson, J., & Kinsbourne, M. (1978). Should you use stimulants to treat the hyperactive child? *Modern Medicine, 46*, 71-80.

Tannock, R., Ickowicz, A., & Schachar, R. (1995). Differential effects of methylphenidate on working memory in ADHD children with and without comorbid anxiety. *Journal of the American Academy of Child and Adolescent Psychiatry, 34*(7), 886-896.

Tannock, R., & Schachar, R.J. (1992). Methylphenidate and cognitive perseveration in hyperactive children. *Journal of Child Psychology and Psychiatry, 33*(7), 1217-1228.

Tannock, R., Schachar, R.J., Carr, R.P., & Logan, G.D. (1989). Dose-response effects of methylphenidate on academic performance and overt behavior in hyperactive children. *Pediatrics, 84*, 648-657.

Taylor, B.M., & Beach, R. (1984). The effects of text structure on middle grade students' comprehension and production of expository text. *Reading Research Quarterly, 19*, 134-146.

Terry, P., Samuels, S.J., & LaBerge, D.L. (1976). The effects of letter degradations and letter spacing on word recognition. *Journal of Verbal Learning and Verbal Behavior, 15*, 577-585.

Thatcher, R.W. (1989). *Nonlinear dynamics of human brain cerebral development*. Paper presented at the international conference Mechanisms of Mind, Havana, Cuba.

Thelen, E., & Smith, L.B. (1994). *A Dynamical Systems Approach to the Development of Cognition and Action*. Cambridge, MA: Bradford Books.

Thoman, E. (1987). Regulation of stimulation by prematures with a breathing blue bear. In J.J. Gallagher & C.T. Ramey (Eds.), *The malleability of children* (pp. 51-70). Baltimore: Brooks Publishing.

Thomas, C.C., Englert, C.S., & Gregg, S. (1987). An analysis of errors and strategies in the expository writing of learning disabled students. *Remedial and Special Education, 8*(1), 21-30, 46.

Thomson, G.O.B., Raab, G.M., Hepburn, W.S., Hunter, R., Fulton, M., & Laxen, D.P.H. (1989). Blood-lead levels and children's behaviour: Results from the Edinburgh lead study. *Journal of Child Psychology and Psychiatry, 30*, 515-528.

Tindal, G., & Hasbrouck, J. (1991). Analyzing student writing to develop instructional strategies. *Learning Disabilities Research & Practice, 6*, 237-245.

Torgesen, J.K., & Young, K.A. (1983). Priorities for the use of microcomputers with learning disabled children. *Journal of Learning Disabilities, 16*, 234-237.

Treiman, R., & Zukowski, A. (1991). Levels of phonological awareness. In S. Brady & D. Shankweiler (Eds.), *Phonological processes in literacy: A tribute to Isabelle Y. Liberman* (pp. 67-84). Hillsdale, NJ: Erlbaum.

Trexler, L.E., & Zappala, G. (1988). Neuropathological determinants of acquired attention disorders in traumatic brain injury, 8(3), 291-302.

Tucker, D.M., & Williamson, P.A. (1984). Asymmetric neural control systems in human self-regulation. *Psychological Review, 91*(2), 185-215.

Uzgiris, I.C., & Hunt, J.M. (1987). *Infant performance and experience: New findings with ordinal scales.* Chicago: University of Chicago Press.

Vallecorsa, A.L., & Garriss, E. (1990). Story composition skills of middle-grade students with learning disabilities. *Exceptional Children, 57*(1), 48-54.

Van Bruggen, J.A. (1946). Factors affecting regularity of the flow of words during written composition. *Journal of Experimental Education, 15*(2), 133-155.

Varela, F.J., Thompson, E., & Rosch, E. (1993). *The embodied mind.* Cambridge, MA: MIT Press.

Vellutino, F.R. (1979). *Dyslexia: Theory and research.* Cambridge, MA: MIT Press.

Venezky, R.L., & Massaro, D.W. (1979). The role of orthographic regularity in word recognition. In L.B. Resnick & P.A. Weaver (Eds.), *Theory and practice of early reading* (Volume 1, pp. 85-107). Hillsdale, NJ: Erlbaum.

Voeller, K.K.S. (1990). The neurological bias of Attention Deficit Hyperactivity Disorder. *International Pediatrics, 5*(2), 171-176.

Voeller, K.K.S. (1991). Toward a neurobiologic nosology of Attention Deficit Hyperactivity Disorder. *Journal of Child Neurology, 6* (Supplement), s2-s8.

von Bertalanffy, L. (1968). *General system theory.* New York: Braziller.

Vygotsky, L.S. (1962). *Thought and language.* Cambridge, MA: MIT Press.

Wagner, R.K. (1996). From simple structure to complex function: Major trends in the development of theories, models, and measurements of memory. In G. R. Lyon & N.A. Krasnegor (Eds.), *Attention, memory, and executive function* (pp. 139-156). Baltimore: Brookes.

Weintraub, S., & Mesulam, M.M. (1983). Developmental learning disabilities of the right hemisphere: Emotional, interpersonal, and cognitive components. *Archives of Neurology, 40,* 463-468.

Welch, A. (1993, April). *Attention Deficit Disorder.* Workshop presented at the annual meeting of the Council for Exceptional Children, San Antonio, TX.

Wender, P.H. (1971). *Minimal brain dysfunction in children.* New York: Wiley.

Wender, P.H. (1988). Attention deficit hyperactivity disorder. In J.G. Howells (Ed.), *Modern perspectives in clinical psychiatry* (pp. 149-169). New York: Brunner/Mazel.

Werry, J.S. (1988). Differential diagnosis of attention deficits and conduct disorders. In L. Bloomingdale & J. Sergeant (Eds.), *Attention deficit disorder: Criteria, cognition, and intervention* (pp. 83-96). New York: Pergamon Press.

Werry, J.S., Minde, K., Guzman, A., Weiss, G., Dogan, K., & Hoy, E. (1972). Studies on the hyperactive child: VII. Neurological status compared with neurotic and normal children. *American Journal of Orthopsychiatry, 42*(3), 441-449.

Werry, J.S., & Sprague, R.L. (1970). Hyperactivity. In C.G. Costello (Ed.), *Symptoms of psychopathology* (pp. 397-417). New York: Wiley.

Wertsch, J. (1985). *Culture, communication, and cognition: Vygotskian perspectives.* New York: Cambridge University Press.

Whalen, C.K., & Henker, B. (1976). Psychostimulants and children: A review and analysis. *Psychological Bulletin, 83,* 1113-1130.

Whalen, C.K., Henker, B., Collins, B.E., McAuliffe, S., & Vaux, A. (1979). Peer interaction in structured communication task: Comparisons of normal and hyperactive boys and of methylphenidate (Ritalin) and placebo effects. *Child Development, 50,* 388-401.

Whalen, C.K., Henker, B., & Dotemoto, S. (1981). Teacher response to the methylphenidate (Ritalin) versus placebo status of hyperactive boys in the classrooms. *Child Development, 52,* 1005-1014.

Whalen, C.K., Henker, B., & Finck, D. (1981). Medication effects in the classroom: Three naturalistic indicators. *Journal of Abnormal Child Psychology, 9,* 419-433.

Whalen, C.K., Henker, B., & Granger, D.A. (1990). Social judgment processes in hyperactive boys: Effects of methylphenidate and comparisons with normal peers. *Journal of Abnormal Child Psychology, 18,* 297-316.

White, N.M. (1989). Reward or reinforcement: What's the difference? *Neuroscience and Biobehavioral Reviews, 13,* 181-186.

Willerman, L. (1973). Activity level and hyperactivity in twins. *Child Development, 44,* 288-293.

Wolf, M. (1986). Rapid alternating stimulus (R.A.S.) naming in the developmental dyslexias. *Brain and Language, 27,* 360-379.

Wolf, M., Bally, H., & Morris, R. (1986). Automaticity, retrieval processes, and reading: A longitudinal study in average and impaired readers. *Child Development, 57,* 988-1000.

Wolraich, M.L., Lindgren, S.D., Stumbo, P.J., Stegink, L.D., Appelbaum, M.I., & Kiritsy, M.G. (1994). Effects of diets high in sucrose or aspartame on the behavior and cognitive performance of children. *The New England Journal of Medicine, 333*(5), 301-307.

Wong, B.Y.L., & Wilson, M. (1984). Investigating awareness of and teaching passage organization in learning disabled children. *Journal of Learning Disabilities, 17,* 477-482.

Wong, B.Y.L., Wong, R., & Blenkinsop, J. (1989). Cognitive and metacognitive aspects of learning disabled adolescents' composing problems. *Learning Disabilities Quarterly, 12,* 300-322.

Wood, D.R., Reimherr, F.W., Wender, P.H., & Johnson, G.E. (1976). Diagnosis and treatment of minimal brain dysfunction in adults. *Archives of General Psychiatry, 33,* 1453-1460.

Wood, F. (1991). *Behavioral aspects of learning disabilities.* Paper presented at the Council for Learning Disabilities international conference, Minneapolis, MN.

Woodcock, R., & Johnson, M.B. (1989). *Tests of Achievement-Revised.* Allen, TX: DLM Teaching.

Yerkes, R.M., & Dodson, J.D. (1908). The relation of strength of stimulus to rapidity of habit formation. *Journal of Comparative and Neurological Psychology, 18,* 459-482.

Zametkin, A.J., Nordahl, T.E., Gross, M., King, A.C., Semple, W.E., Rumsey, J., Hamburger, S., & Cohen, K. (1990). Cerebral glucose metabolism in adults with hyperactivity of childhood onset. *New England Journal of Medicine, 323*(20), 1361-1366.

Zeaman, D., & House, B. (1979). A review of attention theory. In N. Ellis (Ed.), *Handbook of mental deficiency, psychological theory, and research* (pp. 63-120). Hillsdale, NJ: Erlbaum.

Zentall, S.S., Falkenberg, S.D., & Smith, L.B. (1985). Effects of color stimulation and information on the copying performance of attention-problem adolescents. *Journal of Abnormal Psychology, 13,* 501-511.

Zentall, S.S., & Smith, Y.N. (1993). Mathematical performance and behavior of children with hyperactivity with and without coexisting aggression. *Behavior Research Therapy, 31*(7), 701-710.

Zeskind, P.S., & Marshall, T.R. (1991). Temporal organization in neonatal arousal: Systems, oscillations, and development. In M.J.S. Weiss & P.R. Zelazo (Eds.), *Newborn attention, biological constraints and the influence of experience* (pp. 22-62). Norwood, NJ: Ablex.

Appendix A

Simplification of Neurotransmitter Effects

Dopamine (DA)	Norepinephrine (NE)	Serotonin (5-HT)
Activation	**Arousal**	
repetitive motor patterns/control redundancy/repetition persistent behavior tight control sustained focus elaboration detailed analysis on-line holding of information vigilance sustained focal attention sequenced organization of behavior	habituation novelty orientation redundancy reduction broad sweep attention to external events/perception	
Behavior Facilitation	**Behavior Inhibition**	

reward-approach-motivated
  environmental interactions
aggression
extraversion
	suppression of attention to
	  irrelevant stimuli
	social inhibition
		attenuation of noise

	affect-mood regulation	
RELATIVE LATERALIZATION		
left-lateralized; frontal	right-lateralized	
MEDICATIONS		
methylphenidate (Ritalin) d-amphetamine (Dexedrine) pemoline (Cylert)	imipramine (Tofranil) amitriptyline (Elavil) nortriptyline (Pamelor) desipramine (Norpramin)	fluoxetine (Prozac) setraline (Zoloft) paroxetine (Paxil)
PATHOLOGICAL MANIFESTATIONS		
overfocus; stereotypies; obsessive-complusive traits	depression; anxiety; social-withdrawal; hypoactivity	

Index

About the Authors

Miriam Cherkes-Julkowski is a professor of educational psychology at the University of Connecticut. She also has a private practice concerned with diagnosis, assessment, and program development for children with attention deficit disorders and other neurological impairments or learning disabilities. She has consulted with many school systems to develop programs for children with learning problems and to provide continuing education for teachers. Her research has been in the area of attention deficit disorders, learning disabilities, and the implications of cognitive disorders for instruction.

Susan L. Sharp, Ph.D., has been a practicing educator for the past nineteen years. She earned her B.A. *summa cum laude* from Boston College, and her M.A. and Ph.D. in Special Education from the University of Connecticut. Dr. Sharp was a special education teacher for ten years, teaching students with many different types of disabilities in kindergarten through high school. She has taught college courses and supervised teachers in training. Currently, she coordinates the special education department for a small rural school district in Connecticut, has a private practice as as educational diagnostician and consultant, and presents workshops and inservice training. Dr. Sharp's current research interests include reading and written language disabilities, attention deficit disorders, assessment, and school interventions for emotional and behavioral disabilities.

Jonathan Stolzenberg, M.D., is a *summa cum laude,* Phi Beta Kappa graduate of Harvard (1971) and received his M.D. from Albert Einstein College of Medicine in 1974. During medical school and his residency in pediatrics, Dr. Stolzenberg began his ongoing training as a medical and family psychotherapist with Virginia Satir and others and received training in psychopharmacology. As a practicing developmental and behavioral pediatrician and psychotherapist, he realized that children and adults with ADDs had significant problems with learning and living both in and out of school. Noting the cognitive problems that were evident in psychotherapy, he developed a multimodal assessment and intervention that addressed the biological, psychological, and social aspects of this disorder, with a strong emphasis on school interventions at the cognitive/learning level. Dr. Stolzenberg was an early advocate for ADD interventions which focused on the human being and the underlying causes of their coping strategies ("symptoms"), rather than on extinguishing his or her "disruptive behaviors." He and Dr. Cherkes-Julkowski have worked together both clinically, in developing assessment protocols and evaluation of children and adults, and on the formulation and interpretation of the research that formed the foundation for this book.